Toxic Geek Mas

Anastasia Salter · Bridget Blodgett
Toxic Geek Masculinity in Media

Sexism, Trolling, and Identity Policing

Anastasia Salter
School of Visual Arts and Design
University of Central Florida
Orlando, FL, USA

Bridget Blodgett
Division of Science, Information Arts and
  Technologies
University of Baltimore
Baltimore, MD, USA

ISBN 978-3-319-66076-9   ISBN 978-3-319-66077-6 (eBook)
DOI 10.1007/978-3-319-66077-6

Library of Congress Control Number: 2017950719

© The Editor(s) (if applicable) and The Author(s) 2017

This work is subject to copyright. All rights are solely and exclusively licensed by the Publisher, whether the whole or part of the material is concerned, specifically the rights of translation, reprinting, reuse of illustrations, recitation, broadcasting, reproduction on microfilms or in any other physical way, and transmission or information storage and retrieval, electronic adaptation, computer software, or by similar or dissimilar methodology now known or hereafter developed.

The use of general descriptive names, registered names, trademarks, service marks, etc. in this publication does not imply, even in the absence of a specific statement, that such names are exempt from the relevant protective laws and regulations and therefore free for general use.

The publisher, the authors and the editors are safe to assume that the advice and information in this book are believed to be true and accurate at the date of publication. Neither the publisher nor the authors or the editors give a warranty, express or implied, with respect to the material contained herein or for any errors or omissions that may have been made. The publisher remains neutral with regard to jurisdictional claims in published maps and institutional affiliations.

Cover credit: Cover design by Sam Johnson

Printed on acid-free paper

This Palgrave Macmillan imprint is published by Springer Nature
The registered company is Springer International Publishing AG
The registered company address is: Gewerbestrasse 11, 6330 Cham, Switzerland

Preface

Geek-centered and inspired productions have accelerated their march into the mainstream with many recent events—including the success of Marvel's cinematic universe, the rising popularity of video games, and even theatrical screenings of episodes of *Doctor Who*—all bringing geek culture into the spotlight. This rising power and visibility has brought renewed attention to the geek identity's hostility to marginalized groups, including, but certainly not limited to, women. The marginalization of women in geek culture can seem odd when viewed numerically: women compose a large part of the audience of these media. However, they are underrepresented among creators, and mostly invisible or secondary in the works themselves. We examine the state of geek cultural identity and the self-fulfilling prophecy of "geekdom" as a space where women are continually marginalized and instrumentalized instead of given voice. Our focus is on reading digital popular culture as a testimonial and manifesto of geek identity. Examining the identity politics and construction of the geek "hero" can reveal the ways in which these texts across media are encoded with a defensiveness of geek as other that is out of touch with the reality of culture. In turn, this disconnect has grave consequences for the space of women and men both in these texts and communities, as has recently been demonstrated through movements such as Gamergate. These expressions of toxic masculinity and identity policing have given rise to a question from both the media and the community: what aspects of geek culture provide rich fuel for these surges of hostility?

The authors of this work both identify as American geeks and fans as well as scholars dedicated to media studies through different disciplinary lenses.

The franchises, stories, and heroes under discussion here are the same characters that we have grown up with, plastered on office walls, and followed through adaptations and remakes. We have stood in line for the *Star Wars* prequels, attended midnight launch parties for *Harry Potter* novels, and even sat in a theater for a special showing of the extended editions of the entire *Lord of the Rings* trilogy. And yes, we've written fanfiction, obsessively followed shipper tags and fan artists on Tumblr, and engaged in many heated late-night debates over the adaptation choices of *Game of Thrones*. The heroes under examination here are our heroes: the characters we grew up with, and are still growing up with, should not be immune from analysis and critique. While we acknowledge that some critics might be concerned with the positioning of two women-assigned authors of a study on geek masculinity, we believe that this study is not merely concerned with toxic geek masculinity but with the continual rejection and negative framing of femininity within geek spaces: it is impossible to discuss one without addressing both. Throughout, we engage and reject the false binary of masculine/feminine as well as the identities of man and woman: we understand "man" and "woman" to be identity categories including both cis and trans men and women. However, representations of cis men and women dominate geek media, and representation of trans men and women as well as nonbinary, genderqueer, and other gender-nonconforming people remains a distant goal that this discourse of toxic masculinity plays a role in restricting. As we've navigated our own identities as fans, academics, and geeks, we have been continually aware of the challenges of the outsider, and it has informed much of our previous collaborative research on the positioning of non-cis man as other in STEM and the games community.

Our intention is to explore how geek identity has taken assumptions of marginalization as foundational. The perceived status of geek identity as marginalized and threatened even as geek culture has become mainstreamed are contradictory forces at play in the current battle over the renegotiation of the geek identity. To understand this construction, we will look at the very nature of the hero in geek-marketed media, both in spaces marked for science fiction and fantasy and in narratives that seek to reflect geek culture back at itself. These dueling visions of geek-as-victim and geek-as-hero give rise to the hypermasculine geek, an identity forged by rejecting both feminine-marked culture and constructions as well as the traditional athletic male aesthetic. We explore how this identity's relationship to established cultural hierarchies makes it difficult for geekdom to reconcile itself with its new dominant position in pop culture even as it remains dedicated to an identity as the outsider hero: an archetype seen everywhere from

Supernatural to *Firefly* to *Doctor Who*. The challenge to this archetype by those the geek community views as outsiders results in tensions and struggles sending ripples throughout both popular culture and the larger STEM community. These have become more and more pronounced with geek culture's apparent increasing significance and visibility. Over the past few years, we have witnessed the rise of gamer collectives dedicated to excluding women and feminists through movements such as Gamergate, increased attention to hostilities towards women at comic and film conventions, and the continual harassment and threats towards women across geek media who become visible as producers or fans.

Orlando, USA	Anastasia Salter
Baltimore, USA	Bridget Blodgett

Acknowledgements

We are collectively involved in several research communities where we have received feedback on different stages of this project, including the Popular Culture Association, the Society for Cinema and Media Studies, the Modern Language Association, the Foundations of Digital Games Conference, the Association of Internet Research Association, and the Electronic Literature Organization. To name only a few of the colleagues, collaborators, mentors, students, and friends who have offered advice, insight, and inspiration (in alphabetical order): Kathi Inman Berens, David Blodgett, Stephanie Boluk, Julia Bullard, Edmond Chang, Shira Chess, Amanda Cockrell, Joseph Fanfarelli, Jacob Garbe, Todd Harper, Emily Johnson, Matthew Kirschenbaum, Flourish Klink, Carly Kocurek, Adeline Koh, Deb Kohl, Deena Larsen, Liz Losh, Marjorie Luesebrink, Wayne Lutters, Rudy McDaniel, Mark Marino, Nick Montfort, Stuart Moulthrop, Eric Murnane, John Murray, Bonnie Nardi, J.J. Pionke, Aaron Reed, Mark Sample, Adrienne Shaw, Peter Smith, Nick Sousanis, Mel Stanfill, Anne Sullivan, Kathryn Summers, Patricia Thomas, Piper Thunstrom, and Eileen Young.

We feel very fortunate that the world of print still exists and that publishers such as Palgrave Macmillan are keeping academic publishing alive. Thanks to our editor, Shaun Vigil, for his support of the project, and special thanks to Angelia Giannone for her invaluable assistance with preparing the manuscript.

Thanks to our colleagues at the University of Baltimore and the University of Central Florida who were understanding of our woes and penchant for yelling research ideas at each other through the wall. Your words of encouragement and belief that this was a topic worth examination helped us keep pushing through the hard parts.

Deepest love and thanks to our families who have offered both emotional and intellectual support during the writing of this book and our careers. We don't know why we decided looking into divisive, stressful pop culture was a good idea, but we couldn't do it so well without you.

Contents

1 Introduction: Actually, It's about Toxic Geek Masculinity…   1

2 "Dick in a Box": Hypermasculine Heroism in Geek TV and Film   17

3 Beauty and the Geek: On-Screen Representations of Geeks   45

4 Come Get Some: Damsels in Distress and the Male Default Avatar in Video Games   73

5 Through the Boob Window: Examining Sexualized Portrayals in Transmedia Comic Franchises   101

6 Bronies on the Iron Throne: Perceptions of Prosocial Behaviors and Success   131

7 One of Us, One of Us!: Representations and Dialogues with "Fanboys" and "Fangirls"   157

8 Conclusion: That's Not How Geek Masculinity Works!   189

Index   209

List of Figures

Fig. 2.1	Cover of *Captain America* Vol 2#6 (Leifeld 1997). Cover Image: Marvel Comics	24
Fig. 2.2	Milton Waddams in *Office Space* (Judge 1999). Screen capture: 20th Century Fox	33
Fig. 3.1	Chuck and his compatriots in the Geek Squad (McG 2010). Screen capture: NBC	61
Fig. 4.1	A captured woman in *Duke Nukem 3D*	80
Fig. 5.1	Tony Harris's Facebook rant	103
Fig. 5.2	*The Big Bang Theory* promo. Screen Capture from Burlingame (2013)	110
Fig. 6.1	Scott "leveling up" in his pursuit of Ramona	139
Fig. 6.2	Becky as predator in "Time for a Wedding"	151
Fig. 7.1	Watson held hostage by Moriarty in "The Great Game" (McGuigan 2010b)	165
Fig. 7.2	Sherlock's emotional display in "The Final Problem" (Caron 2017)	169
Fig. 7.3	The fan actress versions of Sam and Dean in "Fan Fiction" (Sgriccia 2014)	174
Fig. 8.1	Chuck Tingle responds to his Hugo nomination, 2016	194

1

Introduction: Actually, It's about Toxic Geek Masculinity…

Flip the channels in the early evening and, inevitably, sitcom after sitcom will fill the screen. Surprisingly, one show dominates the current schedule of repeats. *The Big Bang Theory* (Cendrowski 2007–) follows the lives of a group of scientists who spend much of their time in a California apartment filled to the brim with all the hallmarks of geek culture. First-time viewers of the show might be surprised that nearly everyone is even more socially awkward than geeky-friend sitcom characters such as dinosaur-loving Ross of *Friends* (Crane and Kauffman 1994–2004) or architect Ted from *How I Met Your Mother* (Fryman 2005–2014). Unlike the relatively tasteful apartments of the love life-obsessed characters of those other long-running sitcoms, the California dwelling of *The Big Bang Theory*'s central geeks, Leonard and Sheldon, is dominated by technology. Superhero models stare down from the bookshelves, a telescope is clearly visible, and iconic t-shirts of comic heroes and video game characters are a frequent wardrobe choice. In one episode, the exaggerated pixelated breasts of a woman fill the screen of a multiplayer video game as the show's three central young white men, dressed in appropriately geeky shirts and wearing glasses, look on. Their conversation centers on the video game character:

Leonard Hofstadter: We're supposed to be encouraging women to study science. Can you at least play a less sexist game?
Sheldon Cooper: I don't see anything sexist. She can handle a battle-axe as well as any man.

© The Author(s) 2017
A. Salter and B. Blodgett, *Toxic Geek Masculinity in Media*,
DOI 10.1007/978-3-319-66077-6_1

Howard Wolowitz:	And she has mammary glands that can breast feed a family of thirty and have enough milk left over to open a Baskin-Robbins.
Sheldon Cooper:	Mother, warrior princess, small business owner, I see glass ceilings shattering all over the place. (Cendrowski 2013)

In this episode, entitled "The Contractual Obligation Implementation," the show takes on the marginalization of women in the sciences by sending three of its geeky male-scientist leads back to middle school to talk to girls about scientific careers. Their plan is hatched in part over a console game whose hypersexualized avatars reflect the stark realities and entrenched binaries of women's roles in geek spaces. As the conversation above demonstrates, the characters are deeply lacking in self-awareness regarding their roles in a sexist workplace, and this same lack of understanding is constantly played for humor. As the episode continues, the two geeky female love interests are brought in on the phone to be the voice of women mentors speaking to the middle-school girls about their potential future careers in science. However, their words come at a distance, and are undermined by the circumstances shown to the camera: the women are taking a trip to Disneyland, costumed as princesses and re-applying their lipstick even as they share the familiar refrain that brains are just as important as looks. This episode is typical of the type of empty feminism that often shows up in geek culture. Sheldon's words are particularly familiar: "I don't see anything sexist. She can handle a battleaxe as well as any man" suggests that the construction of the woman as avatar to primarily appeal to a masculine gaze is perfectly equitable as long as she has the same strength. Likewise, the show's own geeky women characters are presented as scientific equals to most of the leading geek men, but their protestations of the importance of brains over beauty are undermined by their pursuit of ultra-feminine Disney princess costuming. The point is further undermined when the women are shown shortly after using their princess-ified selves as fuel for sexual encounters with their male counterparts, who in most cases are immediately drawn to the "princess" with a fervor otherwise rarely displayed. In aggregate, the episode's message about women geeks ends with their reduction to objects for the masculine gaze, not unlike the very avatar of the battleaxe-wielding fantasy woman in Sheldon's video game.

The Big Bang Theory has already had an impressive run on television, with ten seasons as of 2017 and no end in sight: as of March 20, the show was renewed for two more seasons (Andreeva 2017). Throughout the show's impressive arc, we see many similar moments that pull into the foreground the construction of the binary of masculine and the feminine in geek culture. *The Big Bang Theory* revolves around four male scientists whose social awkwardness, physical frailty, and obsession with comic books and science fiction mark them as "epic" geeks. On paper, they seem an unlikely crew to fuel one of the more successful television comedies of the past decade. They occupy classic archetypes fully, with continual jokes surrounding their inability to engage in or understand sports and their general lack of attractiveness to women. However, the show's blend of humor and wish-fulfillment in the form of attractive women love interests for the leads has proven a strong draw for viewers and, importantly, captured geek identity at a time of its transitioning headfirst into mainstream culture. Characters on *The Big Bang Theory* are strongly typed as either geek or non-geek, and various guest characters are continually brought in as a reminder of an alternative masculinity that these four (encumbered as they are by all the limitations that go with geek identity) cannot hope to participate in. Leonard's love interest and neighbor Penny, cast in the role of the waitress "beauty" to the scientist geeks "beasts," often partners with men who represent a more traditional hypermasculine ideal as expressed through physical dominance, an interest in sports and beer, and a complete disdain for the intellectual and "geeky" past-times of the main group. The psychological concept of the hypermasculine as defined by Parrott and Zeichner (2003) has its roots in the exaggeration of masculine cultural stereotypes, usually with a corresponding hostility towards the feminine, as chiefly characterized in American popular culture through the jock or "bad boy." The dichotomy of *Big Bang Theory*'s geeks and jocks suggests that this elevation of the hypermasculine is still intact; yet, in the show's cultural clashes, the geeks usually win. In his 2011 update to his book on *Nerds*, David Anderegg noted the show as part of the increasing visibility of nerd and geek stereotypes:

> The show demonstrates that people who are gifted in science and math also love comic books, have no social skills and no sense of humor, and cannot get a girl no matter what … The progress supposedly represented by *The Big Bang Theory* is that nerds and geeks are no longer presented as hateful or disgusting … they're harmless.

The audience is invited to laugh with and at them as they fumble through encounters with women and society and yet still somehow get the girl.

The idea of the extremely geeky male lead flexing his particular form of masculinity to craft social and sexual success is nothing new: one iconic example is *Revenge of the Nerds*, a 1984 comedy centered on a fraternity of geeks trying to gain a place on their college campus (Kanew). *Revenge of the Nerds* continually pitted traditional masculinity in the form of the highly athletic fraternity of "jocks" against its group of nerds, who together represented both a rejection of the traditional hypermasculine and a new form of fraternity, still offering a highly masculine space but with different requirements for entry. The movie takes the battle between geeks and jocks to a next level by looking not just at student conflict but at institutional power struggles, as the jock-turned-university leader wields all the power and the geeks are pitted against the institution itself. This model suggests that geeks are defined by their powerlessness within traditional spaces, and thus have to carve out and build their own institutions and definitions of masculinity in which to excel. Thirty years later, this alternate form of hypermasculinity has manifested much more broadly in popular culture, while keeping its distance from the traditionally feminine. The fundamental concepts of the film are still so resonant that the film provided the foundation for the narrative of Pixar's 2013 *Monsters University*, which featured two young monsters leading a misfit band of unthreatening fraternity brothers through a monstrous version of the Greek Games (Scanlon). Thus, while the geek who gets the girl many not be a new narrative, the geek who gets the sitcom lead and the space of cultural icon does represent a major shift.

That shift represents a geek cultural revolution. In addition to these "geeks" at the center of a mainstream sitcom, we can see top-box office-earning and critically acclaimed comic book movies on an unprecedented scale, British science fiction shows with tie-in clothing lines at Hot Topic, television coverage of video game tournaments, new *Star Trek* and *Star Wars* movies receiving constant attention, and plenty of editorials proclaiming the age of the geek. The consumer aspect of geek culture has grown particularly dominant, as fandom has emerged from being viewed as an outsider culture to an integral part of the experience of media. Social media has particularly enabled this trend, as viewers of the same show gather using hashtags on Twitter, share memes and insider knowledge on Tumblr, and complain bitterly about bad season finales or cliffhangers on Facebook. These are platforms built and powered by geeks that have relied upon geeks as a base of support for building their cultural capital. Visibly consuming and displaying one's love of geek culture is now not only normal but easier than ever before. Some of this can be viewed as an inevitable consequence of the increasing importance of technology and tech-related culture to the success of any individual, particularly in American culture: the web and its influence on business is inescapable. It is significant that devices once associated with geekdom are now not only mainstream but indispensable parts of everyone's daily workflow and social habits. However, this transition reflects more than just the increased visibility of cultural spaces once labeled as the terrain of geeky fans alone.

This mainstreaming of geek culture has followed a similar cycle of recuperation, as Hebdige (1999) observed in his seminal work on subcultures. However, while Hebdige looked at subcultures where subcultural signs of significance were conveyed primarily through things like dress and music, the major mass productions emerging from geek culture have taken the form of media adaptations. Superhero sagas have leapt from comic book stores to morning cartoons to cult films to blockbuster chart-toppers, while video games and even the occasional science fiction or fantasy novel launches at midnight to large groups of fans. The narrative media of geek subculture space, once a way to identify and commune with fellow geeks, has inarguably leapt into mainstream culture. This process of recuperation has inevitably spawned resistance, which is particularly found in the drawing of stricter boundaries around geek identity and geek-coded spaces to keep outsiders out.

Defining the Geek

Geek is a contested term: it is a label that gets applied to others and historically is associated with mockery and outsider status. The term is particularly US centric, and might be understood in other contexts as nerd, fanboy or fangirl, otaku, etc. But over the last two decades it has shifted significantly to become an insider label: a self-identified term that brings with it a connection to an apparent subculture that is increasingly dominant both in popular media and in US economic and cultural structures. The story of geeks and geek masculinity is thus an essential part of the story of masculinity as represented in media more broadly. This popularity and mainstreaming means the term is currently overused and widely applied; however, its origins reveal an essential alignment with a type of toxic straight white masculinity that is rooted deeply in current cultural struggles.

Following the history of increased computer dependency in parallel to the mainstreaming of geekdom leads us back to the young Steve Jobs and Bill Gates, both precursors of today's geek-as-savior and leader tropes. These two geek icons provided the inspiration for their own popular culture spin-off in the form of *The Pirates of Silicon Valley*, a made-for-TV movie that originally aired on TNT and chronicled the birth of the central empires of early Silicon Valley and with it the birth of a tech and start-up culture that would elevate geekdom into something financially desirable and world changing (Burke 1999). The film cast young Noah Wyle and Anthony Michael Hall against one another, taking the stories of Apple and Microsoft's founding and shaping them into mythology. These real-world geek icons became part of the fabric of geek identity, helping to perpetuate the archetype of the geek: socially awkward, glasses-wearing white men—but now with the potential to emerge from their parents' basements and garages to craft the technologies of the future. Like the nerds in *Revenge of the Nerds*, these geeks were heralded as disrupting existing institutions, in this case of business and technology. The narrative of the undesirable, marginalized outsider was becoming the story of tomorrow's tech titans. This film was only one facet of the cultural force that these geeks would represent: other movies, such as *WarGames* (Badham 1983), *Hackers* (Softley 1995), and *Sneakers* (Robinson 1992), featured similar young white male geek heroes in fictional stories.

The web itself is filled with testaments to the formation of geek identity and culture during these early days. In 1994, a website called The Armory launched from a self-labeled "geek house" in Santa Cruz, California. The website was typical of the early web—minimalist in design and assuming a degree of technical interest and competence on the part of the user. The Armory is host to a number of purity tests, a concept that originated from written checklists to determine a person's lack of purity through yes or no questions. As of 2017, the site is still home to several of the first definitive purity tests placed on the web: the Nerd Purity Test and the Geek Purity Test (DuBois 1994). The two tests put into focus the categories of nerd and geek as imagined by the self-labeled group of test creators: while the nerd tests focus primarily on knowledge, the geek purity test consists of a hundred questions. Both tests reflect the contested territory of nerd-versus-geek as social labels, as debated heavily by the early web community. The first twenty-seven questions on the Geek Test are social and include:

- Do you not have a girl/boyfriend?
- Do you relate better to computers than to people?
- Do you like your computer more than life itself?
- Do you treat your computer better than your significant other? (The Armory 1994)

As a testament to geek stereotypes, these social questions remain revealing, suggesting that even if a geek defies odds and manages to have a relationship, that relationship will still be made difficult by the very nature of the geek's obsession and lack of social skills. *The Big Bang Theory*'s Sheldon Cooper acts as a living embodiment of most of the elements identified on this list. The second set of fifty-six questions are more technically focused, covering ownership of technology and knowledge of programming languages and including the memorable and highly gendered question "Is your computer's case size comparitive [*sic*] to your manhood (a phallic symbol)?" (The Armory 1994). The remaining 46 questions devolve further, suggesting that true geeks have poor personal hygiene and questionable public behavior:

- Do you change your sheets less than once a month?
- Do you adjust yourself in public?
- Do you piss all ove [*sic*] toilet seats in public places?

While the nature of purity tests involves progressing to extremes for humor, there's an earnestness to the set of questions and the very idea of the test as determinant. This collection of requirements still offers a glimpse into a common definition of geekdom, even twenty years later. The test ends with the reminder "The more yes answers you give, the more Geek you are. If you got 0%, then you too can work for UCSC" (The Armory 1994). A low Geek or Nerd test purity score (that is, a high level of geekdom or nerdiness based on the test standards) remains a marker of pride and used to be included on forum signatures and profiles. Likewise, Robert Hayden's "Geek Code" evolved as a way to recognize different types of geeks, with the last official version published in 1996, while the concept has lived on. Such tests suggest the quantifiable and shared identifiers that united geek culture with the rise of the Internet as a communal geek space, enabling feelings of exclusivity and power particularly as computers, and thus the tools of geeks, became more essential to everyone's life. The very existence of these tests and quantifiers suggest an anxiety of belonging and identity formation with very structured measures for inclusion and the promise from those on the other side of the computer screen that you are not alone. They also form the basis for an explicit ranking system by which members can measure their own centrality to the community and judge those less aligned.

Users of the Internet have thus been frequently associated with geek subculture despite the fact that everyone who participates in mainstream American culture is now living a life integrated with and by the web. From the early archetypes of the Internet user, a number of on-screen geek and nerd archetypes were born. Lauren Rosewarne (2016) surveys these exhaustively in her examination of media stereotypes of Internet users, suggesting the hierarchy of portrayals has splintered to include the Netgeek, Neckbeard, Cyberbully, Hacker, Cyberpredator, and Cyberperv, with the Netgeek typically portrayed as the most harmless of the lot. All of these stereotypes are associated with masculinity: as Rosewarne observes, "since its inception, the Internet has largely been thought of as male—dominated by men, shaped by men, *understood by men* [original emphasis]. Certainly, as illustrated via the high number of male netgeek characters, the Internet is still frequently presented on screen as gendered" (39).

In her study of masculinity among computer-using men during the era of geek codes and forums Lori Kendall (1999) noted how "nerds" on computer forums—themselves young and mostly white—worked to emphasize their own masculinity while distancing themselves from women and sexuality. Studies of geeks more recently have noted how little has changed: Éva Zékány's survey of the geek in cyberspace noted that across all definitions of "geekiness" masculinity remains a defining quality (Zékány and Cerwonka 2011). While the Geek Test described above made some efforts at gender inclusivity, the masculine-typed behaviors still dominated many of the questions. This is despite the apparent contradiction between geek-signifiers and the expressions identified with masculinity. If anything, computer-aided interactions seem to be an opportunity to perform the hypermasculine (particularly through aggression and violence) without possessing any of the associated physical qualities, as Erica Scharrer's (2004) analysis of gender and aggression in video game advertisements as of 2004 suggests: "male characters were often presented as very muscular … [and] the pursuit of danger as thrill was fairly common. Further, the number of male nonhuman characters in the ad was associated with violence, providing a link between masculinity and physical aggression." Scharrer's analysis suggested only some correspondence with other hypermasculine markers (such as callousness toward sex and the manliness of violence), but those themes find their expression in video games themselves.

This tension between the geek stereotype portrayed in the Geek Test and touted even in self-identified geek culture and the hypermasculine characters geeks embody through popular culture narratives is one site of cognitive dissonance in geek identity. Video game narratives offer heroic male avatars and passive women: Yi Mou and Wei Peng's (2008) examination of video game trailers noted that "female characters are predominantly supporting characters, who are either to be rescued or assistants to the leading male character … the attire and body image of the female characters are often very sexy … yet male characters are portrayed in a normal or masculinized way." This echoes trends in popular culture, particularly the science fiction and fantasy genres often associated with geekdom and included as part of the knowledge and identity sections on many geek and nerd tests. Likewise, pop culture holds recurring examples of the geek turned hero, often through either redefined masculinity or context. In *The Last Starfighter* (1984) a teenage white male arcade game virtuoso is picked up by a head-hunting alien to fight battles in space; in *Captain America: The First Avenger* (Johnston 2011) and *Spider-Man* (Raimi 2002) wimpy, geeky men are abruptly transformed into traditional icons of hypermasculine power. These characters perform the same type of heroism that gamers can embody through avatars like Duke Nukem and Commander Shepard (discussed in Chap. 4), adopting qualities rarely associated with the stereotypes of geekdom.

Playing at Hero

In most of these narratives, geeks either play or are encouraged to identify with the hero. Popular culture reinforces the connection between geeks and heroic icons, particularly superheroes. When Sheldon, Leonard, and the rest of the *Big Bang Theory* crew dress up for Hallowe'en, they don the costumes of the superheroes they worship in comics. Penny's presence in the group (portraying Wonder Woman) along with her current boyfriend (as Superman) aids them in winning a costume contest as the Justice League of America. The episode begins with the four geeks meeting Penny's boyfriend Zack and noting his lack of intelligence:

Zack:	No, I'm almost sure that it was the Discovery Channel. It was a great show. They also said dolphins might be smarter than people.
Leonard:	They might be smarter than some people.
Zack:	Well, maybe we can do an experiment to find out.
Sheldon:	Oh, that's easy enough. We'd need a large tank of water, a hoop to jump through, and a bucket of whatever bite-sized treats you find tasty.
Zack:	I don't get it.
Leonard:	A dolphin might.
Zack:	Oh, I see. You guys are inferring that I'm stupid.
Sheldon:	That's not correct. We were implying it. You then inferred it.
Zack:	Let's go.

Penny: You know, for a group of guys who claim they spent most of their lives being bullied, you can be real jerks. Shame on all of you.

The contrast between Zack and Sheldon suggests a strong dichotomy in hegemonic masculinity-versus-geek masculine stereotypes: Zack is athletic, successful with women, and dumb, while Sheldon is wimpy, socially incapable, and generally marked by his indifference to women. The binary leaves no room for friendship or overlap: Zack and Penny are of value to the group for their physical resemblance to Wonder Woman and Superman in winning the costume contest, but that is where the resemblance and connection ends. As Penny's comment declares, the bullied have become the bullies, secure in the inaccessibility of their references and discourse to an outsider with insufficient knowledge to participate. Sheldon and Leonard are almost gleeful in this display of superiority—a display not unlike those that take place online in forums and social media every day.

If this discussion of bullying and purity tests makes geek identity sound trapped in adolescence, that's only appropriate. It is no coincidence that many of the works dominating geek culture right now belong to the category of "Young Adult," which Patty Campbell (2010) has defined as being primarily concerned with "becoming an adult." The process of becoming an adult in American popular culture is associated with acts of rebellion, with defining oneself against and within society through group identity. The popular image of the geek is adolescent, or arrested adolescent, thanks in part to the assumption of a stunted maturity that accompanies a stronger relationship with a computer than with other people. The worlds of comics are continually rebooting, often with their own adolescent heroes experiencing their rise to manhood as with Peter Parker's lesson that "With great power comes great responsibility." This leaves comics caught in transitional struggles, but with no consequences or maturity waiting on the other side: even the most dramatic development can be rewritten, and characters rarely age to face the long-term outcomes of their decisions. Similarly, the geeks for whom these characters act as role models are left without a figurehead to help navigate the deeper waters of adulthood and its associated responsibilities. This can lead to taking the opposite moral from Spiderman's motto—"With no power comes no responsibility"—a slogan found on posters for Kevin Smith's movie about arrested geeks, *Clerks II* (2006). Lacking in any guidance, they seek out the only path of discovery they really know, rehashing the struggle for adulthood repeatedly instead of leaving it behind for a new type of personal growth. Many of the genres associated with geek culture (primarily, science fiction and fantasy) have been shut out of traditional definitions of literary value. Similarly, the mediums of geek culture include two that are often associated with adolescents and escapism: comic books and video games.

Academics and other gatekeepers of cultural legitimacy have been acknowledging the value of these mediums and genres more seriously with every passing decade. The serious study of comic books and games have become their own academic fields and disciplines. Yet the cultural legacy of the geek's outsider status remains. Works taken seriously as high art are often seen as "escaping" the boundaries or perceived faults of other works in their medium, and the consumers of the mass culture of geekdom (from *Dragonlance* to the latest Marvel reboot to the next *Call of Duty*) have often done so despite criticism of those works as trivial or juvenile. Protectiveness of these mediums thus comes with the territory of geekdom. When several of these mediums have been under attack (historically, as with the Comic Code, or more recently, as with attempts to regulate or censor violence in video games), geeks have been their defenders. Many of these works are mentioned in variants of geek tests and familiarity with core works of the geek canon is essential for entering into the referential discourse of the communities.

Indeed, the defense of geek culture might be as correlated to expressions of masculinity as any of Spiderman's heroics: the narratives within geek culture become the narratives geeks use to define their own heroism, sometimes with dangerous results for groups marginalized by those very narratives. The outsider status of these mediums has diminished significantly: *Angry Birds* (Rovio Entertainment 2009) and other casual games, powered by platforms like the iPhone, have helped to make digital gaming ubiquitous. Comic books themselves may still be primarily the domain of specialty shops, but Marvel's movies are mega-hits, and now those not dedicated to the Marvel continuity have embraced the phrase "I am Groot." Geeks used to the marginalization of their chosen media and fandoms have been given a choice: embrace the new popularity and surge of interest and production of these works, or defend the terrain from those less dedicated, who have never suffered from their geekdom. Many geeks have visibly chosen the latter, playing out a culture war over the turf of geek identity.

Identity Warfare

The construction of geek masculinity has often gone as unremarked as female geek identity has been policed and delineated. Geek identity is a battleground, its territories demarcated by borders both real and rhetorical.

Geek or nerd? Dork or dweeb? Gamer or n00b? (Naturally, purity tests and other clearly quantified surveys exist to determine allegiances.) For women within geekdom, the only available spaces are contested and marginalized: fake geek or fan girl? Sex object or feminist bitch? For women, there's often no answer that doesn't lead to further pigeonholing and silencing, and either extreme can be used as an insult or excuse for marginalization. The increased popularity of once-outsider genres, including comics and video games, has led many within these communities to an increased policing of the borders of their perceived identity spaces. Geekdom is at a crossroads. Once defined by their outsider status and victimization, geeks are now powerful enough as a subculture to make victims out of others, particularly those perceived as lacking the credential earned through suffering that makes one a "true" outsider geek.

Just as the move from bullied to bullies is at first a surprising trajectory for the geeks of *Big Bang Theory* when confronted with a classic hypermasculine jock, it may seem like a far leap from this association of male geek and heroism to the battles that have recently arisen in geek culture. In gaming, the rise of the Gamergate collective—a group dedicated to hunting down and silencing voices in gaming that they view as feminist or as "social justice warriors," often abbreviated SJW—has been masked as concern for the legitimacy of games journalism. In comics, what started as one artists' rant against cosplayers became the fuel for a movement of attacks on "fake geek girls," which in part drew attention to the harassment women already faced for being visible and sexually attractive but perceived as unavailable in comic convention spaces. This obsession with revealing some fans (particularly women) as "fake" comes from what Kristina Busse (2013) has observed as boundary policing within the hierarchies of geek culture: "geek hierarchies border police on two fronts, excluding both those not enough and those too much invested in the fannish object or practices." Such policing recalls the self-testing of The Armory and often takes the form of similar quizzes, issued as a challenge. Likewise, media with many geek hallmarks but an audience of women (such as the *Twilight* series) draws disproportionate attacks and hatred simply for existing and being visible. The rhetoric of all these movements (easily paralleled with outside but geek-correlated groups, such as the Men's Right Activists and anti-feminist segments of atheism) starts to blur together, often with the same message: women—and feminists in particular, an easily defined other to identify as representing the supposed influence of the mainstream—are out to destroy geek culture, and these groups of "true" geeks are ready to defend it.

Overview

As geeks have become more visible, popular culture has taken these geek identities and reflected them back in a consumable form fraught with tension between the hypermasculine and the feminine. Within the rest of these chapters, we will examine the gendered geek as a force in current media. We will primarily addressing geekdom through American culture, where the term "geek" is particularly visible: in other cultural contexts, terms like "nerd" remain popular or are used interchangeably. Thus we will also be focusing primarily on American-made media and relevant examples of other media widely consumed within the USA. We will contextualize both media born of franchises and properties aimed at geeks for consumption, primarily franchises such as *Sherlock*, *Doctor Who*, *Supernatural*, and *Avengers*, and media that offers geeks as objects of consumption to both geek and non-geek identifying viewers, including *The Big Bang Theory*, *Chuck*, and *Silicon Valley*. These themes and identities are woven across multiple media, from movies and television shows to comic books and video games, and we will consider a multitude of forms. Examining these media will allow us to address and understand a fundamental tension of geek culture: the hypermasculine avatar, as demonstrated through comic book heroes and playable characters, versus the decidedly un-masculine geek as character, defined by his scrawniness and lack of success with women. This seemingly harmless focus on wish-fulfillment as dictated by a heteronormative, cisgendered male fantasy has powerful implications for the accessibility not only of geek spaces to women and other marginalized identities but also to the accessibility of those fields characterized as "geek" dominated: computer science, physics, engineering, mathematics, and other "STEM" spaces. To return to *The Big Bang Theory*, this tension has been magnified by popular culture, with the result playing out across social media of not decreased but increased hostilities towards the feminine in geek spaces.

Throughout this book, we will be examining masculinity and hero tropes primarily, but will frequently address the visibility (and marginalization) of femininity and women characters. This is an essential part to establishing and revealing normative and toxic structures at work in geek media: representations of men are shaped and defined in relationship to women as other. Significantly, the mainstreaming of geek culture and the incredible popularity enjoyed now by formerly geek-associated media genres such as comics, science fiction, and fantasy is drawing attention to the unevenness of gender representations within these shows. Often, this criticism focuses on women characters, and thus a considerable portion of the existing discourse on gender and geek media is focused on women and femininity. This is an inevitable side effect of embracing masculine as default: its norms and representations go less interrogated, particularly in popular media discourse surrounding these properties.

To understand the evolution of geek identity as a battleground, we will begin at the top—with the aspirational figures of geek heroes. In Chap. 2, we will consider geek heroes: Doctor Who, Indiana Jones, Tony Stark, Sherlock, and other intellectual yet battle-ready men who embody both geek prowess and hypermasculine ideals. These heroes often have easily dismissed female counterparts, from Amy Pond and River Song to Pepper Potts and Black Widow, whose role in the narrative is defined by the relationship with the hero. We move from science fiction and fantasy to reality, or at least reality through the lens of television: shows including the previously mentioned *Big Bang Theory* and *Chuck* cast geek men as heroes in everyday life. In Chap. 2, we examine the way these aspirational narratives of popular culture use the same models of hero and damsel to fuel formulas of geeky, awkward geniuses surrounded by dumb blonde objects of lust.

In Chap. 4, we move from television and film into video games, which offer a glimpse of the heart of the contradiction at work in geek identity. The majority of video game avatars are male, and many embody the hypermasculine qualities under examination here. Characters such as Duke Nukem present hypermasculinity to the point of self-parody, inhabiting worlds where women are strippers awaiting rescue and all problems can be solved with violence. As we switch mediums once more to comic books in Chap. 5, we further deconstruct the male heroic power fantasy as dependent upon the death and abuse of women as heroic motivator.

After we've deconstructed the narratives of hypermasculinity within the geek cultural canon, we move into the fan culture and communities of geekdom that have formed around these works. In Chap. 6, we examine the concept of "white knighting," or men to the rescue. This concept has emerged in geek communities as a way to place the burden of rescue of marginalized communities on members of the dominant discourse (usually—and appropriately, given the name—straight white men), with the expectation of reward for their good deeds. The impact of white knighting is often greater silencing of marginalized voices, a trend we examine further in Chap. 7. Many geek series (such as *Star Trek*, *Supernatural*, and the BBC's *Sherlock*) invite queer readings and interpretations through the female gaze, but the producers and gatekeepers of geek culture often dismiss such readings even as they profit from the fandom they produce.

Taken in aggregate, these facets of the narrative of masculine versus feminine in geek canon and fandom suggest the impossibility of an integrated geek identity. A more recent version of a Geek Test, written by Yvette Beaudoin and last updated in 2011, is explicitly more gender inclusive (though still very binary in its assumptions) and includes as a final five-point question the statement "I am a female geek" (Beaudoin 2011). This weighting of points could be read in many ways, but perhaps is best understood as a badge for perseverance against the odds of embracing feminine and geek identifiers simultaneously. However, even this token inclusion of women as part of geek culture comes with too many qualifiers to resolve the conflicted relationship of geekdom and femininity. And as we dive further down the rabbit hole of the geek canon, this conflict can seem beyond resolution.

References

Anderegg, David. 2011. *Nerds: How dorks, dweebs, techies, and trekkies can save.* New York: Penguin.

Andreeva, Neelie. 2017. "The Big Bang Theory" renewed for seasons 11 & 12 by CBS. Deadline, March 20. Accessed April 12, 2017. http://deadline.com/2017/03/the-big-bang-theory-renewed-season-11-12-cbs-1202047021/.

Badham, John. 1983. *Wargames.* Beverly Hills, CA: MGM Studios. DVD.

Beaudoin, Yvette. 2011. *The geek test.* Accessed October 5, 2016. http://www.innergeek.us/geek-test.html.

Burke, Martyn. 1999. *The pirates of silicon valley.* Performed by Noah Wyle and Anthony Michael Hall.

Busse, Kristina. 2013. Geek hierarchies, boundary policing, and the gendering of the good fan. *Participations* 10, no. 1: 73–91. http://www.participations.org/Volume%2010/Issue%201/6%20Busse%2010.1.pdf.

Campbell, Patty. 2010. *Campbell's scoop: Reflections on young adult literature 38.* New York: Scarecrow Press.

Cendrowski, Mark. 2013. *The contractual obligation implementation,* 7. CBS, Mary: The Big Bang Theory.

DuBois, John. 1994. Purity tests. The Armory. Accessed February 4, 2017. http://www.armory.com/tests/.

Hayden, Robert. 1996. The geek code. Accessed November 12, 2016. http://www.geekcode.com/.

Hebdige, Dick. 1999. The function of subculture. In *The cultural studies reader,* ed. Simon During, 441–450. New York: Routledge.

Johnston, Joe. 2011. *Captain America: The First Avenger.* Los Angeles, CA: Paramount Pictures. Bluray.

Kanew, Jeff. 1984. *The revenge of the nerds*. Performed by Robert Carradine, Anthony Edwards, and Timothy Busfield.

Kendall, Lori. 1999. "The nerd within": Mass media and the negotation of identity among computer-using men. *The Journal of Men's Studies* 7, no. 3: 353–369. https://doi.org/10.3149/jms.0703.353.

Mou, Yi, and Wei Peng. 2008. Gender and racial stereotypies in popular video games. In *Handbook of research on effective electronic gaming in education*, ed. Richard Ferdig, 922–937. Hershey, PA: IGI Global.

Parrott, Dominic J. and Amos Zeichner. 2003. Effects of hypermasculinity on physical aggression against women. *Psychology of Men & Masculinity* 4, no. 1: 70. https://doi.org/10.1037//1524-9220.4.1.70.

Raimi, Sam. 2002. Spider-Man. Culver City, CA: Columbia Pictures. DVD.

Robinson, Phil Alden. 1992. *Sneakers*. Universal City, CA: Universal Pictures.

Rosewarne, Lauren. 2016. *Cyberbullies, cyberactivists, cyberpredators: Film, TV, and internet stereotypes*. Santa Barbara, CA: Praeger.

Rovio Entertainment. 2009. *Angry Birds*. Espoo, Finland. iOS.

Scanlon, Dan. 2013. *Monsters University*. Performed by Billy Crystal and John Goodman.

Scharrer, Erica. 2004. Virtual violence: Gender and aggression in video game advertisements. *Mass Communication & Society* 7, no. 4: 393–412. https://doi.org/10.1207/s15327825mcs0704_2.

Softley, Iain. 1995. *Hackers*. Beverly Hills, CA: MGM Studios. DVD.

The Armory. 1994. Geek purity test. The Armory. Accessed March 5, 2016. http://www.armory.com/tests/geek.html.

Zékány, Éva and Allaine Cerwonka. 2011. The gendered geek: Performing masculinities in cyberspace. Unpublished master's dissertation, Central European University.

2

"Dick in a Box": Hypermasculine Heroism in Geek TV and Film

A teenager accelerates the stolen car down a desert road, music blasting. We hear sirens and see the cops chasing him even as he speeds towards a cliff. As the car goes over, the young man—James Tiberius Kirk—jumps away from certain death and just makes it to the ledge.

This is the introduction of a classic alpha-male character in J.J. Abram's 2009 reboot of *Star Trek*, one of the two most iconic science fiction series in geek culture. Kirk is the perfect example of a geek-approved hero: an unknowable, all-knowing badass. As William Shatner's classic Captain Kirk says in the opening quote, his type of hero is powerful, able to cheat death, celebrate his victory, and reflect upon his own actions, and, occasionally, hubris. He's continuously successful in his pursuit of women, regardless of their planet of origin, and rarely has committed relationships or serious emotional entanglements. Captain James T. Kirk originated as the womanizing, occasionally rebellious leader on the original *Star Trek*, a show that Ferguson et al. (1997) note was credited with critiquing stereotypes, race and class while remaining entirely traditional in its depiction of gender: "the boundaries that separate racial and class identities, and sometimes species identities as well, were frequently de-neutralized. But conventional gender identity went unchallenged: men were men, and women were women … strength, reason and autonomy were reserved for males." While *Star Trek* has gone through many generations since then, some things remain constant, as the iconic machoism of the 2009 Kirk reminds us. By examining Kirk and his contemporaries, we can develop a compelling portrait of the geek hero and the nature of his masculinity.

© The Author(s) 2017
A. Salter and B. Blodgett, *Toxic Geek Masculinity in Media*,
DOI 10.1007/978-3-319-66077-6_2

Kirk's indestructibility in the face of death-defying scenarios is not unusual. Although many storylines put their heroes within rather perilous straits, the reader can rely upon the fact that they will make it out again alive, if a little bruised. They embody every desirable trait and their negative aspects are often shallow or easily mediated by the remaining cast. This means that the heroes are stronger, wiser, faster and altogether just better. Even their weaknesses can't hold them back and in many cases are the actual source of their strength. From Superman's well-known weakness to shards of his former planet to the Doctor's alien nature and intellect, geek heroes embody and define desirable masculine traits. They are above and beyond our current abilities, but with the superficial weaknesses they are made approachable, open to connection with normal humans. Many geek heroes have transcended their cult media roots to achieve mainstream recognition as cultural icons of masculinity and heroism, most notably Superman himself. Weltzien (2005) notes how Superman can convey epic male heroism through the mere act of removing his suit:

> the pose Superman is most famous for—establishing a kind of Superman iconography—shows him ripping off his shirt, revealing the triangular "S" on the hero suit, instead of a hairy chest that one would see were he not Superman. This is *the* icon of performing masculinity by the changing of dress.

It is no coincidence that Superman's "real" suit is usually found underneath the male power suit, suggesting the raw masculinity and heroism that waits below the crisp fixings of more bureaucratic and civilized power.

With their masculinity and heroism constantly on display, the most iconic of these heroes are humanized through juxtaposition with their compatriots. The audience cannot enter the hero's mind and truly understand how he works, but through the gaze of the supporting characters who know him we can sometimes get a perspective on his thoughts. Very often the hero within these stories is not the character the audience is meant to identify with: that role falls to the secondary, supporting cast. We can view the hero and stand in awe of his deeds and power alongside Rose Tyler, Deanna Troi or Commissioner Gordon, but we are never capable of seeing him beyond the idyllic glow that the secondary characters impart. The secondary cast is an important part of the story, providing a consumer stand-in for interacting with the hero and displaying the proper types of desires we should have when faced with him. Nowhere is this clearer than with Kirk and his crew, which includes his unemotional foil, the Vulcan Spock, with whom he shares a relationship so intense that Kirk/Spock fanfiction became quickly known as one of the definitive examples of a "slash" pairing.

The *Star Trek* universe is one of the most progressive in mainstream science fiction and thus may seem like an odd choice to introduce a discussion of stereotypical and over-the-top masculinity. Certainly, as the universe has expanded, the complexity of character portrayals has correspondingly risen. *Star Trek: Voyager* (1995–2001) has an interesting example of how the gendering of desires and traits are treated by science fiction. Although there are a number of interesting characters within the series, two have similar starting points for their emotional development over the course of the series: Lieutenant Commander Tuvok and Seven of Nine. Tuvok is a Vulcan and second officer of Voyager. He embodies many of the traits of the Vulcan species as laid out by earlier series and is extremely logical and non-emotional, arguing for the most rational course of action against the more hot-headed human members of the crew. Seven of Nine is a member of the Borg Collective that Voyager saved and helped to de-assimilate. Seven begins her time on the ship acting as a very Borg-like entity: mechanical, non-emotional, cold and logical. Despite different starting points, both characters have similar emotional ranges and interests at the beginning of their story arcs. However, during their development they begin to differ greatly. Tuvok goes through numerous experiences and interactions that support his desire for control of his emotions and reactions. Although he learns how to better connect to the more emotional human species, the fundamental aspects of his Vulcan nature are not challenged. When he experiences the challenge of the sudden onset of Pon farr, the Vulcan mating urge, the crew attempts to support his needs and help him overcome the "emotional difficulty" that he is experiencing (McNeill 2000). His inherent Vulcan nature is validated as being good.

Seven of Nine develops along a very contrasting character path. Although her life began as a human, she was assimilated into the Borg Collective at a young age and displays most of the mental traits of a cybernetic species. After her initial introduction, she is pushed very strongly by members of the crew, the Doctor and Captain Janeway in particular, to develop her more human traits. Her arc could be categorized as a "mulatta" narrative, which often serve to reinforce social hierarchies: "by showing women of mixed race who cannot find a place in society, mulatta narratives reify the importance of racial distinctions, even as the figure of the mulatta herself acknowledges the arbitrariness and social construction of race" (Roberts 2000). Of course, Seven of Nine is played by blonde actress/model Jeri Ryan, complicating the construction of her identity and the desirability of her as an object. During story arcs that focus on developing her character there is a strong thematic trait of teaching her how to accept emotions, softness and human frailty. In the latter seasons of the show, Seven is tasked with fostering a group of children rescued from the Borg and must develop her nurturing maternal instincts despite personally disliking the task and suggesting several times that there are crew members more fit for the duty. Unlike Tuvok, Seven's Borg nature is not validated by members of the crew. Her development requires that she take on my acceptable female traits and characteristics to grow as a person. Although some of this could be ascribed to Seven's original birth as a human, the character herself recognizes and identifies more as a member of the Borg, although an individual rather than collective. She knows her human birth name but decides to retain her Borg designation and will willingly identify herself as a Borg when interacting with characters who are not members of the Voyager crew. Due to the gendering of psychological traits, it is important that Seven be distanced from the more masculine emotions that the Borg typically display. While it is only natural that Tuvok, as a prime example of Vulcan masculinity, keep his logical, emotionless nature, Seven, as a woman and character offering a great deal of heteronormative sex appeal, must be distanced from it and taught to embrace the essentialist feminine nature.

To the audience, heroes are the central focus of the story and their interpersonal relationships are the engine that powers the story's action. The secondary cast is developed to highlight the uniqueness of the hero, motivate them to action and reflect upon their triumphs. In order to fill this role properly, the secondary cast is often more identifiable, with very human qualities meant to highlight the exceptionalism of the main character. They also do not often get development beyond their relationship with the main character or what is necessary to drive a particular story arc. The hero must be unknowable but relatable; women must be both desirable and available. So, in the end, we have shallow supporters who serve to provide the hero with relationships that show parts of their personality without the identification or knowledge that would be provided by a first-person viewpoint. Television and film are particularly prominent mediums for this type of hypermasculine hero, who we often associate with genre films such as the macho action movies of the 1980s. However, the more geek-oriented spaces of science fiction, fantasy and comic adaptations hold their own archetypes of this same machismo glorification at the expense of internal development and meaningful relationships, particularly with the women who at best hold secondary roles in the same franchises.

Hero-worship and aspirational hypermasculine role models abound in geek-friendly popular culture. This chapter will examine the construction of male heroism that dominates modern media tagged as geek-oriented, with attention to science fiction. We will expose the silence of women in these same franchises, as characters such as Amy Pond, River Song and Clara Oswald are defined by their relationships with the male main character and exist only to serve his story. Doctor Who, Indiana Jones, Tony Stark, Sherlock and other intellectual yet action-ready figures build on familiar archetypes while epitomizing the dominance of a masculine space to such an extent that fan blogger RoachPatrol (2014) labeled the Doctor as "a predatory dick in a box." This label, which evokes the sexual positioning of these characters, serves as a reminder that while geek heroes often forgo the traditional trappings of action movie masculinity, they still perform a cisgendered, heteronormative sexuality. From these heroes, we will draw a working definition of geek masculinity, with special attention to the outsider status they frequently display.

Defining Hypermasculinity

Within media broadly and science fiction specifically, there is often little range or depth in depictions of masculinity. The 1980s action hero comes to mind as a caricature of an ideal: Susan Jeffords suggests that Reagan is responsible for a particularly American masculinity on display in movies such as *Rambo* (Feitshans and Kotcheff 1982), *Lethal Weapon* (Donner and Silver 1987), and *Top Gun* (Simpson et al. 1986; Jeffords 1994). Although slight traits may vary, by looking at the shared characteristics between different stories and media it is possible to identify trends in defining what it means to be a man and how one acts out that role properly. This pattern of gendered behavior and presentation is threaded through many video games, comics, movies, and television. For those who consume these media, the presented models act as an identifying trait: to be like them is to be a man in an analogous way. Despite the fact that people do not unquestioningly follow the behavior they see within their media, the repeated lack of variation in geek manhood creates a stale cultural well from which people draw comparisons for themselves and their actions. Many people do identify areas of overlap or deviation between themselves and a character show. A favorite activity on social networking sites like Facebook include brief quizzes to "Find out which character of *The Big Bang Theory/Firefly/Star Trek* you are!" While the audience may not be mindless consumers of the mediated identities presented to them, there is a pattern of self-identification with at least specific aspects of the presented identities.

In many cases, the types of masculinity on display as acceptable for geeky men or on display within geeky media is reductionist in its handling of the complexity of identity. Although it has improved, the masculine ideal in much of science fiction has been defined as directly oppositional to the feminine. To be a male is to not be a female. This still leaves a large amount of variation of acceptable activities and interests, but they must be watch carefully to avoid areas of overlap between the groups. Although oppositional identities are not uncommon, they are often overly reductionist and restrictive in how behavior is labelled as acceptable or unacceptable. There needs to be a firm boundary between identities for them to continue in the oppositional format. If there is blurring or overlap between these boundaries it becomes almost impossible to plausibly define one identity from another. This form of constructing masculine identity as presented in geek media today is often labeled with the term hypermasculine.

Hypermasculinity has recently been drawn from the field of psychology by cultural scholars hoping to better understand the gender interactions within various social spheres. This term was originally coined to describe the exaggeration of masculine cultural stereotypes within subcultures (Parrot and Zeichner 2008). It can apply to an overemphasis upon masculine-gendered physical traits and/or behavioral patterns, particularly dismissal or hostility towards feminine displays (Mosher and Sirkin 1984; Mosher and Anderson 1986; Parrot and Zeichner 2003). Hypermasculinity and the systems which construct it rely upon clearly defined gender roles with strong opposing characteristics. For there to be a clear definition of masculinity, and personal execution thereof, the traits which identify male and female must be strictly defined and bounded. These traits become mutually exclusive and all encompassing. Since to be defined as a man under these roles means excluding every possible part of the feminine, little room for variation or alternative presentations of gender is available. Ambiguity is to be avoided at all costs since being unable to be clearly defined as either masculine or feminine breaks the system of traits.

Typically, analysis of hypermasculine characteristics can be broken into two general groupings. The first is the identification of masculine physical traits and acts. The second is behavioral, emotional, and thought patterns. Both groups are essentialist in their identification, relying upon concepts of innate manhood or masculine identity. Embodying these traits is displaying manhood while lacking them is a loss of manhood. For many heroes, this essentialist division plays out as an interesting tug of war between the needs of a story-driven media and the limitations of masculinity as depicted within that media, limiting the variation of characteristics that may be embodied by the cast while still allowing for a recognizable individuality.

A physical hypermasculine presentation focuses upon clearly identifying and emphasizing those traits that separate the cultural concept of man from woman. As the media feeds off from its own presentation these traits often become overemphasized to make the degree of masculinity held by a character stand out against the cultural background. This is particularly true for those that the story identifies as the hero or main character. They must be seen by the audience as being inherently more than the other men present within the story or those from other comparable stories. From simple visual standpoint, this concentration of traits can often be exaggerated to the point of parody, as in the overly muscled bodies drawn by well-known comic artists such as Rob Liefeld (Fig. 2.1).

Those physical traits identified as belonging to men are played up to make the character seem superhuman. They are taller, stronger, more powerfully muscled, lacking in softness or curves, and just physically larger than those around them. But in a media, like comics, where superhuman physiques are rather common, this can be taken to the extreme. From the bulging of muscles, some of which don't exist, to the squareness of the jawline, to the relative size of the chest and shoulders, Liefeld's Captain America has all the individual pieces of a unique specimen of manhood, but much like Dr. Frankenstein's creation their assembled whole is monstrous. Captain America has possessed some of these traits since his origin comics in the 1940s: as Jason Dittmer (2009) notes in his analysis of the first issues of *Captain America*,

> The degree to which his chiseled masculinity permeates the comic book cannot be overstated. Women of all walks of life (at least, of all those portrayed in the comic book—white, generally middle to upper class) find him attractive, including actresses and female secret agents. Captain America's physicality imbues his representation of the nation as a particularly masculine one.

But in this more modern image, he has been pushed so far into the extreme that he isn't entirely recognizable as human. Although this picture is often used to mock the abilities of the artist, it does represent an idea of what the physicality of manhood should be, if only in the most extreme conclusion. There is no feasible way that this figure could be confused with that of a woman.

Fig. 2.1 Cover of *Captain America* Vol 2#6 (Leifeld 1997). Cover Image: Marvel Comics

Yet this physical extremism is only one form of hypermasculine identity performance, and it is in fact the subtler aspects of hypermasculine construction that are strong forces in geek culture. We will examine how psychic hypermasculine ideals are also used heavily within the world of geek media, although they are sometimes more difficult to pinpoint since they aren't often as visually recognizable. For these, manhood is an emotionless state. The best men are cold, calculating, and highly logical, as with Kirk's foil Spock. They rarely let moods get the better of them and if they engage in any emotional display they should be angry, occasionally brooding. The blogger Jen Dziura (2012) observes the effect this type of portrayal has on popular culture expectations, as the emotional range that men are often allowed to engage in is often very limited as the expression of feelings gets typed as feminine. This requires parsing and limiting what becomes defined as emotion or emotional in a way that excludes those states often experienced and outwardly projected by men, as Dziura parodies:

> This is incorrect. Anger? EMOTION. Hate? EMOTION. Resorting to violence? EMOTIONAL OUTBURST. An irrational need to be correct when all the evidence is against you? Pretty sure that's an emotion. Resorting to shouting really loudly when you don't like the other person's point of view? That's called 'being too emotional to engage in a rational discussion. (ibid.)

Due to the construction of masculinity, these items cannot be emotions and more so are desirable traits. For heroes like Spock, Sherlock Holmes, Mal Reynolds, and the Doctor, their inability to give into the weakness of emotions is what makes them great. It often is the key item that allows them to defeat the villain of the week or story arc. And when they must make some display of emotion it typically falls within narrow boundaries and can be "rationally derived" as the only acceptable consequence of what it is happening around them. Although the media presentation of hypermasculine ideals is obvious and often seen as being over the top, this cyclic strengthening makes hiding the less obvious and distorted presentations easier and less likely to receive active examination or criticism. Engagement in media that portrays this extreme type of hypermasculine action has often been linked to a form of expectation shifting (Scharrer 2004; Cohn and Zeichner 2006). It is seen that these stimuli and their implications affect individuals well beyond the period to which they are exposed, setting a higher "baseline" for response in general (Reidy et al. 2009). In general, this connection between player and presentation is seen as desirable. As Anjun Anhuit (2014) says,

> Performing masculinity requires the rejection of the socially accepted opposite: femininity. If we accept the observation that mainstream games are devices for male gamers to perform masculinity, then they need to be devoid of emotions (except anger maybe), they need to be sexist, they need to be

misogynist, they need to be transphobic and homophobic ... and the individual gamer needs to be those things as well.

Geek media can often reinforce hypermasculine stereotypes, despite the continued tension of geek "masculinity" as defined in opposition to athletic masculine norms (Dill and Thill 2007; Taylor 2012). The appearance of characters, their actions, and their perceived role within the media's society have all been addressed as problematic areas in the development of players' masculine identities (Kirkland 2009; Yao et al. 2010). Duke Nukem, a classical figure within the history of gaming, represents this problematic approach to framing masculinity as well as the issues that occur when this type of masculine character is shown as being the player's default character and point of view.

Hypermasculine underpinning within the media positions women into background roles in a man's heroic quest. They exist to admire and define the degree of the main hero's masculinity and act as the reward for the hero's actions, either as a damsel to be rescued or simply an admiring audience for the hero's actions. This subconscious narrative of establishing male geeks as the heroes of their own community requires the establishment of villains and sets up the community's shared ego to be vulnerable. Not only must women and feminine presentations be rejected as a potential hero or member of geekdom, but so must any ambiguous presentation, even in otherwise very masculine characters. In this community, the simple acknowledgement of any non-conforming individual is a direct attack upon all of geek culture, setting up a battlefield upon which "no retreat, no surrender" is the default. Although all feminine-coded items are rejected within a hypermasculine culture, those that transgress traditionally proscribed gender roles often elicit the highest levels of aggressive response (Parrott and Zeichner 2008).

This focus on hypermasculinity has several negative outcomes for the formation of a modern subculture that fosters healthy mental standards for its members. Although women are often the targets of abuse in these subcultures, the men that emulate or surround themselves with these messages also suffer from the impossible standards and inherent emotional disconnect that they foster. Studies of subcultures particularly grounded in masculine ideals taken to these extremes tend to demonstrate certain characteristics:

> Masculine subcultures with high rates of group rape share a core set of social norms, values, and practices. According to O'Sullivan (1998), these include: (a) women being viewed as a threatening "other"; (b) heterosexual sex without intimacy (men who are tender with women are ridiculed as "pussy-whipped");

(c) pervasive homophobia; (d) a sense of entitlement due to their group prestige; (e) cooperation combined with competition, especially competition to perform risky acts; (f) cultural practices of misogyny, such as songs and jokes glorifying sexual violence; (g) sharing of sexuality, for example through mandatory reporting of sexual experiences and through voyeuring, or watching each other have sex; and (h) hazing as a common practice. (Franklin 2004)

We will further explore some of these consequences as demonstrated in geek culture: however, we can also understand these hypermasculine subcultures as on display within geek-targeted works and genres themselves. Geek heroes often construct certain subcultures, or social communities, around themselves. These are demonstrated through the relationships between heroes and the secondary cast. Some of the most obvious consequences can be seen in the idealizing of sex without intimacy (as in Kirk's many conquests) and in continual practices of misogyny and the isolation of women as other from social "in-groups" in geek spaces. We will examine the expression of these types of heroism through several shows currently dominating geek fandom, and we will revisit the theme of this type of hero throughout this book as we address hypermasculinity more broadly as a transmedia phenomenon.

Modern Manhood: Celebrating the Hypermasculine

> Now my Doctor, I've seen whole armies turn and run away. And he'd just swagger off back to his Tardis and open the doors with a snap of his fingers. The Doctor in the Tardis. Next stop, everywhere. —River Song (Lyn 2008)

The Doctor, titular protagonist of the long-running sci-fi show *Doctor Who*, is both a literal and figurative alien. He represents an advanced race called the Time Lords, who have mastery over the flow of time and events within history due to their technology and culture. While the Doctor has a fascination with the human race, he often comes across as being distinctly separate from humanity. One of the unique features of the Doctor's species is an ability to regenerate after taking lethal physical damage. This regeneration imbues the Doctor with a new physical form, set of habits, expressions, and interests. The new Doctor also takes a new set of human companions who will accompany him on his travels through space and time. The companions are always presented in a way to offset the characteristics of the Doctor in some way. If the Doctor is older and world weary, they represent youth and hope for the future. If the Doctor is silly and avoidant of real consequences, they serve to ground him and make him see his actions through to the end. Throughout much of science fiction this cast configuration is repeated. The male hero is surrounded by those who serve to balance them while still supporting their heroic aspects of character. Rose Tyler serves in this humanizing role quite well within the series. As Rose and The Doctor grow close, a love blossoms between them, which serves to strongly show the characteristics of the Doctor as an alien and a hero. Throughout the course of their relationship Rose serves to cause the Doctor to feel new emotions, from the awe of her ability to absorb the core of the TARDIS to the sorrow at her limited lifespan:

The Doctor: I don't age. I regenerate. But humans decay; you wither and you die. Imagine watching that happen to someone that you—[breaks off]
Rose: What, Doctor?
The Doctor: You can spend the rest of your life with me, but I can't spend the rest of mine with you. I have to live on. Alone. That's the curse of the Time Lords. (Hawes 2006)

No human's longevity can match the average Time Lord's lifespan and we do not have the technology to experience the universe in the same way that they do. But through the Doctor's interactions with his human companions and loves, we can feel a connection to that kind of life that allows for the audience to bond with the story and characters. We can hope to find a Doctor for ourselves that will elevate our lives out of the ordinary and humdrum.

This style of character development fits closely with the cycle of the hero outlined in *The Hero with a Thousand Faces* by Joseph Campbell (1949). The hero's journey is a solitary one by necessity. Although they encounter many during their progress, few stay with them throughout the full venture. They arrive within the story when the hero needs to grow, advance, or be challenged, and they leave when the hero no longer needs that source of development. One of the key points Campbell raises is that the hero always returns to their starting point, changed, unable to slip back into the life they had before. For characters like the Doctor, that life literally belongs to someone else. It helps as a way of perpetuating the drama of the story by allowing this cycle to continue in perpetuity. By changing who the Doctor is, we change how he needs to develop and can successfully send him out on another hero's journey at the start of each regeneration.

Doctor Who is one of the longest-running science fiction shows of all time, and it plays a vital role in British culture as a children's show. However, its influence is much broader than that, particularly thanks to its revitalization in 2005 by the BBC with showrunner Russel T. Davies. The rebooted show owes much to the transition of fans to authors: as Matt Hills (2010) notes, in *Doctor Who*, "fandom is not just an audience identity: *Doctor Who*'s fans have officially taken over the running of the show." As the original show aired between 1963 and 1989, it is unsurprising that the new show skews to an older audience that demographically correlates with showrunners and fans who grew up during and after that era. Correspondingly, the Doctor himself has changed and become a more directly hypermasculine and aggressive figure. Within more recent seasons, the character of the Doctor has taken on a more sinister aspect. Although still largely presented within any episode as a jovial, goofy, or harmless person, the lore of the Doctor presented by villains or supporting cast is that of an all-powerful, vengeful demon. Even to the Doctor's main love interest, River Song, acknowledges his stance within the larger galactic community in this section's opening quote. The Doctor projects this power through his interactions with others, and that is really set up as being part of what is attractive about him, the danger. Although the Doctor doesn't engage in violence within the view of the camera there are many stories shared by secondary cast where he decimates his enemies. This view of the Doctor aligns closely with the classic presentation of the hero within modern media. The stories about the Doctor shared within the individual episodes sound more akin to Rambo's blood rage than a congenial British chap.

The companions in many geek media also serve to highlight the unique nature of the hero. Through building his story, they underline the aspects of the hero that simply do not fit with normal human life. Lando Calrissian has many similar qualities to Han Solo, but his responsibilities keep him from filling the same hero status as Solo (Kershner 1980). He must contend with the requirements of running a city during wartime and having to put the needs of many people above his own desires. Lando's choice to betray the crew of the Millennium Falcon for rather utilitarian reasons shows off Han Solo and Luke Skywalker's more heroic qualities. Because they are the heroes of the story line they are not tied down by the regular connections and obligations and can make their decisions based upon what they feel is best instead of being forced to assess the tradeoffs of living in a complex world. Similarly, the connection between the Doctor and Rose and the human qualities this exposes makes many of the Doctor's decisions stand out as harsher and more alien to the human mindset. Because we can see that he is a caring individual who has both shame and pride in his race and a long history of interaction with others in the universe, the Doctor's choices can come across as more monstrous. From actively capturing and sealing away his entire civilization to allowing Amy Pond to be captured and experimented with during a season, we can see the alien thought patterns and behaviors that simply do not align with the more human characteristics that he displays. With the controversial 2017 casting announcement placing a woman in the shoes of the Doctor, it is possible these patterns will change as new gendered expectations are brought to the role.

Beyond a stunted emotional range, hypermasculine identification of characters also limits the interests that are acceptable for men in the media. Within the cult classic *Firefly* (2002–2003), three of the male leads are good examples of how variety in interests is capped. Jayne displays the most stereotypically masculine interests, liking guns, booze, and looking at women. Mal is focused on fighting, his pride and honor, and being the hero or leader of those around him. Simon is interested in medicine, displaying his intelligence, and acting as a protector for his sister. All three characters' interests are embodied in the gendered expectations of what men are naturally drawn towards. Beyond a strong focus on heterosexual desire among the male members of the cast, each is seen as being unable to separate their interests from their inherent identification as men. Mal can't help but pick a fight about the Brown Coats in a bar because that's just who he is as a man (Whedon 2002). Simon can't help but squash others intellectual inputs in a conversation because to know more than others is important to his manhood. Jayne is Jayne, because, really, it's Jayne. The potential exceptions to this are Shepard Book, a peaceful religious preacher who in the early series is more focused on keeping the other characters from coming to blows than typically masculine pastimes, and Hoban 'Wash' Washburne, the pilot and husband of First Officer Zoe. Shepard Book is portrayed as seeming to embody more feminized traits and interests at the series start, but as the story of the show is developed his background shows a history of gendered actions and violence which would make even Jayne feel proud. Even at the end of the series, Book represents a natural leader and hero, fighting off invading forces at his commune and managing to survive long enough to give the crew of the Serenity vital information. Shepherd Book embodies the toughness, wisdom, and vitality of an ideal man. Wash, on the other hand, loves to fly, still plays with toys, and adores his wife. Overall, he is presented as an amazing pilot, but his character is developed entirely in relation to his marriage. He demonstrates the value of a devoted man, but is often shown as being weaker and lesser psychologically than the unattached male cast members. Much like Book, Wash's moment of masculine triumph, successfully pulling off a very dangerous and technical landing, occurs directly before his death (Whedon 2005). Wash manages to get the rest of the crew to relative safety at the expense of his life. Both deaths are emotional moments within the series and serve to drive the remaining cast forward, motivating them towards the final conflict with stronger convictions because of the sacrifices. While these presentations add interesting diversity to the masculinities of the cast, it is very apparent that they also receive the harshest punishments. The deviations of Wash and Book from the traditional masculinities needs to be dealt with harshly by ultimately ending the characters for plot devices that drive the development of the more traditionally masculine members of the crew.

In *Firefly*, the women central characters are offered some freedom and feminine spheres are critiqued, but Christine Rowley (2007) notes that:

> the utopian and dystopian representations of gender relations in F/S [Firefly/ Serenity] focus on changes in and to feminine identities, leaving masculinities unchallenged … likewise, the concept of the (female) companion may be radically different from contemporary western society's representation of sex work, but there are no unfamiliar masculinities in S/F that function in a similarly critical way.

This is a recurring problem of imagination in science fiction, particularly those mainstream works that dominate television airwaves: dystopias tend to echo, rather than test or challenge, the boundaries of gender representation.

Hypermasculinity and the Cultured Noble

Amy Pond: 'I thought … well, I started to think you were just a madman with a box.'
The Doctor: 'Amy Pond, there's something you better understand about me,'cause it's important and one day your life may depend on it. [he smiles] I am definitely a madman with a box.' (Smith 2010)

Throughout modern media's history there has been a dichotomy portrayed between the different masculinities that occur within our culture. Although the most oppositional portrayal of these diverse types is represented within artifacts aimed at the tweens, teens, and young adult age groups, the general identification can be made in media of all types, targeted at all age groups. This dichotomy is often identified within geek media as the jocks vs. nerds.

The jocks are portrayed as filling all the required boxes of the masculine identity. They are handsome, good with women, and physically talented. Within media presentations, this often comes alongside increased social standing and general popularity and respect. Even when aimed at children, the jock identity is a natural born leader of men, the type of person who just naturally arises in a crisis to take control of the situation and lead their team to success. This is often portrayed, even in geek media, as being the better masculinity. It best fills the roles of men as they are defined by modern culture and is held up as being the type of masculinity that all men must strive for within their lives. Failure—if one member fails to conform properly—is held as an unacceptable weakness or emasculation that should be purged by the community.

This forced conformation is often focused upon the other major masculinity presented: the geek or beta male. Much like femininity is defined oppositional to masculinity, the beta male is defined oppositional to the alpha masculinity. The geek is physically weak, typically unattractive or unconventionally attractive, extremely intelligent, and socially poor or awkward. The mythos of the geek male is established to make that identity fulfill an outsider status. While general society rewards the alpha male for his innate abilities, it punishes the geek for not living up to those same standards. Persecution is a key part of the formation of this cultural definition. To be a beta is to have suffered throughout for not being man enough. Women will reject betas and find them unattractive, or simply use them for their few assets. Because they lack the social skills to network and stand up for themselves, they often fill low power positions or roles that will help to reinforce this mentality.

When seen from within a geek-oriented viewpoint, these struggles are what adds value to the geek identity. To have suffered is to understand what it means to not fit it. Interestingly, geek media often follow the standard story arc of a revenge fantasy. The plot of the movie *Office Space* is that of several nerds getting revenge on those they feel have taken advantage or otherwise used them through their superior technical knowledge. One of the most nerd-typical, Milton (shown in Fig. 2.2), illustrates every stereotype from pocket protector to poor social skills (Judge 1999). Usually, these stories show the geek as being a critical although often overlooked member of their organization. They are the ones who are smart enough to make everything work, but the rewards go to others who better embody the traits that society values.

The characters in *Office Space* might seem like an odd choice for an argument on hypermasculinity as the principal heroes of the film are physically

Fig. 2.2 Milton Waddams in *Office Space* (Judge 1999). Screen capture, 20th Century Fox

unintimidating, put-upon, and in many ways appear to be losers at the game of life (Judge 1999). However, they do demonstrate several of the characteristics we see in masculine subcultures, and by the "geek" hypermasculinity yardstick of intelligence they are (in their own perception at least) privileged. The three heroes of the film form—Peter, Michael, and Samir—form their own exclusively male inner circle with their boss as an enemy. When Peter's girlfriend is found to have previously had a relationship with said boss, social shunning erupts, as Peter accuses her: "He represents all that is soulless and wrong! And you slept with him!" (ibid.). Likewise, discussions of sex and its availability factor heavily in their decision to conspire against their company:

Peter Gibbons: [discussing the possibility of going to prison] This isn't Riyadh. You know they're not gonna saw your hands off here, alright? The worst they would ever do is they would put you for a couple of months into a white-collar, minimum-security resort! Shit, we should be so lucky! Do you know, they have conjugal visits there?
Samir: Really?
Peter Gibbons: Yes.
Michael Bolton: Shit. I'm a free man and I haven't had a conjugal visit in six months. (Judge 1999)

According to Hunter (2003), the *Office Space* approach to masculinity is particularly, dangerously, relatable: "the depictions of masculinity in 1990s office movies were possibly even more 'dangerous' (that is to say, dependent on characteristics like aggression, physicality, competition, dominance over women, and so on) than those of the Reagan-era action films because they invite so much comparison with the elements of 'real life.'" This lends a credibility to the call-to-action delivered by Office Space's "hero," Peter: "It's not just about me and my dream of doing nothing. It's about all of us together" (Judge 1999). Hunter (2003) points out that, given the absence of women in the movie, "all of us together" might as well read "all of us men together," as "Peter not only determines specific causes of the crisis of masculinity[;] he encourages all of the men together to make a change before it's too late." The plight of white middle-aged masculinity thus becomes a rallying cry for change, a position statement not unlike that you might encounter in a Men's Rights Activist Subreddit.

In fact, it is this focus on being intelligent and knowledgeable that often serves as comfort to the geek male when he feels like an outsider to the cultural identities of masculinity. Although geek males do not represent the alpha-male version, they have an extreme intelligence that is valuable as an asset and tool to both society and the geek himself (Chamberlin 2012). Those who find themselves on the wrong side of this intelligence will be forced to deal with the consequences of their poor decisions once the real value of manhood is better understood.

> Last week I left a note on Laura's desk
> It said I love you, signed, anonymous friend
> Turns out she's smarter than I thought she was
> She knows I wrote it, now the whole class does too
> And I'm all alone during couple skate
> When she skates by with some guy on her arm
> But I know that I'll forget the look of pity in her face
> When I'm living in my solar dome on a platform in space

As Jonathan Coulton's (2008) song showcases, what the beta masculinity yearns for within these revenge fantasies is not the removal of an unbalanced social system that benefits one type of masculinity, but simply the inversion of the system to support their form of masculinity. This fantasy leaves the cultural norm of unequal power in place but changes the form of masculinity that benefits from high societal standing. Within this power structure, the perceived rewards and placement of everyone outside of the traditional masculinities remains the same, not truly creating a fairer world but only making minor adjustments to the inequality of the current one.

The power structure defined within geek revenge fantasies is reminiscent of times before modern media. The worship of the intellectual aloof and the disdain for the physical engagement mirrors the traits valued within Western aristocracy up until the early twentieth century. Within this role, the geek and jock are now new masculinities manufactured by modern media, but simply inverted rebranding of older social roles. The dominance of the geek-aligned masculinity can be seen within the media of the nobility during the Enlightenment and Victorian eras. To be a man of value was to have the time to pursue higher intellectual goals and to be deeply grounded within a number of subjects. The noble could see things from afar and understand their implications given their superior intellect and social standing. They were not involved in the everyday politics of survival, but had the ability to engage in the larger topics of governance, philosophy, and science because of the social standing their wealth afforded them.

Alpha masculinity, accordingly, was devalued within this system. To be physically strong was to be a laborer. Someone whose talents were best suited to the factory or the field had not time or inclination for intellectual pursuits. These were men who were too involved in living their day-to-day lives to provide a valuable contribution to their society. This was a boon due to their inability to reach the proper emotional distance that was needed to govern or pursue knowledge. Often, being relegated to the role of laborer was seen as being beneficial to these men, because it kept them from getting too involved with their uncontrollable urges and baser natures. They may be physically gifted, but they were given to violence, anger, aggression, and if not distracted would cause problems through interfering too much in matters above their heads.

> Basically, the whole "geeks versus jocks" thing that gets drilled into us by media and the educational system isn't about degrees of masculinity at all. It's just two different flavours of the same toxic bullshit: the ideal geek is the alpha-male-as-philosopher-king, as opposed to the ideal jock's alpha-male-as-warrior-king. It's still a big dick-measuring contest—we're just using different rulers. (Prokopetz 2015)

Although modern media has inverted the powers within the system, both identities are based upon a test for dominance in which men are placed at the top of the hierarchy and vie for control and power. The hypermasculine definition of manhood is not challenged within a geek identity but simply redefined to be focused on slightly different traits. It is still seen as being oppositional to femininity, but instead of physical strength and weakness the distinction is based upon intellectual ability. The geek hypermasculine ideal is found in Batman, not Superman: while physical prowess is still lauded and demonstrated, intellectual achievement, technical mastery, and other skills are perhaps even more important. Prokopetz's admittedly crude suggestion that intellect and insider knowledge is the "ruler" for measuring this type of masculinity plays out clearly in many geek cultural contexts.

Within several episodes of *The Big Bang Theory*, Sheldon and Amy's intellectual identities are pitted against one another. Sheldon brings with him the mental baggage of the geek masculine mentality and often ridicules the challenge, quality, and value of Amy's work within neurobiology. Although Sheldon isn't often successful in these challenges, he doesn't seem to be able to learn from them either. He is wedded to the idea that to be a valuable geek man is to be smarter and engaged in more difficult intellectual work than those around him. To admit that Amy's work is more valuable or simply as valuable as his own is threatening to his identity. This hierarchy of knowledge being the arbiter of value is seen throughout the show and the relationships between the main characters, with Sheldon and Leonard being the main males, Howard being constantly criticized for his lack of doctorate-level degree, and Raj for his disinterest in really applying his intellect and display of more feminine interests in his social life and romantic partners.

When the typical hierarchies of athleticism or physical prowess are replaced with these intellectual and social measures, what results can become the gatekeeping mechanisms of a culture. We will address these consequences more directly in Chap. 3 when we look at comic books and the identification of the "fake geek girl."

In the long view, the different forms of masculinity represented with modern geek media are still as restrictive and built upon harmful hierarchies of power as the traditional hypermasculine definition. The application of hypermasculinity to geek media is as important as its application to traditional media. Geeks fall into a unique area where they are actively being sold two definitions of manhood: the traditional definition of the hypermasculine, physically oriented leader and the alternative inverse of the intellectual, distanced noble (O'Malley 2013). While individual consumers are often acknowledged within geek-centric media to be lacking in physical definition, they are still marketed many products that allow them to embody that experience. As game designer and blogger Anjin Anhut (2014) says:

> Mainstream game developers/publishers capitalize on that desire for status and foster an environment through marketing that has performing cis straight male as the top of the social hierarchy. They encourage social anxiety around

that ranking system and provide the remedy for that anxiety by creating most of their content in a way that is all about performing masculinity, from the way protagonists are designed, the heavy emphasis on combat gameplay and conquest, to the rejection of anything feminine.

By extending the definition of hypermasculinity to include these non-physical traits that support the existing harmful hierarchies of power it becomes possible to really examine how the relationships between men and women within geek media are defined according to deeply gendered beliefs despite existing as a response to traditional masculinity.

The Geek Hero and His Band of Admirers

Pepper Potts: Am I gonna be okay?
Tony Stark: No, you're in a relationship with me, everything will never be okay. But I think I can figure this out, yeah. I almost had this twenty years ago when I was drunk. I think I can get you better. That's what I do, I fix stuff.
Pepper Potts: And all your distractions?
Tony Stark: Uh … I'm gonna shave them down a little bit. (Black 2013)

Tony Stark's relationship to the other Avengers and his main romantic partner, Pepper Potts, is a prime example of how the modern geek hero is both larger than life and incapable of acting as a normal person. The very interests and abilities that make them ideal candidates for admiration is what must necessarily distance them from anyone who could get too close. Tony wouldn't be Tony Stark, let alone Iron Man, without his all-consuming fascination with technology and drive to understand how things work. If he didn't lose himself in this desire to tinker and understand, he would not have been as successful as he was in the creation of his inventions. And if he hadn't been the brilliant, distracted, sometimes sweet person this allowed him to become, he probably would not have been successful in his wooing of Pepper Potts. The support characters within the Iron Man series of movies serve to humanize Stark, who left to his own often comes across as hostile or megalomaniacal. The obvious love and tolerance shown by Pepper and Rhodes, Tony's two main friends and supporters, as well as their interactions show that there is more to Tony than his money and genius. Beyond helping to advance the storyline at a few critical points, these characters are the humanizing forces within the plot line. They draw Tony out of his distant shell, make him express his approachable human emotions and allow the audience as viewers to connect to his motivations and actions as a reasonable extension their own. Very few people have the technological genius that Stark displays, but many can empathize with having a friend or family member who is just a little bit out of touch or out of control. We can easily see ourselves within the role of the secondary characters, doing our best to make sure that those we love are safe and happy, even while we dream about being the hero himself.

Our main quality for defining heroes within geek media is elusive: they must somehow be larger than life. They are more intelligent, faster, bigger, stronger than your average person. Even when they experience troubles or anxieties, they are somehow more. Stark's drinking issues and womanizing seem more interesting than their real-life counterparts. Steve Roger's issues fitting into a new century is well beyond our capabilities to grasp, even if we have struggled with surviving in a foreign culture. Because the hero must stand out from the average person to be an aspirational figure to the audience, he must be pushed towards the extremes. While we live in a culture saturated with hypermasculine traits and advertisements, many people do not have strong personal connections to these types of identities. After all, if they did, an extreme would not be extreme. But this does pose a difficult problem for the creation of media that rely upon this viewpoint. If the main character must be so far beyond everyday experience, how can the audience connect with him and care about the story being presented? Within our capitalist culture, this connection is vitally important. It allows not only for the presentation of a story, but for the creation of a mythos and marketing platform. If I as a consumer do not feel a connection to the main hero of a story, I will not be likely to seek out the media that story is in, nor will I purchase related media or platforms that build upon that story's characters and plot.

The construction of Stark's suit as a weapon that projects a masculine identity is essential to this discourse. Without it, the difference in muscular strength between Steve Rogers and Tony Stark is noticeable: with it, the suit is constructed in a way that is suggestive of some physical strength. However, it is very different from the suits it spawns: in the first *Iron Man* movie (Favreau 2008), Stark's rival Obadiah Stone builds his own suit, one far more massive and traditionally intimidating, while Iron Man's sometimes ally Rhodes dons a noticeably bulky and muscular War Machine suit in *Iron Man 2* (Favreau 2010). The first *Iron Man* also establishes Potts' reluctance in the role of superhero comic girlfriend. As Tony Starks suggests when propositioning her to fill the role, "If I were Iron Man, I'd have this girlfriend who knew my true identity. She'd be a wreck. She'd always be worrying I was going to die, yet so proud of the man I've become. She'd be wildly conflicted, which would only make her more crazy about me" (2008). These sequences (along with Stark's playboy credentials, which are established when a reporter asks if he went 12 for 12 with this year's Maxim models), cement Stark as a perfect wedding of geek intellectual credibility with hypermasculine sexual prowess, attitude, and skills.

In a memorable moment of *The Avengers*, Tony Stark is confronted by the more traditionally masculine Captain America, who aggressively suggests that Stark is nothing without his technology: "Big man in a suit of armor. Take that off, what are you?" Undaunted, Tony Stark replies: "Genius. Billionaire. Playboy. Philanthropist" (Whedon 2012). Notably, his self-descriptor starts with the measuring stick of geek masculinity—his intellect—then proceeds through more traditional masculine traits, including wealth and prowess with women, before unexpectedly ending with social generosity. Captain America continues to hold Stark to a more traditional hypermasculine standard and finds Stark lacking: "I know guys with none of that worth ten of you. I've seen the footage. The only thing you really fight for is yourself. You're not the guy to make the sacrifice play, to lay down on a wire and let the other guy crawl over you" (ibid.). Tony Stark's reply is a perfectly calculated testament to geek masculinity: "I think I would just cut the wire" (ibid.). The tension on screen between these two characters takes Steve Roger's traditional military masculinity and puts it in contrast with Tony Stark's "brain-over-brawn" approach to the world, a mindset that would make the scientist behind Captain America's transformation more of a hero than the man himself. As Stark puts it, "Everything special about you came out of a bottle." Predictably, Steve Rogers retaliates by suggesting violence, telling Stark: "Put on the suit. Let's go a few rounds" (ibid.).

Stark's manliness is confirmed later in the movie when he goes alone to confront Loki with a warning. His robots remove his armor as he enters, buying time before he can launch his next weapon. In the exchange, Loki questions Stark's ability to threaten him without his weapon, and Stark admits to Loki's advantage in a physical conflict:

Loki:	Please tell me you're going to appeal to my humanity.
Tony Stark:	Uh, actually I'm planning to threaten you.
Loki:	You should have left your armor on for that.
Tony Stark:	Yeah. It's seen a bit of "mileage" and you got the "glow-stick of destiny." Would you like a drink?
Loki:	Stalling me won't change anything.
Tony Stark:	No, no, no, threatening! No drink? You sure? I'm having one. (ibid.)

Tony's relationship with his suit is explored more thoroughly in *Iron Man 3* movie (which follows *The Avengers* in the Marvel Cinematic Universe sequence). The film separates Tony from his armor for most of the film, forcing him to again demonstrate the type of scrap-metal and personal ingenuity that shaped his identity in the first *Iron Man* (Black 2013). In that film, he literally forged his armor, while in *Iron Man 3* he instead must fix his suit and fight a new supervillain.

Iron Man 3 ends with a voiceover from Tony Stark after he destroys many of the automated Iron Man suits he has been working on for much of the film: "My armor was never a distraction or a hobby, it was a cocoon, and now I'm a changed man. You can take away my house, all my tricks and toys, but one thing you can't take away—I am Iron Man" (Black 2013). The comparison of the suit to a "cocoon" suggests that Tony Stark has emerged into a hero at a new level, fully integrated with the identity of Iron Man as superhero that he had previously only "worn" as another costume. It's worth noting that this separation of man from armor has consequences to Iron Man's identity: as Hogan (2009) notes, "Iron Man is one of the few characters in the North American comic book industry whose costume can change on a regular basis without causing a fan outcry." This is very different from the way in which "the suit makes the man" for a character such as Superman. For Stark, his brain is the essential ingredient to his success, and his most hypermasculine scenes are not found in the donning of armor, but in his exchanges of wit and clever plans.

The hypermasculine presentation of the hero within geek media is a careful balancing act of presenting the larger than life alongside the humanized and intimate. The audience must be able to feel that they connect with these characters and story, while also being in jealous awe of the fantastic lives that they get to live. The more humane supporting cast often takes on the bulk of this work by providing the main character with opportunity for development and emotional connection, while also highlighting their extraordinary nature. Be it Sherlock's intelligence in relation to Watson's approachability or Captain Mal's impulsive bravado to Zoe's stoic calculation, geek media relies upon the hypermasculine definition to shape and present characters across all its platforms.

References

Abrams, J.J. 2009. *Star Trek*. Paramount Pictures. DVD.

Anhut, Amos. 2014. Beyond fantasy–Gender performance & games. *How not to suck at game design*, December 7. http://howtonotsuckatgamedesign.com/2014/12/beyond-fantasy-gender-performance-and-games.

Black, Shane. 2013. *Iron Man 3*. Marvel Entertainment. DVD.
Campbell, Joseph. 1949. *The hero with a thousand faces*. Princeton, NJ: Princeton University Press.
Chamberlin, Tim. 2012. While discussing the trouble with finding a girlfriend … Our Valued Customers, December 12. http://ourvaluedcustomers.blogspot.com/2012/12/while-discussing-trouble-with-finding.html.
Cohn, Amy M., and Amos Zeichner. 2006. Effects of masculine identity and gender role stress on aggression in men. *Psychology of Men & Masculinity* 7 (4): 179–190. https://doi.org/10.1037/1524-9220.7.4.179.
Coulton, Jonathan. 2008. The future soon. *Where Tradition Meets Tomorrow*. MP3.
Dill, Karen, and Kathryn P. Thill. 2007. Video game characters and the socialization of gender roles: Young people's perceptions mirror sexist media depictions. *Sex Roles* 57 (11–12): 851–864. https://doi.org/10.1007/s11199-007-9278-1.
Dittmer, Jason. 2009. Fighting for home: Masculinity and the constitution of the domestic in Tales of Suspense and Captain America. In *Heroes of Film, Comics and American Culture: Essays on Real and Fictional Defenders of Home*, ed. Lisa M. DeTora, 96–116. Jefferson, NC: McFarland.
Donner, R., and J. Silver (Producers), and R. Donner (Director). 1987. *Lethal Weapon* [Motion Picture]. United States: Warner Brothers.
Dziura, Jen. 2012. Bullish life: When men are far too emotional to have a rational argument. *The Gloss*, November 12. http://www.thegloss.com/career/bullish-life-men-are-too-emotional-to-have-a-rational-argument-994/.
Favreau, Jon. 2008. *Iron Man*. Marvel Entertainment. DVD.
Favreau, Jon. 2010. *Iron Man 2*. Marvel Entertainment. DVD.
Feitshans, B. (Producer), and T. Kotcheff (Director). 1982. *Rambo: First Blood* [Motion Picture]. United States: Orion Pictures.
Ferguson, Kathy, Gilad Ashkenazi, and Wendy Schultz. 1997. Gender identity in Star Trek. In *Political science fiction*, ed. Donald M. Hassler, and Clyde Wilcox, 214–233. Columbia: University of South Carolina Press.
Franklin, Karen. 2004. Enacting masculinity: Antigay violence and group rape as participatory theater. *Sexuality Research and Social Policy* 1 (2): 25–40. https://doi.org/10.1525/srsp.2004.1.2.25.
Hawes, James. 2006. School reunion. *Doctor Who*, season 2, episode 3. April 29, BBC.
Hills, Matt. 2010. Doctor who. In *The essential cult TV reader*, ed. David Lavery, 97–103. Lexington: University Press of Kentucky.
Hogan, Jon. 2009. The comic book as symbolic environment: The case of Iron Man. *ETC: A Review of General Semantics* 66 (2): 199–214. http://www.jstor.org/stable/42578930.
Hunter, Latham. 2003. The celluloid cubicle: Regressive constructions of masculinity in 1990s office movies. *The Journal of American Culture* 26 (1): 71–86. https://doi.org/10.1111/1542-734x.00075.
Jeffords, Susan. 1994. *Hard bodies: Hollywood masculinity in the Reagan era*. New Brunswick, NJ: Rutgers University Press.

Judge, Mike. 1999. *Office space*. Twentieth Century Fox. DVD.
Kershner, Irvin. 1980. *Star wars: Episode V—The empire strikes back*. Lucasfilm. DVD.
Kirkland, Ewan. 2009. Masculinity in video games: The gendered gameplay of Silent Hill. *Camera Obscura* 24 (271): 161–183. https://doi.org/10.1215/02705346-2009-006.
Leifeld, R. April 1997. *Captain America Vol. #2: Industrial Revolution*. New York, NY: Marvel Comics.
Lyn, Euros. 2008. Forest of the Dead. *Doctor Who*. Season 4, episode 9. June 27, BBC.
McNeill, Robert Duncan. 2000. Body and soul. *Star Trek Voyager*, November 15.
Mosher, Donald L., and Ronald D. Anderson. 1986. Macho personality, sexual aggression, and reactions to guided imagery of realistic rape. *Journal of Research in Personality* 20 (1): 77–94. https://doi.org/10.1016/0092-6566(86)90111-x.
Mosher, Donald L., and Mark Sirkin. 1984. Measuring a macho personality constellation. *Journal of Research in Personality* 18 (2): 150–163. https://doi.org/10.1016/0092-6566(84)90026-6.
O'Malley, Harris. 2013. The selling of masculinity: Paging Dr. *Nerdlove*, March 18. http://www.doctornerdlove.com/2013/03/selling-masculinity/.
O'Sullivan, C. 1998. Ladykillers: Similarities and divergences of masculinities in gang rape and wife battery. In *Research on men and Masculinities: Masculinities and violence* vol. 10, ed. L. H. Bowker, 82–110. Thousand Oaks, CA: SAGE Publications Ltd. https://doi.org/10.4135/9781483328010.n5.
Parrott, Dominic J., and Amos Zeichner. 2003. Effects of hypermasculinity on physical aggression against women. *Psychology of Men & Masculinity* 4 (1): 70–78. https://doi.org/10.1037/1524-9220.4.1.70.
Parrott, Dominic J., and Amos Zeichner. 2008. Determinants of anger and physical aggression based on sexual orientation: An experimental examination of hypermasculinity and exposure to male gender role violations. *Sexual Behavior* 37 (6): 891–901.
Prokopetz, David. 2015. Untitled. *Prokopetz*, January 4. http://prokopetz.tumblr.com/post/107164298477/i-think-my-biggest-huh-moment-with-respect-to.
Reidy, Dennis E., Steven D. Shirk, Colleen A. Sloan, and Amos Zeichner. 2009. Men who aggress against women: Effects of feminine gender role violation on physical aggression in hypermasculine men. *Psychology of Men & Masculinity* 10 (1): 1–12. https://doi.org/10.1037/a0014794.
Roach. 2014. Untitled. *To Live and Die Before a Mirror*, August 20. http://roachpatrol.tumblr.com/post/95270108077/god-damn-and-like-gallifrey-has-some-deeply.
Roberts, Robin A. 2000. Science, race, and gender in *Star Trek: Voyager*. In *Fantasy Girls: Gender in the New Universe of Science Fiction and Fantasy*, ed. Elyce Rae Helford, 203–222. Lanham, MD: Rowman & Littlefield.
Rowley, Christina. 2007. Firefly/Serenity: Gendered space and gendered bodies. *The British Journal of Politics & International Relations* 9 (2): 318–325. https://doi.org/10.1111/j.1467-856x.2007.00286.x.

Scharrer, Erica. 2004. Virtual violence: Gender and aggression in video game advertisements. *Communication and Society* 7 (4): 393–412. https://doi.org/10.1207/s15327825mcs0704_2.
Simpson, D., and J. Bruckheimer (Producers), and T. Scott (Director). 1986. *Top Gun* [Motion Picture]. United States: Paramount Pictures.
Smith, Adam. 2010. The eleventh hour. *Doctor Who*, series 5, episode 1. April 3.
Taylor, T.L. 2012. *Raising the stakes: E-sports and the professionalization of computer gaming*. Boston, MA: The MIT Press.
Weltzien, Friedrich. 2005. Masque-ulinities: Changing dress as a display of masculinity in the superhero genre. *Fashion Theory: A Journal of Dress, Body & Culture* 9 (2): 229–250. https://doi.org/10.2752/136270405778051374.
Whedon, Joss. 2002. The train job. *Firefly*, season 1, episode 2. September 20, Fox.
Whedon, Joss. 2005. *Serenity*. Universal Pictures. DVD.
Whedon, Joss. 2012. *The Avengers*. Marvel Entertainment. Blu-ray.
Yao, Mike Z., Chad Mahood, and Daniel Linz. 2010. Sexual priming, gender stereotyping, and likelihood to sexually harass: Examining the cognitive effects of playing a sexually explicit video game. *Sex Roles* 62 (1–2): 77–88. https://doi.org/10.1007/s11199-009-9695-4.

3

Beauty and the Geek: On-Screen Representations of Geeks

In the opening of *Ten Things I Hate About You*, released in 1999, new kid and slight geek Cameron gets a campus tour from uber-geek Michael along with words of wisdom on the impossibility of dating the hot blonde Bianca, who Cameron immediately insists is less shallow than Michael thinks. A Shakespearean plot ensues, first with Bianca using Cameron to get a shot with the conventionally hot and masculine Joey, and finally with Bianca realizing the appeal of "nice guy" Cameron. This type of story is classic, particularly in modern romantic comedies, which tend to reward a different type of masculinity than the conventional action film or other genre pieces. Indeed, attractiveness seems not to be required at all for a modern lead (with Seth Rogen being a prime example), and many films suggest that any geek should be able to overcome awkwardness, introversion, and even ugliness to find the beautiful woman they deserve. In Judd Apatow's *Knocked Up* (2007), for instance, gorgeous and successful Allison Scott (portrayed by Katherine Heigl) finds herself tied to Seth Rogen, playing a stoner, after a one-night stand ends in pregnancy. Stories like these aided the rise of a new variation of the trope, often called "Ugly Guy, Hot Wife" (TV Tropes 2017). The new variation was based upon assumed natural traits of both women and men. The man was a full-sized child, often selfish, wrapped up in his hobbies and friends, with low levels of attentiveness to physical attractiveness, while the wife was hot, driven, organized, and generally patient with her spouse's flaws. As Carter Soles (2013) asks when surveying the current spectrum of romantic comedies, "Nowadays, schlubs play schlubs and audiences are expected to accept that geeky males can win over classically beautiful women. What does it tell us about the state of gender relations, sexual fantasy, and desire that a physically average geek like Rogen can trump an iconically attractive and glamorous star like Grant?" It certainly suggests something about the state of masculinity and indeed the aspirational masculinity that pop culture has chosen to present.

Reality television takes a slightly more mercenary approach to the pairing of beauty and schlub. The show *Beauty and the Geek* (Smith 2005), which aired from 2005 to 2008, recreates misogynist expectations by casting women as beauties and men as geeks. The show's summary emphasizes this division between the mentally and physically gifted:

> Once upon a time, there were attractive women who got by on their appearances, and intelligent men with limited social skills, who lived in a house together, learning from each others' weaknesses and strengths. By the end of their journey, these diverse men and women received lessons in confidence, equality, and dignity. No longer were they just the Beauty and the Geek. (TV. com 2015)

This description puts particular weight on geeks as defined by a combination of brains and limited social skills while the women were not expected to offer much other than attractiveness. The couples were not explicitly encouraged to date—the show described itself as a "social experiment" rather than a relationship-driven show—but much of the tension came from the highly gendered, heteronormative set-up and challenges. The show relied on several strange conceits, including forced cohabitation by a beauty and a geek, who were paired as a team for a series of challenges involving both intellect and social skills. Each member of the cast was labeled by some defining feature: the first season included "Computer Programmer," "Mensa Member," and, tellingly, "Has never been kissed," while the women included "NBA Dancer" and "Life-Sized Barbie Doll" (Smith 2005). These shallow labels suggest the roles each gender was invited to fill in this fantasy.

This phenomenon has made its way into the popular consciousness in many ways, including lowering standards for masculine attractiveness. One of the most notable of these was the circulating of the "Dad bod" concept, popularized in an editorial by Mackenzie Pearson: "We love people saying "they look cute together." But we still like being the center of attention. We want to look skinny and the bigger the guy, the smaller we feel and the better we look next to you in a picture" (2015). While Pearson associates the look with frat boys (not geeks), geek culture is also associated with a privileging of intellectual life and focus over physical habits and attention to exercise routines. The lifestyle demands of jobs in geek-haven Silicon Valley leave little time for exercise for those competing in the work-focused rat race of masculinity. Considering work–life balance among technical professionals, Joan C. Williams (2010) cites Marianne Cooper's study, which demonstrated that "white-collar work is clean, gender-neutral knowledge work unrelated to physical strength. This leaves white-collar men searching for ways to imagine their work as proving their manliness. In Silicon Valley … they do so by interpreting long work hours as a heroic activity." In his examination of marginalized and hegemonic masculinity, Cliff Cheng (1999) notes that the definition of hegemonic masculinity relies upon the presence (and exclusion) of marginalized performances of masculinity. Geek masculinity, with its absence of hypermasculine qualities and apparent association with "un-masculine" traits, is often cast in popular culture as a marginalized masculinity. Many of the shows examined here invite viewers to embrace that dichotomy by repeatedly contrasting their geek leads with embodiments of traditionally understood hegemonic masculinity: physically active, sexually successful, white men. However, the dichotomy is false: geek masculinity is not marginalized. It is instead an inevitable evolution of hegemonic masculinity in a culture where dominance and technical mastery are increasingly interwoven.

Stories of geeks and their relationships to "hot" women reinforce a number of stereotypes embedded in geek masculinity: a Google image search for the word "geek" returns as its top hits images and photographs of white men with glasses (Geek Google Image Search 2016). Of the top hundred results, nearly all of the pictorial images are coded as male and feature a white man; among the few pictures of women, sexualized poses are common, while none of the male geeks appear in sexualized poses. They are, however, primarily costumed to suggest a physical type: collared shirts, bow ties, suspenders, wide-rimmed glasses, and high waist pants are all frequent occurrences. The suggestions embedded across these images are clear, even if actual real-world encounters with anyone dressed in these fashions are unlikely: geeks still possess a form of masculinity that is separate from the aspirational, physically governed world. Images such as these are a reminder of the power that these stereotypes still hold and of the importance of physical presentation in identity establishment and recognition.

In this space, bounded possibilities are offered for models of geek identity and particularly geek masculinity as expressed through media in a gendered, heteronormative space. Examining the state of nerds in 2011, Lori Kendall observes that "the masculinity of nerds is still somewhat in question, protecting a form of hegemonic masculinity which continues to give primacy to aggressiveness and physicality" (512). As the media roles reflected to us play a strong role in shaping group identity, we will consider geek identity as constructed through television depictions. *The Big Bang Theory* and many similar franchises revolve around the stereotype of a beautiful but stupid (if often "street-savvy") woman pursued by socially inept but brilliant men. We will deconstruct the tension of the "un-masculine" geek as opposed to the hyperfeminine bimbo and the narrative of geek wish fulfillment it constructs in which women serve as rewards and audiences for male brilliance. The heroes of these franchises, with their combination of socially awkward presentation and geek stereotypical quirks, offer a perfect parallel to the aspirational narratives of the pop culture on which these very characters feed, as the relationship of Sheldon with Spock perfectly epitomizes. R.W. Connell and James W. Messerschmidt (2005) surveyed the concept of hegemonic masculinity in 2005 and observed that it is a mutating and evolving concept in both theory and practice. Writing in 1999, Lori Kendall suggested that "nerd imagery can … either challenge or reinforce hegemonic masculinity." Nearly two decades later, the promise of this challenge is unfulfilled. The mainstreaming of geek subculture has certainly brought with it an increased visibility of geeks as characters who might not at first seem to reflect the dominant masculinity in US culture. These depictions are part of negotiating the new American masculinity, which is heavily influenced by the reliance upon technology of all cultural participants. We will contrast these geek icons and their masculinity with the definition of the hypermasculine hero drawn from our examination of geek-driven popular culture narratives.

A Big Bang

The Big Bang Theory premiered on September 24, 2007 and is still running as of 2017, with two more seasons at least already forthcoming. This is a fairly long run for a sitcom: for comparison, NBC's *Friends* ended after ten seasons, and CBS's *How I Met Your Mother* ended after nine. CBS's chairman called *The Big Bang Theory* "the biggest comedy force on television" (Goldberg 2014). As we introduced earlier, the show's main cast has matured to include seven primary characters, which resembles the sitcom formula of *Friends* (three men and three women, alternating as roommates and partners throughout the seasons, with one "geek," Ross) and *How I Met Your Mother* (three men and two women, including a married heterosexual couple and one "geek," Ted). The shows employ geek culture to different extremes: *Friends* is infamous for using Ross's geekdom as a pretense for his sexual fantasy involving Princess Leia, which Rachel fulfills while most of the other characters pass judgment. The same trope of Leia as fantasy object occurs in *That '70s Show*, but in this case initiated by a woman (Donna) who offers herself as Leia as a going away present to her geeky partner, Eric (Trainer 2005). By contrast, *How I Met Your Mother* (perhaps in part thanks to its more recent air-dates) uses geek culture more freely among its cast, causing *Den of Geek* to give the show a positive recommendation:

> [The show] is often a celebration of the nerdier things that many of us hold dear. While over on *The Big Bang Theory*, the writers have made a habit of poking continuous fun at geek habits and constantly reminding the audience that "girls don't date guys who watch *Star Trek*/collect comic books/play *Dungeons & Dragons*", *HIMYM* revels in such a culture, and not just with its male characters. (Stansfield 2013)

These formulaic comedies rely on the romantic tensions between characters and often use gender stereotypes to construct situational comedy. They also feature predominately white casts despite being set in an urban context, and those casts rarely interact for long with any character outside the main circle. For example, *Friends* relies on what Phil Chidester (2008) terms as a "closed circle," which is highly driven by the shared belonging that is visually reinforced as the characters continually gather on the couches of their living room and coffee shop. But the characters of *Friends* and for that matter *How I Met Your Mother* are not only white: they are also primarily not geeks. They inhabit public spaces, such as the living room and bar, and present the same mannerisms and behaviors in those spaces as they do at home. Thus they demonstrate a hegemonic unity to the world, together as a distinct cultural group and isolating outsiders with their tightly knit social structures (Marshall 2007).

As a formulaic sitcom, *The Big Bang Theory* similarly creates a circle around its characters, and in doing so pulls together five geek-identified characters with one non-geek woman, Penny. This is a precise reversal of the other shows examined here, in which the token geek serves as the outsider to the other's more confident social interactions. In *Friends* (Mancuso 1996) and *How I Met Your Mother*, the love life of the geeky character is the most challenged: Ross is mocked for his obsession with dinosaurs and opens the series divorced from a wife who now identifies as a lesbian, while Ted is ostensibly the narrator of his show telling the story of how he met his children's mother, but instead seems to be chronicling hopeless relationships one after another. The main casts of each show might also have rotating relationships and romantic problems, but their exploits are not considered as laughable or challenged as the two white male geeks who occupy the stereotypical position. *The Big Bang Theory* likewise employs the outsider as a foil, but does so through the geek's hot next-door neighbor, Penny. In this dynamic, Penny presents the outsider perspective, and is offered as an audience stand-in when reacting to the extremes presented by the geeks themselves:

Penny: I mean, who even reads *Scientific American*?
Leonard: It's kind of a big deal.
Penny: If it's such a big deal, how come the biggest celebrity they could get for the cover is a molecule? (Cendrowski 2007)

In this collision of science geek and aspiring actress, the tensions between Penny's world and the geeks' world are continually played for laughs. For instance, the above conversation about *Scientific American* magazine contrasts the geeks' reverence for being featured in the leading science magazine with her participation in and idealization of celebrity culture. As a participant in non-geek coded culture, Penny serves as the straight man (or rather woman) to the geeks' wise guys. The straight man and wise guy pairing in comedy can be traced back to the early days of vaudeville and remains a staple of many sitcom pairings today. As the name implies, the trope was originally used to describe two male comedians and many times even modern interpretations make use of two men to run a joke in this fashion. It recalls the "hot wife" trope of recent romantic comedy, but with a decidedly geek-focused twist that puts Penny in the friend/wife/mother role to all the geeks. Within television an alternative formulation is used in sitcoms starting in the early 2000s with the straight man, ironically, being a woman, often the main romantic interest of the male comedic lead.

The piqued television interest in geek-related stories in the early 2010s also modified the now more popular male/female comedic pairing by providing the men with a geeky background and interests and the woman being more traditionally popular and beautiful. This helped to both further infantilize the role of the wise guy by grounding the defining part of his identity is culturally coded as child-like, collecting comics and video games, and cast the women as both disinterested in geeky pursuits and naturally less funny and passionate than their male counterparts. Within these shows, the joke that was set up by the actors usually either painted the female lead as clueless and ignorant of very important geek things or the male lead(s) as social outcasts from normal society. This spate of comedic pairings helps to paint a broad picture of the expectations of both men and women and geeky men in particular. Although the shows were more sympathetic in their portrayal of geeks than they had been in earlier decades, they were still regulated to the role of lesser than. They are not adults in their own right but man-boys that must be taken care of, inviting the audience to wonder how the characters have survived this long without a sensible contact point in their lives. Often the characterizations represent a major difference between these media portrayals and ones from earlier decades focused more on showing these men as attractive partners who simply need a 1990s make-over montage to finally grow up and understand adult social relationships. Although this may not represent the real diversity of male and masculine-identifying geeks, and largely leaves the female-identifying group in the cold, they do help to shape the cultural background and repository of shared knowledge from which real people draw when shaping their own identities and expectations about life.

By twisting the formula for a sitcom and casting geeks as the main group, *The Big Bang Theory* presents a closed circle in which social norms are set by geeks. It is significant that the geeks do not routinely occupy any public space with the same frequency as the casts of comparable sitcoms: they instead are primarily shown within the apartment, in the lunch room or rarely the labs of the university, or in a comic book shop, a safe geek-coded public. The most commonly shown exterior traditional public (a physical public space) favored by the cast is The Cheesecake Factory, where Penny initially works, and while she is shown there in a service role it is implied that this is one location where she can set some of the norms, occasionally refusing to serve or acknowledge Sheldon following conflicts.

Penny: Hi, you guys ready to order?
Howard: Hang on, honey. Shiva and Ganesh? The Hindu Gods against the entire Union army?
Leonard: And Orcs!
Penny: I'll be back.
Raj: Excuse me, Ganesh is the remover of obstacles, and Shiva is the destroyer. When the smoke clears, Abraham Lincoln will be speaking Hindi and drinking mint juleps.
Penny: Alright, my boss says you either have to order, or leave and never come back.
Howard: What do you recommend for someone who worked up a man-sized appetite from a morning of weight training and cardio-funk?
Penny: A shower.
Howard: I'll take the heart smart platter. (Weyman 2007)

These scenes emphasize the difference in dynamic with a group of geeks versus a group of non-geek-coded characters. We are invited as the audience to join Penny in her judgment and laughter at the characters, and to understand her frustration with their refusal to break up their speculative conversation to place an order. Some geek-identifying watchers have noted that this distancing makes it difficult or impossible to enjoy the show:

> the humour in The Big Bang theory relies on the audience siding with and relating to Penny, the character coded as "normal" in comparison to the main four guys. It also relies on the audience having a sense of superiority over Leonard, Raj, Sheldon and Howard. We're supposed to feel like we're cooler than them and that we're better than them. (Butmyopinionisright 2012)

The Big Bang Theory and Televised Masculinity

Within her book *Cable Guys*, Amanda Lotz (2014) looks at televised masculinity throughout the late 1990s and early 2000s. Lotz describes the presentation of male homosocial groups as the place in which it becomes possible to see men exploring what masculinity is through the deep bonds of friendship and trust. It is within these social groups that the different types of manhood that are acceptable can be looked at and critiqued within the world of the show (2014). And through the use of cross-textual analysis an examination of a multitude of masculinities can be made. Lotz writes, "The homosocial enclaves created in these series allow for performance of a masculinity that is much different from the way these men are depicted when they enter mixed-gender or 'civilian' spaces and also reveal a particular type of men's talk that is uncensored by norms of social propriety" (2014). This holds particularly true for geek shows as well. The male cast members interact with each other in a manner that establishes what the expected power and social conventions within the group are. For geeks, these include arguments about the details of shows, scientific discussions, playing games together, whereas the interactions between the geeks and the non-geeks acts as a marker to how geek masculinity is othered from the more common and expected presentations. The geek cast is made to feel awkward, unsure of what is going on around them, having discussions with one another that sound like people jointly playing a role-playing game or occasionally like Sir David Attenborough describing an exotic animal species. In those cases where the geek men bring up a topic of their interest, there is usually one of three responses in heterosocial but homogendered groups: disinterest, mockery, or stupidity. The geeks are unable to participate in traditional masculinities and find that others outside of their group are not interested in joining their appreciation of their hobbies.

Geek-centered television is one of the few categories where comedies outweigh other genres of production, which may be in part because of the role geeks have typically played as figures for mockery and pity. This choice for genre production is very interesting in its intersection for presenting the development of a modern masculinity. Lotz draws upon Brett Mills' discussion of identity formation within the genre, saying "comedy creates a space for the incorporation of non-dominant ideologies and disenfranchised identities because of its ability to contain difference through its narrative imperative to 'laugh at'—this is what, in the terms of the literature on humor, is classified as 'superiority theory'" (2014). Although these identities are presented as being ones that exist, they are shown as being something that is often the hinge upon which a joke swings. While geeks as an identity are given more screen time the differences highlighted between the homo and heterosocial interactions are still highlighted in a way that is clearly meant to portray the geek identity as that of an outsider. The shows validate the geek as an identity that does exist but also places them implicitly within a social hierarchy where their identity is devalued in comparison to more normative masculinities. Television studies further look at this type of comedy and the technical production in relation to presenting the characters as being more or less available to the audience as potential identities. The reliance of geek television upon the comedy genre with multiple cameras and a laugh helps to underscore that the geek identity is one that should be seen as laughable more often than it is seen as acceptable. Within *The Big Bang Theory* the boys' hobbies, thoughts, and actions are often the butt of the joke instead of being presented in a more sympathetic light. Often the only times we see these identities presented in a more sympathetic way is when they are played across genders in the interactions between the male leads and women.

Leonard: Once you open the box it loses its value.
Penny: Yeah, yeah. My mom gave me the same lecture about my virginity. I gotta tell you, it was a lot more fun taking it out and playing with it. (Cendrowski 2012)

The deep bond shared between the men within the homosocial group does raise the potential for sexual tension to develop. This tension is still presented as an othered expression of intimacy and often results in fear among the group. Within many shows this is set up and knocked down through humor and interactions between the different characters. It is interesting how *The Big Bang Theory* approaches the homosexual panic Lotz speaks of by simply acknowledging the fluid boundaries of sexuality between Raf and Howard. At least twice in the series it is implied that these two engage in sexual activities with the other present. Although they show a bit of discomfort with the topic, they also address it in a rather frank and straightforward manner. Sadly, it is still often the set-up or punchline for a joke about how strange the two characters are. It is also interesting that these explorations are occurring for the sideline characters who are at least partially othered through the additional cultural identities which they display. Raj, the only character of color on the main cast, is the one who seems most comfortable expressing alternative sexual standards or interests. This can be tied back to the exoticization of both Raj's Indian culture and alternative sexualities. It gives the show an easy way to relieve the sexual tension between male members of the cast without having to take a clear stance on any potentially controversial topics. Given that Raj and Howard are othered so strongly within the show it also serves to safely protect the heterosexual relationships of Leonard and Sheldon the white leads.

As with most sitcom set-ups the characters are presented in the minimal amount of depth needed for them to develop over the series without being so complex that setting up the basic jokes of the show becomes impossible. Character identities in commercial television are the fast food hamburger, just varied enough to provide a veneer of choice but meant to be palatable to the widest audience possible. In many instances, the male characters are presented as being just slightly different takes on the inherent characteristics of geekiness. They are intelligent, well versed in their chosen fields of geekiness, socially awkward. They can fall within culture's expectations of male beauty but often in non-traditional fashions. Often, they have a strong focus on physical goods and will collect or display their hobbies externally. Across most of these characters and series these common traits hold consistent, presenting a view into how geeks are viewed by the media creators. When there are deviations from their standard formula, such as when working with an ensemble cast, it's often those geeky traits being modified by other identity signifiers like Howard's Jewishness or Raj's Indian background. Taking away those other identifiers leaves a core idea of geeky identity that has little to no variation among the men. At their core, all the main male cast of *The Big Bang Theory* hold the same viewpoints, interests, hobbies; their geek nature is more core to them than any other cultural differences. To be a geek within this circle is to express these traits without modification or genuine difference. All other identity elements are superficial aspects that coat the true, shared geeky core: the bond of shared structure that encloses the circle around the four male leads that the women can never fully penetrate, even if they occupy some of the same physical spaces on the show. Leadership and agency within the group discourse is as reserved as Sheldon's spot on the couch, and when a character such as Penny tries to occupy it, it is always temporary. Cultural and religious identities are often cores upon which individuals build their sense of self, but for the TV geeks it is more of a mask that can be held up when appropriate to tell a joke or differentiate characters.

Within the halls of television geeks are characters that can be largely reduced to a checklist of like and behavior traits. With few exceptions, these are shown as being the core aspects to the main characters identities and the items by which the audience identifies them as othered from the rest of the cast. Other parts of their individual identities are more of a veneer over the essentialized nature of their geekhood, although perhaps that essential geekhood is part of the show's appeal: Robert Sullivan speculates it has:

> benefited from the rise in Comic-Con culture and the virtual takeover of Hollywood by comic-book franchises. Even if some people can't identify with sci-fi geekery, there are similar obsessive societies all over America—fantasy sports leagues, gun owners, foodies. (Leonard and Sheldon arguing over the merits of superhero movies isn't so different than Frasier and his brother jousting over wine vintages.) (Sullivan 2013)

Viewed through that lens, the characters are simultaneously objects of mockery and of potential self-identification for the male viewer.

Amy and Penny or How to Woman

While much of the attention of *The Big Bang Theory*'s narrative is focused on and powered by the four male friends, women characters do occupy increasing roles of agency within the show that provide an opportunity to reflect and provide foils for the dominant masculine drive. Sadly, much like the "hot wife" trope examined at the opening of this chapter, many women on geek TV typify some of the worst stereotypes about women. *The Big Bang Theory* presents a dichotomy between the two major presentations in the form of Penny and Amy Farrah Fowler. The differences between the female characters paint an interesting contrast with the identities presented for the male cast. For the first several seasons of the show, only Penny appeared as a developed recurring female character. Two more educated, geek-coded women characters were introduced at the end of season three to expand both the cast and the dynamics of the relationships: Amy Farrah Fowler, a neurobiologist chosen by an online dating site as Sheldon's only possible match, and Bernadette Rostenkowski, who starts out working at Cheesecake Factory while she earns a PhD in microbiology, providing a model for a working-class woman with aspirations realized more fully than Penny's dream of acting.

Penny, last name unknown, was introduced in the pilot episode as the beautiful blond next-door neighbor to Leonard and Sheldon. Since she is one of the most frequently recurring cast members and a central one to the main love story that holds the narrative structure of the multi-season show together, it would be easy to believe much is known about her. After all, for the male cast we could list not only their full names but their likes and dislikes, personal schedules, childhood traumas, and psychological hang-ups. It wasn't until the ninth season that Penny even had a last name, taking Leonard's after marriage. She is presented as a typical woman for California: a pretty, not very bright girl from the Midwest who moved to the coast to find a job in acting and is working as a waitress. She is treated as only a bare sketch of a person, a McGuffin in human form that is presented to act as a foil to the boys' personalities but also as a love interest to keep the tension of the show raised. She acts not only as the straight man for Sheldon and Leonard's antics, but also embodies what the show writers seem to typify of normal female desires. She is the norm that the other cast members are measured against for humorous effect and her own perceived failings as a woman are held up for scrutiny and laughter.

Amy Farrah Fowler is one of the standout female characters of *The Big Bang Theory*. She is an interesting character for illustrating the problems with women's representation in geek media. Amy is often portrayed as being as smart as Sheldon (the acknowledged intelligence powerhouse) in an area that is just as difficult and therefore as serious a science. But when we see her as a character, one of her defining traits has been her lack of female friends and the "real" experiences of womanhood.

Amy consistently shows an enthusiasm for stereotypical female experiences that she never received in her early and formative years. Those that she had were usually ones that could be understood as being either masculine or geared towards masculinized hobbies and her interest in science. This connects and reinforces a strong cultural theme that women who engage with technology and science are unfeminine. It acts to inherently gender these interests and activities and as a group softly push women and feminine acts to the outside. These thematic trends play alongside and help to reinforce cultural beliefs that have real world implications for women interested in the sciences and technology. Nobel laureate Dr. Tim Hunt resigned after comments about his "trouble with girls" in the lab, focused on the problems he perceived with them as either objects of desire, attracted to him, or crying at criticism (Bilefsky 2015). Similarly, an NPR interview with Shrinivas Kulkarni featured the scientist describing fellow practitioners as "boys with toys," placing an emphasis on both words that made it clear how he gendered STEM (Clancy 2015). It spawned the #girlswithtoys Twitter tag, a feminist protest of Kulkarni's demeaning remarks that featured many women doing science (Palca 2015). Science and scientific-like activities are culturally gendered as a "boys' only" area where a female participant is either a detriment to the activity or simply an anomaly that should be discarded when making observations about the field.

Amy is also often shown as being underdeveloped during her early appearances, much like her male geek colleagues. She is engaging in online dating in order to keep her mother happy and generally acts more like a teen with an overbearing parent than an independent adult woman. Overall, her portrayal can largely be seen as a gender-swapped version of Sheldon. She even takes up a role of acting like a foil to Penny, similar to Sheldon's relationship with Leonard. During these early episodes Amy is an object of conversation for many members of the cast as they express disbelief in her apparent realness and horror at the realization that there are more people in the world similar to Sheldon. Slowly, Amy's character is developed into more than just the trope of Rule 63 (the opposite-gender counterpart) Sheldon and takes on her own quirks and habits. In particular, she begins expressing a great deal of sexual desire, although in more clinical terms than we see the other female cast using. In this way, Amy and Penny are shown as being similar based upon a common female trait: sexual desire. Penny is typically dismissed within the show for her apparent willingness to engage in casual dating and sex.

Sheldon:	Simple extrapolation. In the three years that I've known you, you were single for two. During that time, I saw 17 different suitors. If we work backwards, correcting for observation bias and postulate an initial dating age of 15 …
Penny:	Whoa, wait, wait, wait. I did not start dating at 15.
Sheldon:	I'm sorry. 16?
Penny:	14.

Sheldon: My mistake. Now, assuming the left side of a bell curve peaking around the present, that would bring the total up to 193 men. Plus or minus eight men.
Amy: Remarkable. Did you have sexual intercourse with all of these men?
Penny: No.
Sheldon: Although that number would be fairly easy to calculate.
Penny: Oh.
Sheldon: Based on the number of awkward encounters I've had with strange men leaving her apartment in the morning, plus the number of times she's returned home wearing the same clothes she wore the night before …
Penny: Okay, Sheldon, I think you've made your point.
Sheldon: So we multiply 193, minus 21 men before the loss of virginity, so 172 times 0.18 gives us 30.96 sexual partners. Let's round that up to 31. (Cendrowski 2010)

This exchange continues in a different manner as the conversation moves on.

Sheldon: This is an interesting topic. How many sexual encounters have you had?
Amy: Does volunteering for a scientific experiment in which orgasm was achieved by electronically stimulating the pleasure centers of the brain count?
Sheldon: I should think so.
Amy: Then 128. (Cendrowski 2010)

We never hear Amy's number outside of a scientific experiment, but this positions Amy early on as a very interesting juxtaposition between the clinical and distant scientist and the sexually active woman. Somehow Amy's use of orgasm within a clinical trial is less socially judged than Penny's engagements with men, condemning the very human interaction as being dirty or baser than what could occur within a laboratory setting. To stimulate the pleasure center through electrodes is one thing, but to do it through physical contact is another matter entirely.

Amy also serves to highlight the perceived essentialized traits for women. She secretly yearns to experience the activities and trappings of womanhood, most of which Penny engages in unthinkingly. The most successful and smartest woman presented on the show really just wants to be one of the girls and go out dancing and looking at boys. Her identity is halved and strongly compartmentalized; we never see the strong confident scientist at the same time that we see the woman interested in fashion or clubs. When Amy expresses these desires, it is often played against Penny, the "good" woman of the group. Amy's interests in female-oriented activities are shown as being overbearing and largely a joke. Although Penny is shown as participating in all of them herself, to reach out to Amy by including her is cast in the light of charity and comedy meant to actually keep Penny and Amy from bonding. Amy's apparent sexual interest in women is also used to keep distance between her and Penny as characters, as the target of her poor attempts at flirting result in Penny typically physically distancing herself within the scene. They also occur during moments where real female bonding could occur between these two characters and is instead reduced to a joke about the physical role that beautiful women like Penny are meant to play.

At the end of season 8, Amy dumps Sheldon after he finally says that he loves her. This is shown as being a bit of a character development for Amy, since she realizes that there are many people out there who could be interested in her as a partner. Given the show's focus on Leonard and Sheldon, this situation gets more airtime as a tragedy than real development for one member of a cast. Many of the jokes after their break up focus on the impact that it has on the male cast members. Sheldon sees himself as having jumped through all the correct hoops to achieve his goal, but the princess instead left him. He quickly reverts to an explicit woman-hating attitude in an attempt to distance himself from the pain of a break up. The affective portrayal is that this is the logical conclusion and a rational decision for him to make given the circumstances under which it happened. Although there is a bit of humor at play in how overboard Sheldon tends to go in any emotional upsets he has, it is done in a very forgiving way.

Stuart: Well, I know more women are buying comics than ever, but for some reason, I can't get'em in here.
Penny: All right. Well, what have you tried so far?
Stuart: Uh, I've been stocking more female-oriented titles. In the bathroom, I folded the end of the toilet paper into a triangle. And, uh, you are now sitting in the official breastfeeding area. (Cendrowski 2015)

(We revisit the comic shop as a geek-coded, gendered zone in Chap. 4.) Penny and Amy are depicted as opposed but essentialized women. Neither gets the personal development of who they are or what drives them outside of their relationship with the male leads. When played off one another the roles and boundaries open to women become apparent. While some nerdiness is acceptable, these are not women who will ever really be geeks. There is simply too much of their inherent female nature showing through for them to be accepted as one of the boys. Women within these shows are reduced to very stereotypical portrayals. Instead of addressing the harassment and discomfort that many women feel in geek spaces Stuart instead focuses on breastfeeding and fastidious toiletry requirements, because it is only in those highly gendered ways that women and men differ.

Like most sitcoms, the casts of geek shows evolve only a bit during their time on the air. The cores of the characters are important for the plot and jokes within the show, so development must be minimal to avoid having the character change too dramatically. The fact that Amy is one of the few characters who has had significant character development during the seasons following her introduction underscores the childlike and undeveloped nature assigned to the geeky characters. In this way, she reflects the male characters of Raj and Howard, who also experience significant development. All three characters have protective, visible parents within the series. Their parents attempt to control them through a variety of means in order to prevent them from growing up in certain ways. Howard literally lives at home with his mother. Raj is beholden to his parents for the money they send him to live. Amy's mother doesn't have as clear a hold on her as the other characters, but it is also likely that she is the only strong female interaction Amy experiences prior to the character's introduction in the series.

Across the varied women that are present in these shows there is this strange set up. The men are shown as being different from normal guys, clearly in the social "other" category. But the female leads can't help but be intrigued by them. Socially, many aspects of the men's personality should be repulsive to them, but the women can't help but find themselves drawn in deeper to the men's lives. Their behaviors are set up as being both their weakness and their strength; their otherness is the allure that gets them the women they should desire. These characterizations reinforce the show's determined division of masculine and feminine, as "the various male and female characters identified as geeks reify dualistic and misogynistic constructions of gender and intelligence, tying pursuits of the mind to the false ideal of masculinized abstraction" (Sartain 2015, 96). These divisions are most clearly noted in the Sheldon–Penny dichotomy, as Sartain notes: "Penny is the female side of the Cartesian gender binary that Sheldon epitomizes. She is beautiful, embodied, sexual, and unintelligent" (100). However, they are further reflected in every character thanks to a mind/body

Fig. 3.1 Chuck and his compatriots in the Geek Squad (McG 2010). Screen capture: NBC

divide that Butler (2002) notes will tend to create false binaries: such binaries "ought to be rethought for the implicit gender hierarchy that the distinction has conventionally produced, maintained, and rationalized."

Chuck: From Geek to Hero

Co-existing with *The Big Bang Theory*'s sitcom rein, the NBC series *Chuck* (Levi) ran from 2007–2012 and offered an even more elaborate contrast between its geek male cluster of characters and a set of dynamic foils, including, of course, an attractive blonde woman. *Chuck* features an unusual dynamic, existing in a liminal space between geek reality shows (such as HBO's *Silicon Valley* and *The Big Bang Theory*) and action-oriented fantasy shows. Chuck himself represents in many ways a case of failure to launch, a term that is commonly associated with an extended adolescence and a failure to achieve the culturally imposed standards of adulthood. We come to learn early on that Chuck was exceptionally bright and had a future as an engineer with a Stanford education until he was thrown out for cheating. Now, he lives with his sister and works in information technology, or glorified tech support, with no greater hopes for future success than moving up to an assistant manager position.

Chuck is a member of the "Nerd Herd" and appears at the start of the first episode playing at spy to escape a boring party with his best friend, Morgan Grimes. The uniforms and design of the "Nerd Herd" (see Fig. 3.1) recall that of Best Buy's Geek Squad. Lori Kendall (2011) describes the Geek Squad look as conforming to the essential elements of the nerd stereotype and notes that attempts to "allay the unmasculine aspects of nerd identity" lead to continual contradictions that "demonstrate the strength of the nerd stereotype" as white and male. The workers of the Nerd Herd are primarily male and embody geek stereotypes similar to those of *The Big Bang Theory*, but without the same redeeming intellectual qualities or financial resources. Because of this, *Chuck* has been critiqued for its harsh, stereotyped representations of geeks: as Darowski (2012) observes, "for a show that in many respects celebrates nerd culture, the members of the Nerd Herd are shown to be inferior in many ways to the medical doctors. Chuck's fellow Nerd Herders are socially inept and, in the case of the recurring characters Jeff and Lester, mentally inferior to the average human."

In the pilot episode of the show, Chuck is living an ordinary life prior to an email from an old friend that causes him to download a database of spy secrets directly into his brain. When the CIA and NSA realize that he's apparently stolen their database, they send an attractive woman agent, Sarah, to investigate. Their first interactions occur through a veil of Chuck's suspicion as he tries to figure out why a physically and conventionally attractive woman is apparently interested in him.

Sarah:	That's funny.
ChuckChuck:	Well, I'm a funny guy.
Sarah:	Clearly! Which is good, because I am not funny.
ChuckChuck:	Is that your big secret, by the way? Cause I've been sitting here trying to figure out what's wrong with you …
Sarah:	Oh, plenty … believe me.
ChuckChuck:	I was thinking "either she's a cannibal, or she's really not that funny," and I was pulling for cannibal 'cause I'd never met one before …
Sarah:	Uh, not a cannibal, but I did just come out of a long relationship, so I may come with baggage.
ChuckChuck:	Well, I could be your very own baggage handler. (McG 2010)

The gap between the two characters only widens when Sarah is revealed to be a CIA agent and ends up undercover as Chuck's girlfriend, positioning the characters for an awkward sitcom-esque dynamic of putting up the pretense of being in a relationship even as they begin to form a real one. The first episode of *Chuck* ends with Chuck watching Sarah, his new CIA agent handler, walk through the store with a distinctive ring on her finger. Seeing the ring gives Chuck and immediate memory flash, pushing him to see images of her recorded on video fighting multiple men and shooting a gun towards a surveillance camera with a smile. This moment is a reminder that, unlike her textual counterpart Penny, Sarah serves as a prototypical strong female character behind her disguise of dumb blonde. The series gradually reveals that Sarah was previously involved with Chuck's former friend-turned-rival-turned-CIA agent Bryce Larkin, a character who is shown as demonstrating both mental and martial arts prowess.

Chuck's sister and her boyfriend, often referred to by Chuck and his friends as "Captain Awesome," further provide clear foils as non-geek established adults with a clear path forward. Both are doctors employed in the medical field. Captain Awesome (Devon Woodcomb) provides a particularly valuable foil as a character with both intellectual prowess, as a cardiothoracic surgeon, and physical capabilities, as an athlete involved in sports and other activities. By contrast, Chuck fulfills many geek stereotypes: he is decidedly not athletic and he takes no active physical role in missions until a download gives him an instant, *Matrix*-esque, knowledge of martial arts. However, he is provided with an even more insidious foil for masculinity in the form of Morgan, his best friend and sidekick in the Nerd Herd. Interactions between Captain Awesome and Morgan emphasize the very different types of masculinity they represent:

Awesome: Morgan? Why don't you let me handle this? No offense, but I've had my fair share of ladies.

Morgan: That's because you live in a bubble. Okay? Take a look at yourself. Go ahead. It's a freakish bubble of handsomeness. Now look at me. No bubble, no bubble. I've gotta be completely verbal. (Chechik 2010)

Again, we see in this depiction a strong emphasis on the mind/body dichotomy: Morgan believes that his lack of physical attractiveness has forced him to develop compensatory skills with verbal and mental prowess, although his life circumstances and relationship history suggest that the opposite is the case. Awesome's attempts to help Morgan through the "crossroads" of his masculinity provide one of the show's more comic episodes, as he tries to assist Morgan with strategies like tucking in his shirt and using product in his hair while ultimately drawing even more attention to Morgan's relatively scrawny stature and arrested adolescent demeanor. After the transformation, Morgan shows up to work on Hallowe'en in a sweater vest, but ultimately reverts quickly to his old self. In that same episode, Morgan impresses his colleagues at the Nerd Herder by eating unidentifiable expired food out of the company refrigerator (McNeill 2007).

Throughout the evolution of the show, more of the characters from Chuck's regular life become involved in his new life as secret agent, providing an aspirational narrative of geek-to-hero transformation without any real costs to his social life or connections with familiar friends. But throughout, Chuck never loses his fundamental identity, despite becoming more physically capable and wielding weaponry (including a gun). He routinely performs his moments of competition and heroism through computer skills. Lauren Rosewarne (2016) notes that scenes like Chuck's competition with Freddie over hacking speed is part of an attempt to "reassert masculinity that has been somehow diminished," suggesting that hacking can be part of "regressive" performances of masculinity (50). We are constantly invited to compare him to his NSA agent foil, Casey, a man who directly embodies traditional masculinity and is shown as very capable of killing—a line Chuck, as geek hero, never crosses.

Imagining Silicon Valley

Both *Chuck* and *The Big Bang Theory* ignore realism in favor of comedy: in their imaginary worlds, a waitress can afford the same apartment as two Caltech scientists, and a tech support guy can defuse a computerized bomb with a porn site virus. Few geek-focused shows have taken a strongly realistic bend: among these, one of the most famous is the short-lived *Freaks and Geeks* (Feig and Kasdan 1999–2000). The 1999 show depicted a group of easily recognizable "freaks" and "geeks" in high school in 1980 and became a cult favorite (despite only twelve episodes airing) in part thanks to its acceptance that one could be simultaneously freak and geek:

> the central tension of the series is between mathlete Lindsay and Freak Lindsay, and where many other shows would buy into Kowchevski's argument that Lindsay is wasting her natural gift in favor of hanging out with a bunch of burnouts, *Freaks And Geeks* holds that tension in its head nicely. Lindsay probably stands a better chance of getting into MIT if she's first block on the mathletes, but [the freaks] in many ways, give her the confidence to be more truly herself. (VanDerWerff 2013)

A decade and a half later, the show still remains remarkable for inviting those tensions and honesty in character portrayals even as more modern geek-centered fare rejects complexity.

3 Beauty and the Geek: On-Screen Representations of Geeks

One of the most notable recent examples of geek portrayals on television goes straight to the heart of geek power: *Silicon Valley* (Altschuler et al. 2014–). HBO's *Silicon Valley* is a relatively new show, premiering in 2014, with a premise straight out of *Wired* cover articles—six young men struggling and triumphing as they found a Silicon Valley start-up. Lauren Rosewarne notes that the characters in *Silicon Valley* perceive themselves as part of a category of netgeek heroism, or as the "geek-made-good," which includes financial as well as social success (147). The show opens with what could easily work as a modern geek dream sequence: young programmer Richard Hendricks is trying to pitch his music app, Pied Piper, for funding from a venture capitalist. After his app is recognized for having brilliant underlying software algorithms, Hendricks finds himself with a new partner and funding to take his start-up to the next level. The episodes follow their struggles with shady business deals, lawsuits, publicity stunts, and other pitfalls straight out of the history of companies such as Facebook and Snapchat.

In the first episode, CEO Gavin Belson comments on the homogeneity of Silicon Valley's many teams: "It's weird. They always travel in groups of five. These programmers, there's always a tall skinny white guy, a short skinny Asian guy, fat guy with a ponytail, some guy with crazy facial hair and then an East Indian guy. It's like they trade guys until they all have the right group" (Judge 2014). His statement is intended humorously, but it instead draws attention to how little variance the show allows its characters in their masculinity and diversity: the central characters reflect a fairly similar distribution, although they at least lack some of the characteristics of the "brogrammers" that provide them with foils.

From the very first moments, it is made abundantly clear that women have little place in the powered in-circle of *Silicon Valley*. Women hover at the outskirts at a high-powered party while networking takes place man-to-man, and the amount of wealth is clear. In this world, Kid Rock is an accessory brought into give a party gravitas, then ignored, and masculinity is measured in technical prowess and status (Yang 2014). Reviewers have criticized the show's apparent willingness to reflect Silicon Valley's own poor gender ratios by rendering women mostly invisible on the show:

> The near-total invisibility of women in the show doesn't problematize the valley's lack of gender diversity so much as it simply replicates it and dials it up to ten. A more successful strategy for highlighting the dearth of women in tech would be to actually show us some interesting female characters, and have them play a part in critiquing the current reality. (Bacon 2014)

The show's leading men are depicted as simultaneously anxious about the lack of women and anxious about appearing to have hiring preferences for women, as one exchange captures:

Jared: There's a distinct over-representation of men in this company. Look around. I think it would behoove us to prioritize hiring a woman.
Gilfoyle: I disagree, OJ. We should hire the best person for the job, period.
Dinesh: And Carla is one of the best.
Jared: Right, let me rephrase: I think having a woman in the company is important but hiring someone only because they're a woman is bad. I would never compromise Pied Piper.
Richard: Okay, just to be clear, our top priority is to hire the most qualified person available, right?
Jared: Of course.
Dinesh: But would be better if that someone was a woman even though the "woman" part of that statement is irrelevant?
Jared: Exactly. It's like we're the Beatles and now we just need Yoko.
Dinesh: That's the worst example you could have used. (Berg 2015)

Likewise, when women are portrayed on the show, they often fall victim to some of the worst assumptions of geek masculinity:

> [I]t seems the greatest effect of Silicon Valley sexism and gender disparity is how hard it makes it for these guys to hook up with women. The jokes' target is the pathetic, emasculated dudes, sex-starved nerds busy with dick-measuring contests—not the troubling system they're a part of. Instead of skewering the tech world, the show merely reproduces its toxic mythologies. (Breger 2014)

Thus, the depictions of women on the show offer few counterparts to the persistent masculinity at its center, and a tendency towards tokenism in portrayals of geek culture not only continues but is reinforced by its own character's words.

Silicon Valley has drawn mixed reviews for its accuracy as a show, although the show's creators have emphasized their connection to tech culture: as executive producer Alec Berg notes, "I've been very immersed in socially awkward nerd culture my entire life. Mike's the same way. The rhythms and idiosyncrasies of those guys are very familiar to us" (Jurgensen and Rusli 2014).

Stephanie Chan investigated parallels between the show's depictions of clothing and noted that they seemed to have accurately captured brogrammer 'drag':

> If watching HBO's "Silicon Valley," which paints brogrammers as code-typing, conniving bullies in tight T-shirts with the wrong kind of Valley accent, hurts a little, it's because it cuts too close to the truth. Take a stroll around San Francisco's South of Market district, though, and you'll see fewer fist bumps and spandex tees and more men who look like the show's main character, Richard, in his button-up shirt and slacks. (Chan 2014)

This clash of uniform between the "brogrammer" and the more conventional geek serves a deliberate role in the series: it offers a visual reminder that even among geek men there are "cool" bullies, who are more successful at occupying a traditional position of hegemonic masculinity than their less "masculine" counterparts. These characters, who simultaneously succeed by the definitions of both categories, are the ultimate example of geek masculinity's impact on hegemonic masculinity.

Conclusion

Geek television depicts an interesting view of identity. While centering an entire series on geeks shows a surprisingly level of acceptance from previous decades, there remains the reliance on older tropes and viewpoints about the unsuitability of the geek in the masculine hierarchy. They are shown as being powerful, perhaps even attractive, within certain realms, but they can't dominate the social structure that they live under. Their stance is still that of the outsider who cannot fit in with a normal society and should be viewed with mild pity and humor.

Many of the classic geek characters of television were tokens within groups of non-geek coded characters, from *Saved by the Bell*'s Screech to *Family Matters*' Urkel. These characters were not presented as aspirational, and were usually limited to providing foils for their starring counterparts. However, the balance of power has shifted in some shows, with *The Big Bang Theory* the most direct example of what happens when geeks are presented as dominant within a grouping. Meanwhile, shows such as *Silicon Valley* recast classic narratives of business and power with geeky residents of a space that bears little resemblance to Wall Street, except perhaps in the clustering of money and power available. Alongside the popularized geek heroes of culture (with Mark Zuckerberg and Steve Jobs as the most recognized), these characters are reshaping the popular perception of geekdom. In some ways, these retellings are broadening definitions and possibilities: however, the range of masculinities expressed remains relatively narrow, and the spaces afforded to women to occupy these narratives are limited.

In the attempt to classify a singular geek identity, television comes closest to presenting an inter-textual consistency. Current geek shows draw heavily upon existing media representations of geeks but gives them a bit more shine and depth than had previously been presented. Instead of being the beleaguered outsiders, geeks can run the show, and perform hegemonic masculinity even while apparently expanding its boundaries. This reflects the changing role of geek-coded activities within our society. Before the early 2000s technology was difficult to use and expensive to purchase, but today technology is everywhere and the computer savvy are a valuable asset. As culture shifts to align with economic and social pressures the interpretation of those who embody those values will rise. However, not enough time has passed for there to have been significant changes. The geeks are shown as being more relatable to the common person and more desirable within a modern setting, but they are still outsiders, the weird kids who don't fit in. This positions geek masculinity upon a precipice of identity. There must be some acknowledgement of their power over technology and cultural interests, but they still do not feel that they have the control and respect that traditional masculinities saw attached to these things. Meanwhile, more traditional masculinities are looking to shore up their cultural power and are happy to continue making other identities feel disconnected from popular support. Much like the break within the Democratic Party along racial lines in the 1948 election, more traditionally presenting geeks, white, middle-class, educated men are being pulled towards supporting the traditional power structure. Those who fall outside of the traditional presentation (women, geeks of color, alternative sexualities, poor geeks) are being forced further away from the potential of the cultural shift in progress: geek masculinity has become part of hegemonic, white, male masculinity.

References

10 Things I Hate About You. 1999. Directed by Gil Junger. Buena Vista Pictures. DVD.

Altschuler, J., M. Judge, D. Krinsky (Writers), and M. Judge, A. Berg, J. Babbit (Directors). 2014–. *Silicon Valley*. Los Angles, CA: HBO.

Apatow, Judd. 2007. *Knocked Up*. Directed by Judd Apatow. Universal Pictures. DVD.

Bacon, Lauren. 2014. You know what's more sexist than Silicon Valley? Its HBO version. *Quartz*, April 15. Accessed July 19, 2015. http://qz.com/199337/you-know-whats-more-sexist-than-silicon-valley-its-hbo-version/.

Berg, Alec. 2015. The lady. *Silicon Valley*, season 2, episode 4. May 3, HBO.

Bilefsky, Dan. 2015. Women respond to Nobel Laureate's "trouble with girls." *The New York Times*, June 11. Accessed July 12, 2015. http://nytimes.com/2015/06/12/world/europe/tim-hunt-noble-laureate-resigns-sexist-women-female-scientists.html?_r=0.

Breger, Esther. 2014. The boring sexism of HBO's "Silicon Valley." *New Republic*, May 30. Accessed June 2, 2015. https://newrepublic.com/article/117963/hbos-silicon-valleys-boring-sexism.

Butler, Judith. 2002. *Gender trouble*. New York: Routledge.

Butmyopinionisright. 2012. The problem with *The Big Bang Theory* ... *Tumblr*, September 7. Accessed January 8, 2015. http://butmyopinionisright.tumblr.com/post/31079561065/the-problem-with-the-big-bang-theory.

Cendrowski, Mark. 2007. The leftover thermalization. *The Big Bang Theory*, season 8, episode 18. October 22, CBS.

———. 2010. The robotic manipulation. *The Big Bang Theory*. September 23, CBS.

———. 2012. The transporter malfunction. *The Big Bang Theory*. March 29, CBS.

———. 2015. The perspiration implementation. *The Big Bang Theory*. October 19, CBS.

Chan, Stephanie. 2014. HBO's "Silicon Valley" tech uniform is unbellievably accurate. *Business Insider*, May 4. Accessed August 23, 2015. http://www.businessinsider.com/tech-uniform-2014-5.

Chechik, Jeremiah S. 2010. Chuck versus the American hero. *Chuck*, season 3, episode 12. March 29, NBC.

Cheng, Cliff. 1999. Marginalized masculinities and hegemonic masculinity: An introduction. *Journal of Men's Studies* 7 (3): 295–315. https://doi.org/10.3149/jms.0703.295.

Chidester, Phil. 2008. May the circle stay unbroken: Friends, the presence of absence, and the rhetorical reinforcement of whiteness. *Critical Studies in Media Communication* 25 (2): 157–174. https://doi.org/10.1080/15295030802031772.

Clancy, Kate. 2015. Girls with toys: This is what real scientists look like. *Slate*, May 18. Accessed May 21, 2015. http://www.slate.com/articles/health_and_science/science/2015/05/girls_with_toys_on_twitter_feminist_hashtag_shares_images_of_women_doing.html.

Connell, R.W. and James W. Messerschmidt. 2005. Hegemonic masculinity: Rethinking the concept. *Gender and Society* 19 (6): 829–859. https://doi.org/10.1177/0891243205278639.

Darowski, Joseph J. 2012. Chuck versus the machine: The intersection of biology, technology, and identity on *Chuck*. *The Journal of Popular Culture* 45 (4): 712–726. https://doi.org/10.1111/j.1540-5931.2012.00954.x.

Feig, P. (Writer), and J. Kasdan (Director). 1999–2000. *Freaks and Geeks*. United States: Paramount Worldwide.

Geek Google Image Search. Google. Accessed January 24, 2016.

Goldberg, Lesley. 2014. *Big Bang Theory* renewed through season 10. *Hollywood Reporter*, March 12. Accessed June 5, 2015. http://www.hollywoodreporter.com/live-feed/big-bang-theory-renewed-season-687949.

Judge, Mike. 2014. Minimum viable product. *Sillicon Valley*, season 1, episode 1. April 6, HBO.

Jurgensen, John and Evelyn M. Rusli. 2014. There's a new geek in town: HBO's "Silicon Valley." *The Wall Street Journal*, April 3. Accessed August 9, 2016. https://www.wsj.com/articles/SB10001424052702303987004579479244213599118.

Kendall, Lori. 1999. Nerd nation: Images of nerds in U.S. popular culture. *International Journal of Cultural Studies* 2 (2): 260–283. https://doi.org/10.1177/136787799900200206.

Kendall, Lori. 2011. "White and nerdy": Computers, race and the nerd stereotype. *The Journal of Popular Culture* 44 (3): 505–524. https://doi.org/10.1111/j.1540-5931.2011.00846.x.

Lotz, Amanda. 2014. *Cable guys: Television and masculinities in the 21st century*. New York: New York University Press.

Mancuso, Gail. 1996. The one with the Princess Leia Fantasy. *Friends*, season 3, episode 1. September 19, NBC.

Marshall, Lisa Marie. 2007. "I'll be there for you" if you are just like me: An analysis of hegemonic social structures in "Friends." Unpublished PhD Dissertation, Bowling Green State University.

McG. 2010. Pilot. *Chuck*, season 1, episode 1. March 29, NBC.

McNeill, Robert Duncan. 2007. Chuck versus the sandworm. *Chuck*, season 1, episode 6. October 29, NBC.

Palca, Joe. 2015. 'Playing around with telescopes' to explore secrets of the universe. *NPR*, May 16. Accessed April 12, 2017. http://www.slate.com/articles/health_and_science/science/2015/05/girls_with_toys_on_twitter_feminist_hashtag_shares_images_of_women_doing.html.

Pearson, MacKenzie. 2015. Why girls love the dad bod. *The Odyssey Online*, March 30. Accessed April 1, 2015. http://theodysseyonline.com/clemson/dad-bod/97484/.

Rosewarne, Lauren. 2016. *Cyberbullies, cyberactivists, cyberpredators: Film, TV, and internet stereotypes*. Santa Barbara, CA: Praeger.

Sartain, Jeffrey A. 2015. Geeksploitation: Gender and genius in *The Big Bang Theory*. In *Genius on television: Essays on small screen depictions of big minds*, ed. Ashley Lynn Carlson, 96–112. Jefferson, NC: McFarland.

Smith, Brian. 2005. Episode 1.1. *Beauty and the Geek*, season 1, episode 1. June 1, CW.
Soles, Carter. 2013. Team Apatow and the tropes of geek-centered romantic comedy. *Bright Lights Film Journal*, October 31. Accessed April 10, 2017. http://brightlightsfilm.com/team-apatow-and-the-tropes-of-geek-centered-romantic-comedy/.
Stansfield, James. 2013. The geek credentials of *How I Met Your Mother*. *Den of Geek*, August 29. Accessed February 14, 2015. http://www.denofgeek.com/tv/how-i-met-your-mother/27074/the-geek-credentials-of-how-i-met-your-mother.
Sullivan, Robert David. 2013. *The Big Bang Theory*'s character and cast progression earns its viewers. *AV Club*, September 25. Accessed August 9, 2015. http://www.avclub.com/article/ithe-big-bang-theoryis-character-and-cast-progress-103291.
Trainer, David. 2005. Short and curlies. *That '70s Show*, season 7, episode 24. May 18, CBS.
TV Tropes. 2017. Ugly guy, hot wife. *TV Tropes*, April 11. Accessed April 12, 2017. http://tvtropes.org/pmwiki/pmwiki.php/Main/UglyGuyHotWife.
TV.com. 2015. *Beauty and the Geek* show summary. https://www.tv.com, February 9. Accessed February 9, 2015. http://www.tv.com/shows/beauty-and-the-geek/.
VanDerWerff, Todd. 2013. Looks and books. *Freaks and Geeks*. *AV Club*, August 14. Accessed February 19, 2015. http://www.avclub.com/tvclub/freaks-and-geeks-looks-and-books-101384.
Weyman, Andrew D. 2007. The hamburger postulate. *The Big Bang Theory*, season 1, episode 5. October 22, CBS.
Williams, Joan. 2010. *Reshaping the work: Family debate*. Cambridge, MA: Harvard University Press.
Yang, Jeff. 2014. Pilot: TV recap. *Silicon Valley*, season 1, episode 1. *The Wall Street Journal*, April 6. Accessed March 12, 2015. http://blogs.wsj.com/speakeasy/2014/04/06/silicon-valley-season-1-episode-1-pilot-tv-recap/.

4

Come Get Some: Damsels in Distress and the Male Default Avatar in Video Games

In 2012, science fiction author John Scalzi (known to geeks for novels such as *Redshirts* [2012b], a send-up of the disposability of minor characters in *Star Trek*) decided to address what he perceived as a lack of awareness of privilege in the geek community by drawing a metaphor from gaming: "straight white male," he explained, is the lowest difficulty level setting you can choose in the game of life (2012a). He further elaborated on the idea of life as a role-playing game, noting that the truly hardcore players at the game of life (i.e., a poor, lesbian woman of color) were those who started with none of the systemically advantageous categories, and in doing so built a concept of the world as a game where all of these identities were represented. The piece immediately caused a stir within the gaming community, particularly after it was published on Kotaku, a games journalism site notorious for attracting trolling and misogynist discourse. However, the piece did not trigger the type of self-reflection on privilege that Scalzi had perhaps set out to inspire. Another science fiction writer, Erin Hoffman (2012), pointed out that the metaphor was unlikely to ever be successful in reaching gamers because it suggested that most gamers are, in life, "casual players," and "to be 'casual' takes away everything about their primary self-identification, and is not going to remotely elicit a rational response." The very term hardcore gamer suggests intensity (and inevitably draws an association with "hardcore" versus "softcore" in other spaces including pornography and punk music), although there is really no set definition of the term: it is an identity label whose boundaries are set by those who chose to adopt it. In a 2011 Kotaku piece on the myth of hardcore gaming, journalist Tim Poon noted that even he isn't sure what the real distinction is between hardcore and casual gaming: "Perhaps much like US Supreme Court Justice Potter Stewart in Jacobellis v. Ohio, there is no intelligible definition of a casual or hardcore game, but 'I know it when I see it' … hardcore gamers generally find casual games too simplistic and not true video games, and for that reason, they find it inappropriate and possibly offensive that the casual players dare file themselves under the same banner as the 'true' gamers have taken so much pride in." Even the apparently negative aspects of the hardcore label are often embraced as definitive parts of the identity, as TL Taylor (2006) commented in her study of players in the Everquest massively multiplayer online role-playing game (MMO): "the casual gamer is often seen as someone 'with a life' who invests only moderate amounts of time in a game, while the power gamer appears as an isolated and socially inept player with little 'real life' to ground him … it dichotomizes and oversimplifies the much more complicated social experience of players in each category." Given that tension, it's easy to use the term casual gamer as an insult, particularly for the very audience of hardcore gamers to which Scalzi's metaphor attempted to appeal.

This conflict over privilege (particularly when related to gender) is nothing new to the gaming community, but over the past several years an increased visibility of gaming thanks to in part to the rising industry of casual gaming has made the internal war over gamer identity more visible than ever. Scalzi's article served as just one catalyst for a broader discussion that included many expressions of outrage over the apparent equation of straight white male to an "easy" life, a characterization that a subset of hardcore gamers rallied to reject. In 2013, satirist Luke McKinney drew on the rage and privilege demonstrated in comments and related gaming discourse for his follow-up article to Scalzi's piece, "5 Gamer Comments that Give Straight White Guys a Bad Name." He identified (and, through his labeling, parodied) five common protests used to counter the description of straight white male privilege:

#5. Sexy Hot Babes Have it Easier!
#4. Everything-ism Is Over!
#3. My Life Sucks, So There's No Bias
#2. Never Mind Other People, You Hurt My FEELINGS!
#1. White Males Are the Only Minority Left! (McKinney 2013)

This list of assumptions could in some ways be applied to forum conversations and social media discourse surrounding feminism and misogyny across the web, but in gamer culture it takes on a particular focus that is in clear dialogue with the construction of identity within gaming texts. Scalzi's choice of metaphor was only part of the problem in his attempt to reach gamers: using gamespace to explore diversity in privilege falls flat in part because of the incredible lack of diversity within gaming. In life, straight white male might be the easiest difficulty level: in gaming, straight white male is the default avatar, which brings with it a different set of assumptions and consequences that make it difficult for games to break out of the straight white male gaze. Indeed, a disproportionate amount of attention in game studies and culture is focused on minority and marginalized game characters and players (including women) while the "default" identity of gaming goes relatively unremarked. This attentiveness to representations of the other is valuable, but it also allows the assumptions of white male identity as telegraphed in games to become invisible. The default becomes normal, unmarked, and thus difficult to challenge or contest.

Luke McKinney's satire of the responses from white male gamers to discussions of privilege reveals some assumptions that can also be analyzed in the larger context of video game culture. Perhaps most crucially, the top comment cluster called out by Luke McKinney suggests that the straight white man is an endangered species, and indeed that men are under attack within culture and thus the identity and power of white men must be protected from the incursion of dominant others (2013). In most video games, particularly in genres associated with the hardcore title, straight white male is often the only avatar presented. At the same time, those white males are often presented as marginalized, set against a world where everyone is out to thwart them and their desires—literally, game worlds where white men are a persecuted "minority." The others out to attack white men can take the form of invading aliens, zombies, and other monsters against which the lone white male hero is often cast as humanity's only hope: an all-too-familiar trope from science fiction and fantasy at large, as we discussed in our earlier analysis of male heroes in genre fiction. In games, this distinction becomes even greater: if marginalized characters are primarily presented as villains, sidekicks, or absent, the white male hero is the only character who gets to be embodied as a person. Everyone else's identities are scripted by the programmer and delivered by the computer's mediated interface, while the avatar is the player's character, and the agent of change and action in the game. This type of heroism is not unlike that presented by Neo in *The Matrix*: he is the only one who is above and outside the system, and thus the only one whose actions can change the world (Wachowski and Wachowski 1999). We will revisit some of the consequences of this association of white masculinity with agency later, in our discussion of "white knight" syndrome.

Avatars occupy a complex space in our discussions of geek masculinity more broadly, as games are simultaneously "macho" and passive, representing the ultimate space for fantasy play and dissonance between geek and character. Gaming embodies many of the contradictions between geek culture and masculinity, as avatars are often hypermasculine (athletic, militant, and violent) while the act of playing a video game is not inherently physical or masculine. Despite the rise of a few gaming systems that rely on mimetic interfaces, or interfaces in which the interaction mimics play, there remains a fundamental disconnect between the player's actions and the actions and physicality emulated within the gameworld. In this chapter, we will examine the construction of the male geek avatar, from the sexually challenged Leisure Suit Larry to the stripper-rescuing Duke Nukem, and consider the roles that these games offer for male wish fulfillment and play. The focus on male as actor in these games allows us to consider the woman as passive, and that passivity holds consequences for the perception of feminine in geek identity. Games are already a highly charged space for gendered discourse, and while the female avatar has often been considered, the ubiquitous white male warrior avatar has gone relatively unremarked thanks to his status as "default." We will probe the very notion of the white male hypermasculine as neutral by focusing on the most generic of avatars, as exemplified by the face of Doom's space marine staring up at the player even as the player controls a first-person shooter, and further explore the implications of these avatars for gaming culture and gendered discourse within the community. In examining these avatars, we can come to understand how gamer identity has come to be defined by a state of being always under attack, and how the defense of gamer identity against "others" has sparked an unprecedented scale of viciousness in the ongoing Internet culture wars. The most publicized of these clashes, "Gamergate," demands particular attention as it has brought the limitations and consequences of marginalization in gamer identity into focus as a defining battlefield of geekdom.

Game Characters and Masculinity

In surveying the terrain of straight white male characters in search of a better understanding of the default identity in gaming, we can easily become overwhelmed by the illusion of diversity among the many avatars that have captured critical and popular attention. As expected, many of the most iconic characters in video games fall under these identifiers, from the mustached Mario, a plumber on a constant quest to rescue his blonde princess in distress, to Gordon Freeman, the geek turned hero of *Half-Life* (Valve 1998) and *Half-Life 2* (Valve 2004). It is helpful to group some of these characters into categories based on common traits and genres, as particular genres of games lend themselves to avatars that express different masculine ideals. The arcade genre often features childlike or cartoony characters: Mario is of course the most iconic (and, thanks to transmedia and merchandising, one of the most recognizable even to non-gamers) but heroes such as Mega Man (an android introduced by Capcom in 1987) and Bomberman (Hudson Software 1983) are likewise heroes in action-packed cartoon worlds. Nintendo has also brought us one of the most recognizable blond male heroes, Link, who has his own princess, Zelda, to save (Nintendo 1986), and Pit, star of the *Kid Icarus* series, who has to rescue the Queen of Light Palutena in very similar circumstances (1986–2012). These characters have more in common with obvious warrior hypermasculine avatars such as biker Francis (*Left 4 Dead* 2008), SEAL Lieutenant Commander Sam Fisher (*Splinter Cell* 2002), fugitive cop *Max Payne* (2001), engineer-turned-survivalist Isaac Clarke (*Dead Space* 2008), and the many other heroes of shooter and horror games than first meets the eye when placing them side by side: all offer different entry points into a white male savior narrative of video games, in which the white male hero plays out a classic narrative of save the world and rescue the girl.

Crafting a portrait of the white male avatar is difficult in part because of the proliferation of such avatars: from Link to Mario, from Max Payne to Sam Fisher, male avatars apparently represent meaningful diversity in everything but those primary signifiers. Some of these notably break from expectations of the hypermasculine depiction, particularly in games in which violence is either less central or handled differently than in classic shooters. For instance, Ewan Kirkland's (2009) analysis of the characters of the *Silent Hill* series notes that while the game is dominated by masculine depictions and play, "the men of *Silent Hill* frequently contrast with the assured, unquestioning, militarized hypermasculinity regarded as standard across the industry; instead, they are ordinary, flawed, even neurotic to the point of psychosis" (178). Rather than contradicting our understanding of gaming as a hypermasculine space, however, such characters can instead be understood as demonstrating how the dominance of male avatars allows for a diversity of expression that minority and marginalized characters (thanks in part to their relatively low numbers) are rarely afforded within gaming narratives.

The relationship of these avatars with the game world is most essential to our understanding of their role in developing game identity. To recall Luke McKinney's satire of the white male as the only minority left, many games in fact build this concept into the development of the character's relevance and quest. In his examination of post-9/11, post-apocalyptic videogames, Ryan Lizardi (2009) notes that the protagonists of these games often refer to aliens and others using derogatory language "reminiscent of 1980s masculine action films" and demonstrate hypermasculine contempt and an insider mentality against the other. Such language and actions also reminds us of the intersectional element of race in these representations, as only the white male is afforded this level of personhood, and just as in many action films the role of villain is left to the racial other and their presumed threat (with fears of immigration and terrorism translated into tales of alien invaders and other "bad guys"). Games in this genre include *Gears of War* (2006), *Resistance* (2006), and *Halo* (2001), although the mechanisms and conceit of the genre recall earlier genre games, including even more abstract narratives such as *Space Invaders* (1978). These genres include a number of what Kishonna L. Gray (2014) refers to as white messiahs of shooters. Marcus Fenix of *Gears of War* (Epic Games 2006) is leader of primarily non-white characters and plays out a typical white messiah narrative: "his character succeeds against impossible odds against villains saving town after town" in a manner that "reaffirms the fantasy of an autonomous individual" even as his team members sacrifice themselves in his service (ibid., 21). Jessica Aldred and Brian Greenspan (2011) similarly explore dystopian game worlds, and note that in *Bioshock* the player takes on the role of a white male savior, Jack, on a journey that can end in one of two ways:

> a downward spiral of greed and malevolence, in which ... you take over the underwater city [or] you become the benevolent patriarch who brings the Little Sisters safely to the surface, where they are guided through a montage of compulsorily heterosexual life rituals that incrementally bind them to the patriarchy itself.

Bioshock is a complex text: it is a first-person shooter with an interwoven narrative of a doomed city and experimental technology that invites the rethinking of humanity in the context, and allows players to make decisions about the value of life in a way that other games in this genre rarely allow. However, it falls very strongly into the genre of white male as actor, with a white male antagonist, Andrew Ryan, standing in as an Ayn Rand figure inviting further discourse on race, class, and superiority. As Grant Tavinor (2009) notes, the entire game parallels and satirizes the objectivist philosophy advanced in Ayn Rand's *Atlas Shrugged*. Aldred and Greenspan's interpretation of the ending points out that the fate and assimilation of the Little Sisters into "normal" society is again placed into the hands of the player, with an outcome not unlike that of any other damsel in distress game conceit. These readings invite us to consider how these characters have created expectations and narratives that have bled out into the larger discourse of gaming culture, often with inflammatory results.

Duke Nukem, Leisure Suit Larry and the Problem of "Parody"

The characters of today's post-apocalyptic dramas owe a great debt to earlier avatars and particularly to the heroes of early first-person shooters. The appropriately named Duke Nukem, one of the most brazenly straight white male avatars who is routinely cited as one of the greatest video game characters of all time, arose, unsurprisingly, out of the first-person shooter genre. Duke Nukem is masculine to the point of self-parody, usually depicted wearing a tank top and military ammunition vest that shows his steroid-enhanced muscle mass, with guns in both hands and sunglasses at night. *Duke Nukem 3D* (3D Realms 1996) brought Duke Nukem to life as a stripper-rescuing, alien-slaughtering hero complete with a ready arsenal ("50 Greatest Video Game Characters" 2015; Winegarner 2009). Throughout play, he repeated a range of appropriately hypermasculine catch-phrases, including "Nobody steals our chicks … and lives!" "Come get some!" and "Hail to the king, baby!"—the latter two both borrowed from the similarly hypermasculine horror-humor film *Army of Darkness* (Raimi 1992). The juxtaposition of Duke Nukem with the over-the-top action of parodic horror film *Army of Darkness*, in which experienced "evil dead" fighter Ash is teleported back to 1300 AD to fight an army of skeletons, invites us to read Duke Nukem's phrases humorously. However, there is no subtlety or self-awareness to the construction of Duke Nukem's identity, as his catchphrases are followed up with literal actions that convey a consistent objectification of women and exaltation in violence with no irony.

As the hero of the apocalypse-in-progress during *Duke Nukem 3D*, Duke Nukem is almost an embodiment of McKinney's (2013) first highlighted gamer outcry—"white males are the only minority left." Duke Nukem drops into Los Angeles for a vacation and instead finds that all the men are dead and the city is overrun by pig-faced cops (literally, not metaphorically, pig-faced) and aliens. Other men are invisible in the game, with the exception perhaps of the corpse of a space marine in one of the levels, an homage to

Fig. 4.1 A captured woman in *Duke Nukem 3D*

another white male avatar from *Doom* (id Software 1993). Duke's mission takes him through strip clubs and alien ships with captured mostly naked women held for fiendish alien plots (see Fig. 4.1). The game ends with Duke Nukem killing the alien leader and retiring for "more action" in bed with one of the many rescued women. As an avatar, Duke Nukem is an endangered white man with the entire world against him, and a collection of (primarily) white women to save. These women are objectified throughout: without prompting, Duke shouts things like "Shake it, baby!" and "You wanna dance?" to strippers he encounters throughout the game. Inevitably, all the women in the game are either strippers or mostly nude women encapsulated in alien pods: stripper and hostage are the two roles offered to women in Duke's world. These echoes of the "damsel in distress" theme have carried forward from Mario's princess-rescuing onwards.

It is thus only appropriate that Duke Nukem himself has survived as an avatar at the center of many gaming gender controversies. *Duke Nukem Forever* (3D Realms and Gearbox Software) was finally released after years of pushbacks to poor reviews in 2011. The game itself included a mode called "Capture the Babe," in which teams could fight over women by capturing them and slapping their behinds to calm them down so they can carry them away. Any anger at the inclusion of the "spank" button was parodied by Mike Krahulik and Jerry Holkins in their gaming webcomic *Penny Arcade*, with the two white male gamers having an exchange: "Did you know there's a mode in *Duke Nukem* where you slap a woman's bottom?" / "Did you know there's a mode in *Call of Duty* where you murder, like, a million people? It's called *Call of Duty*" (Krahulik and Holkins 2011). This false equivalency is a common argument in gaming: why, after all, should we be offended by playful sexism when playful violence remains at the center? The "Capture the Babe" mode perfectly captures the Duke Nukem complex, as all players within the battle play as Duke Nukem seeking to "out-score" the other team through their acquisition of women. In an interview by John Callaham (2010), developer Randy Pitchford noted that the character had evolved beyond satire thanks to their refusal to give his worldview any complexity:

> Many imagine that Duke began as a cliché or amalgamation of the prima-facie heroes during a great era for action heroes. Since then, we've sort of witnessed a pussification of our heroes in action movies. They have become complex, emotional characters. Duke, being incredibly one-sided and super badass, now stands out, not as a cliché, but as a unique and fresh character rising through a tide of emo.

The use of the word "pussification" is particularly telling, as it suggests strong negative associations with any move towards behaviors coded as feminine. Pitchford suggests that their disinterest in granting Duke Nukem any depth is thus part of his power, and it is certainly what makes him such an uncomplicated choice for analysis as a hypermasculine ideal (ibid.).

The marketing for the game reflected a broad embrace of Duke Nukem's ideals. The game was promoted at Penny Arcade Expo, or PAX East, a gaming convention that officially has a no "booth-babes" policy. Despite that policy, the *Duke Nukem Forever* booth featured models wearing revealing schoolgirl outfits sitting next to a garish throne in which gamers could pose with the women as props. The use of the throne and implied subservience of the women took on a particularly garish tone given the presence of chandeliers and banners with catchphrases including "Come Get Some" welcoming gamers to the booth. The convention is run by the same team behind the Penny Arcade webcomic, which made light of the spanking mode in *Duke Nukem Forever*. In a similar dismissal of the potential consequences of this type of display to the women attending the event, Penny Arcade argued that as the women were dressed as characters from the game, their outfits were allowable and they would not be removed as booth-babes. Coverage in the gaming media was more upfront, with Stephen Totilo (2011) posting photos to *Kotaku* under the heading "Duke Nukem Draws Them in with the Ladies, and the Chandeliers," noting "Some game booths here at PAX East turn heads because of their posters or their people dressed in mech suits. That's too classy for Duke Nukem Forever." As a leading force in the gaming community, Penny Arcade and PAX have already been central to gaming gender controversy. The comic itself features the two male avatars of the writer and artist, and often uses sexist humor as part of the punchline. In 2010, a comic was posted that depicted rape as a game mechanic for humorous purposes, causing a broader discussion on gaming's engagement with rape culture and the questionable status of PAX as a safe space. The events that followed included Penny Arcade's decision to sell a team jersey themed shirt around the rapist creature from their comic, a "dickwolf," and a subsequent dispute that demonstrated how the "increasing presence of female gamers is met at the contentious boundary by pushing femininity to the outskirts of gaming spaces, thus reaffirming the role of the masculine with hardcore gamer identity" (Salter and Blodgett 2012).

Duke Nukem is an extreme case of a gaming avatar, as his actions and identity perfectly embody the ideal definition of the hypermasculine. However, he is the perfect starting point for our consideration of gaming avatars as spaces where cisgendered, straight, white male identity has become a default setting. The original Duke Nukem could be dismissed as a figure of parody, an extreme macho man with a muscular build that only steroids or computer animation could even make possible. He drew on his origins, particularly Bruce Campbell's *Army of Darkness* fighting action hero, and delivered deadpan lines with no trace of irony or self-awareness. Nearly fifteen years later, his same persona might seem out of touch with modern humor and sensibilities, but in reality he serves as a valuable reminder of the limits of parody: Duke Nukem is too close to the white male character ideal to be dismissed as satirical, and in a world of battling space marine descendants Duke serves not only as an iconic character but as a totemic hypermasculine avatar. His struggle is the struggle of a white man as marginalized victim made outsider by a world of aliens who can only be overcome by violence. The prize for his successful fighting always takes the form of women, as in the final scene of *Duke Nukem 3D*.

The difficulty settings for *Duke Nukem 3D*, *Doom*, and other iconic first-person shooters often feature different levels with greater implied macho and masculine attributes associated with higher difficulty levels, while easy levels often include some derision towards the player for even selecting the option. For instance, in *Duke Nukem 3D*, difficult levels included "Piece of Cake," "Let's Rock," "Come Get Some," and the nightmare difficulty "Damn I'm Good." Doom's difficulty skill levels ranged from "I'm Too Young to Die" and "Hey, Not Too Rough" to "Hurt Me Plenty," "Ultra-Violence," and "Nightmare." The sentiment remained even as we switch contexts, with a fantastical follow-up to *Doom* (id Software 1993), *Heretic* (id Software 1994), including a difficulty level entitled "Thou Needeth a Wet-Nurse." The difficulty levels across these early games were primarily distinguished by the quantity, distribution, and quality of enemies, and occasionally involved the distribution of resources such as ammunition and health flasks. The very labelling of these difficulty levels (and the shaming corresponding with "easy" mode) is a reminder of why Scalzi's (2012a) metaphor failed: no self-respecting hardcore gamer wants to view themselves as the person struggling through the "Wet-Nurse" difficulty setting of life. The very implication that a gamer is playing life on easy mode is an offense, particularly given the interpersonal struggles that are a defining backbone of geek identity.

Duke Nukem is not merely a hypermasculine macho avatar: he is a metaphorical embodiment of the struggles of a white male gamer. And even his most apparently contradictory counterparts, such as Leisure Suit Larry, hold similar positions. Characters such as Leisure Suit Larry (Sierra On-Line 1987) and Guybrush Threepwood (Lucasfilm Games 1990) are the geeks of the gaming universe, awkward around women and incapable of handling themselves in physical combat. Leisure Suit Larry is as extreme as Duke Nukem in his relationship with women, but his skills and machismo appear to be the exact opposite. As a polyester-lounge suit-wearing bar rat with no assets, his mission is always to get laid, but his ability to achieve that mission is questionable at best. Guybrush Threepwood is more noble (and in constant pursuit of one woman, the highly capable pirate-turned-governor Elaine Marley) but equally inept, and the player is in both cases invited to try to guide these failure-prone men through the challenges that accumulate on the way to a woman's bed and/or heart. It is notable that both of these characters are from adventure games, a classic genre that incorporated very little action and thus very few action heroes, with even the most potentially macho of characters (such as investigator Gabriel Knight in the games of the same name, or Indiana Jones in early Lucasfilm adventure games) typically not involved in combat.

The adventure games in the *Leisure Suit Larry* series span several years: the original game was released in 1987, with sequels as late as 2009. The fundamentals of Leisure Suit Larry's methods have not changed over the years:

in 2013, *Leisure Suit Larry Reloaded* (Replay Games 2013), a Kickstarter-funded remake of the original, was released. The Kickstarter campaign was appropriately titled "Make Leisure Suit Larry come again!" and included reward levels including the Lefty's Bar Pack (complete with a "reveal" pen of one of the game's women characters) and the high-tier "Pervert's Edition," which offered backers the chance to be included as judgmental customers during Larry's purchase of a condom in a convenience store (Replay Games 2012). The game still opens with Larry outside the seedy Lefty's Bar. Progression requires Larry to head to a casino and win more than US $10,000 at the in-game Blackjack tables. One of the women Larry pursues, "Fawn" at Club 69, will only dance with Larry after he first gives her a rose, candy, and a ring. Larry can marry Fawn in a quick Vegas-style wedding after giving her his wallet, although ultimately he ends up in bed alone, tied down, with his wallet missing. This scene is at best cynical of the motivations of both parties: Fawn is drawn as an animated, Jessica Rabbit-esque, pin-up girl, and she is very clear on her own intentions when confronted with Larry's attempts to get her into bed. Throughout the series, Larry's single-minded quest often ends in similar failure, as when his courting of Rose in *Leisure Suit Larry 6* (Sierra Entertainment 1993) ends with Larry getting an enema, or when his attempt in the same game to win over the dominatrix Thunderbird ends with Larry on a leash as a "puppy dog."

Thus as an avatar Larry Laffer is a man with a simple quest to get laid, and he is forever thwarted by the standards of women who are sexually desirable but not available to him, or, if available, turn out to be sexually "flawed" in some way that thwarts his conquest. In his constant attempts to manipulate the situation and "beat the boss" by getting laid, Larry is if anything a perfect counterpart to the pick-up artist community, which likewise views women in terms of conquest and obstacles. As Amanda Denes (2011) analyzes in her study of classic pick-up artist texts, such strategies involve ignoring, subduing, or subverting women's conversation in the pursuit of a "biological" reaction that will result in a sexual encounter. Such strategies and metaphors equate easily to games as they involve reductionist views of women as targets, not unlike AI opponents in a video game. It is thus unsurprising that the discourse surrounding the pick-up artist community (which has strong overlaps and ties to sections of the gaming community) is filled with a vocabulary not unlike gaming's, with a Kickstarter project entitled "Above the Game" attracting huge support from Reddit with advice such as "Don't ask for permission. Be dominant" (quoted in "'Above the Game,' A Guide" 2013) eerily recalling both the occasional tactics of Larry and the "Capture the Babe" mode of *Duke Nukem Forever*.

While Leisure Suit Larry and Duke Nukem both present physical extremes, their hypermasculinity is inherent both in their pursuits and in the "man-versus-world" mentality they represent. And, of course, both are ultimately rewarded: both *Duke Nukem 3D* and the first of Leisure Suit Larry's adventures end with the characters in bed with conventionally attractive women. In the case of *Duke Nukem 3D*, the woman was "earned" through victory over the final alien bad guy, while in Leisure Suit Larry, a progression of gifts and money are primarily used to "overcome" obstacles and reach the desired target. (In *Leisure Suit Larry in the Land of the Lounge Lizards*, a prostitute is available early on as a way to stop the virginity timer countdown, but sleeping with her will cause Larry to pick up an immediately fatal STD unless a condom is acquired first. And, of course, the game doesn't end until he acquires a woman through a less obvious financial transaction.) The equation of victory in *Leisure Suit Larry* games with "scoring" with a woman in a hot tub is not unlike the "Capture the Babe" mode in *Duke Nukem Forever*: both suggest to gamers that the world is hostile to their desires, but through the right strategies or use of force their avatars can still "score."

Gender in Gamer Identity

The simple equation of Duke Nukem or Leisure Suit Larry's patterns and identities to the broader development of gamer identity is an uneasy line to draw, as we risk oversimplifying the impact these texts have had. Attempts to understand the relationship between avatars and player attitudes are complicated: an experiment conducted by Karen Dill, Brian Brown, and Michael Collins (2008) suggested that long-term exposure to game stereotypes and attitudes could lead to a tolerance of sexual harassment and more significant attitude changes over time, but proving this sort of correlation in a complex environment is difficult and can lead to oversimplification. Many studies have focused on women characters thanks in part to their relative invisibility in gaming titles, which can lead us to overlook the environments that have constructed those stereotypes, and the resistance to change that characterizes gaming as an identity. We will first consider the visibility and representation of women as characters and avatars within gaming environments, then move to examine the inclusion of women in constructions of gamer identity and communities.

Christopher Near (2013) examined the relationship of female characters with video game sales in a study of 399 game boxes from 2005 to 2010, finding "sales were positively related to sexualization of non-central female characters among games with women present. In contrast, sales were negatively related to the presence of any central female characters (sexualized or non-sexualized) or the presence of female characters without male characters present." However, this may in part reflect the fact that 41.6% of the games only showed male characters, while only 6.8% of games had only female characters and the remainder had either both (27.1%) or no human characters at all (24.5%; ibid., 260). It is hard to generalize anything from representation on covers, but of course such figures make it even easier for marketing and sales organizations within the game industry to avoid expanding their representation of characters. An analysis of avatars, or playable characters, across 150 games over 9 platforms in 2009 found that of all characters 86.09% were male and 13.91% were female (Williams, Martins, Consalvo, and Ivory 2009). By comparison to the US population, these numbers suggest a dramatic overrepresentation of men (along with skewed ethnicity and other values). These figures of representation echo discussions in the broader media space about representation: one study noted that men perceive a crowd that is 17% women (the standard in Hollywood crowd scenes) as 50/50, while a crowd that is 33% women is perceived as having more women than men ("Casting Call: Hollywood Needs More Women" 2013). This ratio is echoed in games-based publicity and in play, where avatars can be of the player's chosen gender, but the non-player characters (NPCs) are often the visible actors within the main storyline, quests, shops, and leadership organizations within the game.

This trend of representation continues in virtual worlds, which in theory should provide the most diverse landscapes as explorable large-scale simulations. T. Franklin Waddell et al. (2014) examined characters encountered in twenty hours of play of *World of Warcraft* (2004), *Guild Wars* (2005), *Dungeons and Dragons Online* (2006), and *Runescape* (2001). Of the characters encountered who presented or were identifiable as gendered, 87.22% were male characters (7). Aside from recalling the distribution of women in Hollywood crowd scenes, these numbers must make us wonder how the assumption of the male default translates to the construction of worlds (which themselves echo the demographics of development teams at typical AAA studios.) In virtual worlds, these demographics are particularly troubling because they imply the presence of invisible women, playing domestic roles in the imagined homes of *World of Warcraft*'s urban hubs Stormwind or the Undercity, relegated to an insignificant status in building the population of what is supposed to be an immersive environment. Of course, these demographics can be changed by player avatar creation, but when the world is unoccupied by players the designer-built characters form the consistent population and the impetus for most player actions.

These numbers have a recurring similarity that demands examination: whether on game covers or in the "crowd" scenes of virtual worlds, women occupy a marginal space not unlike that they hold in the game development community itself. Indeed, that space seems calculated to keep women from even appearing to hold equal roles, as it usually falls below the 17% cut-off that the previously cited Hollywood study observed as the moment at which male viewers perceive equity. Given that expectation of gaming as a male space, and the potentially low threshold at which the space can be perceived by men as including a disproportionate number of women, it is perhaps unsurprising that the rise of casual gaming and the influx of visible women players that has come with it has been perceived as a potential assault on male gaming spaces. The game industry's marketing suggests an awareness of this need to put men front and center: a study of 225 console video game box covers from 2005 found that men were twice as likely to be portrayed, and "female characters were significantly more likely to be physically objectified than the male characters were," with large breasts a key part of most portrayals (Burgess, Stermer, and Burgess 2007). While male characters could (and have) been argued to present similarly unrealistic standards, they are not sexualized for a desiring gaze but instead offered as bodies for habitation. Projects such as "The Hawkeye Initiative," a satirical movement based on a concept from comic artist Noelle Stevenson, perfectly demonstrate the difference between the two types of objectification (Skjaldmeyja 2012–present). The initiative features the hypermasculine and macho Avenger Hawkeye in the poses offered to women in comics and results in spine-breaking body configurations that are very different from his typical posing or portrayals. A similar conflict between the two types of objectification played out when a woman working on *Hawken* (Meteor Entertainment 2012), a mechatech piloting and combat game, was uncomfortable with the company's pin-up picture of the woman mechanic (shown in the poster wearing cut-off shorts and a strip of fabric around only the center of her breasts) and decided to draw attention to it by replacing it with an image of the game's male mechanic wearing only briefs and displaying his abdominal muscles (Hudson 2013). The manager responsible for placing the original poster in the office responded by keeping both images side by side, according to the woman responsible for the substitution: "That was a brilliant prank. You called me on exactly the bullshit I need to be called on. I put up pictures of half-naked girls around the office all the time and I never think about it. I'm taking you and Sam to lunch. And after that, we're going to hang both prints, side by side" (AnonymousFan8675309 2013).

The impact of sexualized characters in office environments and in games themselves is difficult to measure in concrete terms. Elizabeth Behm-Morawitz and Dana Mastro (2009) used such sexualized and non-sexualized female heroines as a way to judge agency and their findings "cautiously" suggested that playing the sexualized characters negatively impacted the player's beliefs about women's abilities. However, their study was conducted focusing on women gamers, not men. Likewise, it is difficult to generalize about correlations or preferences of avatar gender among gamers: Carol Stabile's study (2014) of avatar gender choice (particularly in the form of gender-swapping) among MMO players noted that the flexibility of gender in such games "allows for some interesting examples of resistance… many of the players I played with brought into play critiques of what they understood to be the dominant forms of masculinity in these persistent virtual environments." This dominance of masculinity continues into the real-world offices where these virtual environments are built. The 2014 "Gamasutra Salary Survey" found that men are 95% of programmers, 91% of artists, 87% of designers, and 78% of producers. These numbers are remarkable even by the already low standards for gender representation in STEM fields, and become particularly troubling given even professions within the industry that are traditionally more diverse (such as artist) suffer from such extreme underrepresentation. The lack of representation among programmers is far less surprising, particularly as masculinity and programming have become more entwined: The term "brogrammer" was popularized in 2012, with an emphasis on rape jokes and a frat boy culture that "lay bare the conceptual problems with the recurrent 'boys and their toys' view of computing" (Hicks 2013). The very word "brogrammer" brings to mine office games of beer pong alongside late-night competitive deathmatches in first-person shooters, a combination of geek masculinity and hypermasculinity that leaves little room for diversity in the office. The working conditions of the game industry encourage the development of "brogrammer" culture and contribute to hostile work environments for women who do venture into the boys' club of the industry. These microaggressions and exclusive environments attracted particular attention in November 2012, when the hashtag "#1ReasonWhy" arose on Twitter as a way for women in the industry to chronicle the reasons why they felt marginalized and harassed (Blodgett and Salter 2013). The trolling and harassment of women using that hashtag only contributed to the portrait of a hostile space.

There is an assumption of a universal gamer identity experience that is both problematic and pervasive, as Adrienne Shaw (2013) noted in her interviews with game-players: "interviewees who fit the standard image of a gamer assumed that their viewpoints were 'a dime a dozen.'" In the context of a study of hardcore board gamers, Björk and Åresund (2009) noted the importance of considering gaming activity in its own context: "games can become social microsystems where each participant's role is that of a player. When we engage ourselves in games we thus tend to set aside who we are in other situations" (121). The emphasis here is on player, but the same might be said of the larger video game community, in which adopting the identity of a gamer can become a dominant identity. There is decidedly a difference between the identity of gamer (and the cultural role that comes with it) and the identity of a player, which implies a more limited and immediate social microsystem.

A survey of gamer attitudes conducted by Jesse Fox and Wai Yen Tang (2014) observed that "participants who endorsed masculine norms were more likely to report sexist attitudes about women's participation in video games," judging based on a sexism scale that included such statements as "Video games are a man's world, and women don't belong" (317) If hardcore gaming is its own microsystem, as the attempts of gamers to use it to construct a marginalized identity suggest, the hard numbers of representation from characters to women in the industry certainly seem to echo the assumption that this system is a "man's world." And, just as the inclusion of 33% women in a crowd scene may be to the male viewer a sign that women are abruptly dominating a space, so too is the increased visibility and participation of women in gaming threatening the very foundations of that microsystem.

Anita Sarkeesian and Gamergate

If we embrace gaming as a microsystem, we must with some uneasiness embrace the term gamer, which is a charged identity marker not unlike the very term "geek" and comes with community backing. Adrienne Shaw (2012) points out that studies tend to apply the term "gamer" to anyone who plays games, but this does not reflect its cultural usage: "How people identify as gamers, is a different question from who counts as a gamer… identification allows us to parse how one might be externally placed into a category from how one actually describes one's own identity" (29–30) Women are often considered well represented among gamers, with a 2014 study of British gamers suggesting women are now 52% of game-players (cited by Stuart 2014), but Shaw's study found that males were much more likely to adopt the label of gamer: "no other category, including race, sexuality, religion, education, age or type of gaming platform, demonstrated such a striking disparity between who identified as a gamer and who did not" (33). Sean Duncan (2013) suggests we think about the boundaries between games and designers, and game play and gamer communities, as dissolving: "there is an appealing connection to be made between a designed element of games (contestations over some form of space) and the practices that are negotiated and discussed in online affinity spaces" (44). If we embrace that assumption, particularly where game communities are concerned, then we can understand characterizations such as Duke Nukem and Leisure Suit Larry as existing within the current battlefield over gamer identity.

This tension over gamer as an identity label has played a significant role in the importance of "hardcore" and "casual" as distinguishing identity markers which allow primarily male gamers to mark certain titles and game players as unwelcome in the "true gamer" clubhouse. John Vanderhoef's (*Kotaku* 2013) analysis of conversations on video game sites including *Joystiq*, and *Destructroid* noted that hardcore gamers other casual games as "games for girls," and:

> despite the co-presence of dissenting voices that critique these gendered attacks, the core gamers I highlight utilize hegemonic conceptions of gender to degrade casual video games, employ post-feminist sarcasm that ends up reifying the hardcore/casual binary even as they critique it, and evoke a protest rhetoric of victimization by positioning the casual games movement as a dominating, oppressive force bent on destroying and replacing traditional, masculinist games.

This rhetoric has existed since casual gaming became a marketing force, but it has risen significantly over the past five years.

An unexpected catalyst in the hardcore/casual gendered discourse took the form of a YouTube video series funded by a Kickstarter. *Tropes vs. Women in Video Games*, Anita Sarkeesian's video series on the role of women in games, has generally attracted threatening and violent resistance among a segment of male gamers, but her video suggesting that most women in video games are cast as the "damsel in distress" awaiting rescue by a male hero attracted vitriol (2013). The attacks towards Anita Sarkeesian have taken many forms, from threats and violent comments to sexual harassment to games. Notably, the "Beat Up Anita Sarkeesian" game was published in

July 2012 on Newgrounds by Bendilin Spurr with the description Anita Sarkeesian "claims to want gender equality in video games, but in reality, she just wants to use the fact that she was born with a vagina to get free money and sympathy from everyone who crosses her path." This vicious comment gets straight to the heart of the creator's attitude: Sarkeesian's gender and support have, in his mind, invited him to make her into a literal virtual punching bag. The escalation of online threats over the past two years suggests that social media and games of this kind provide venues for the same type of simulated violence, in both cases with Sarkeesian as a target and usually with the lack of consequences that action through anonymous avatars provide. Whether her attackers are playing "Beat Up Anita Sarkeesian" or sending tweets with descriptive threats of sexual violence, they are engaged in the same game, and she is cast as a voiceless NPC enemy.

Aaron Trammell and Anne Gilbert (2014) suggest that as we incorporate our understanding of play with a critical analysis of media we can see that gaming communities are impacted by the most "ugly and barbaric aspects of play," including prejudice and discrimination (402). Certainly, the "Beat Up Anita Sarkeesian" game and the other harassment that has followed are an example of precisely that ugliness. Nowhere has this played out so clearly as in the use of identity as a weapon through the practice of "doxing." This tactic demands that anonymity be eliminated for any women in the gaming community and makes it difficult for women to participate safely in discourse:

> While many feminist bloggers choose to use their real names anyway, most still suggest that pseudonymity must remain a choice anywhere where one seeks to have conversations about issues of import… while real name policies are purportedly enstated to protect the safety of online conversations, many bloggers, pseudonymous and otherwise, suggest that real name policies make women and minorities of all kinds less safe, both online and off-line, and have other negative effects on these groups as well. (Moll 2014)

This use of identity as a weapon took center stage in 2014 thanks to the rise of Gamergate, a movement organized first on 4Chan and Reddit and later primarily on 8Chan that started with the doxing and harassment of a woman game developer, Zoe Quinn (Lee 2014). Gamergate has been defined by its continual attacks on any woman who speaks out against them or attracts their ire for bringing feminist discourse or views into gaming, including, of course, Anita Sarkeesian. With the release of personal information about their identities, workplaces, and addresses, several female developers and public figures have been forced to leave their houses due to threats of violence against them or their families.

Sal Humphreys and Karen Orr Vered (2013) suggest that we need to consider the framing of outbreaks such as the attack on Sarkeesian, particularly as these attacks themselves echo a game in which Sarkeesian is the "enemy," but in which the ultimate outcome "may be to silence other women who are thinking of speaking out against oppressive and sexist behavior" (4). However, in the wake of Gamergate, Anita Sarkeesian (2014) has suggested that those attacking her are in fact fighting because of the understanding that they have already lost: "Those who police the borders of our hobby, the ones who try to shame and threaten women like me into silence, have already lost. The new reality is that video games are maturing, evolving, and becoming more diverse." However, the individuals within the community are still policing their borders. Jennifer Allaway's (2014) experiences conducting social research during Gamergate reflect the challenge the community can present to researchers: a survey she was conducting on diversity and representation in game content was found by the Gamergate community, listed on 8chan, and abruptly received four hundred responses in four hours: "they ranged in their degree of racism and misogyny, but they all ridiculed the project with dishonest mockery. It appeared that less than 5% of the new responses had actually come from developers."

Writing in 2012, Mia Consalvo noted that "The 'encroachment' of women and girls into what was previously a male-gendered space has not happened without incident, and will probably only become worse before it (hopefully) improves"—a prediction that has proven quite accurate with the rise of Gamergate and the subsequent increased visibility of hostility both to women and to feminist discourse in gaming. In a biting piece for Deadspin, a sister site to Kotaku, Kyle Wagner (2014) suggests that Gamergate is another step towards the future of social media as a primary stage for culture wars:

> All culture wars strike these same chords, because all culture wars are at bottom about the same thing: the desperate efforts of the privileged, in an ever-pluralizing America, to cling by their nails to the perquisites of what they'd thought was once their exclusive domain.
>
> What we have in Gamergate is a glimpse of how these skirmishes will unfold in the future—all the rhetorical weaponry and siegecraft of an internet comment section brought to bear on our culture, not just at the fringes but at the

center. What we're seeing now is a rehearsal, where the mechanisms of a toxic and inhumane politics are being tested and improved.

However, what this analysis misses is an even more frightening aspect of Gamergate as a site of culture wars: Gamergate represents players who have for years been playing as marginalized victims of others (from aliens to zombies) with the expectation that victory can be won by destroying the other. Gamergate rhetoric has embraced the gaming metaphor completely, but with women such as Anita Sarkeesian and Zoe Quinn recast as "boss monsters" between themselves and their score. The larger cultural critiques raised during the ongoing fight is often dismissed through heavy use of social media branding. From #NotYourShield, meant to show support among minorities for the Gamergate ideals, to the creation of Vivian James, a female mascot for the movement, social media has been used to show that not just the individuals targeted by Gamergate are wrong but any criticism leveled against the industry is unjust. Through this lens, gaming identity and gaming narratives are merged, and the face of the straight white male is the face of "true" gaming identity.

In the wake of the 2016 election, Gamergate surfaced once more in popular discourse as analysts looked to toxic masculinity and online spaces to understand their role in the outcome. Analyzing the connection, Matt Lees observed:

> The similarities between Gamergate and the far-right online movement, the "alt-right", are huge, startling and in no way a coincidence. After all, the culture war that began in games now has a senior representative in The White House. As a founder member and former executive chair of Breitbart News, Steve Bannon had a hand in creating media monster Milo Yiannopoulos, who built his fame and Twitter following by supporting and cheerleading Gamergate. This hashtag was the canary in the coalmine, and we ignored it (2016).

These connections run deeper than names alone: the discourse of exclusion and marginalization is rampant in so-called alt-right media, which draws on existing communities such as Men's Rights Activists and other movements targeted at men who believe the past offered them more benefits (and privilege) than the present. Likewise, the discourse of GamerGate was fueled by nostalgia. Even though it was powered ultimately by one man's vendetta against his ex-girlfriend, it spawned a narrative of reform: a call to make gaming great again.

Conclusion: Playing the Savior

Adrienne Shaw (2013) has suggested that attempts to broaden the definition of gamer to be more inclusive are doomed to failure and instead we might focus our efforts on thinking beyond the "identity" of gaming:

> Rather than argue that the gamer identity is too narrow or blissfully democratic (it is neither), I assert that critical perspectives, such as feminist and queer theory, offer an approach to video games that can focus more attention on the lived experiences of those who engage with these games outside the dominant audience construction—indeed outside of identifying as gamers—and make an argument for representation that takes seriously those perspectives.

However, the identity of gamer has become as much a battleground as any city Duke Nukem has entered. It has been argued that this increased level of hostility, threats, and violence represented most recently by Gamergate is a reaction to the decreased significance of gaming as an identity. Leigh Alexander (2014) suggests that gamers as traditionally defined are no longer a major force:

> Developers and writers alike want games about more things, and games by more people. We want—and we are getting, and will keep getting—tragicomedy, vignette, musicals, dream worlds, family tales, ethnographies, abstract art… "Gamer" isn't just a dated demographic label that most people increasingly prefer not to use. Gamers are over. That's why they're so mad.

While this reading of events suggests cause for optimism, the reality of those who can financially sustain themselves creating games offers less cause for hope: women and other marginalized creators are coming into game creation at the fringes, often through creating free games or works supported tenuously through independent creative content creation and distribution. The face of the mainstream industry and the face of the AAA game still recall Scalzi's definition of easy difficult: straight, white, and male. And, like Duke Nukem and Leisure Suit Larry, these "defaults" defy parody or exaggeration, reacting to invading others through assertions of privilege and dominance that have now risen to include extreme threats of violence. In the larger construction of geek masculinity, gamer identity has perhaps proven best at maintaining its own sense of marginalization and cohesion, reacting even to analysis of its own construction as to a threat. This defensiveness is not unlike the core mechanics of a first-person shooter game, which presents the players with a world of unambiguous morality. It is impossible for Duke Nukem to reason with the aliens who are invading his city. The only option is to shoot first, and leave conversation and discourse for the occasional cut scene or one-liner.

The label of "gamer" is often used in popular culture as shorthand for a particularly anti-social type of geekdom. Despite the incredibly social nature of most games and the gaming community, gamers and gaming have been dragged out and associated with impetus for school shootings, with basement-dwelling loners, and with an arrested adolescence that the content of some AAA titles certainly seems to reflect. However, the great tragedy of such simplification is in everything it excludes, from the more complex portrayals and dimensions of masculinity that games have embraced to the incredible range of games and game-players (if not "gamers") on the margins. The mainstream identity of the gamer, from the boys of *The Big Bang Theory* to *Chuck* to *South Park*'s obese and "life-less" *World of Warcraft* power-gamer, is a hollow default, but it is one the gamer community continues to don as an avatar through the struggles and conflicts currently defining this generation in gaming. The outcome of this conflict might seem easy to dismiss as a battle over labels, but in fact it is a battle over who will hold agency within gaming.

References

50 greatest video game characters. 2015. *Empire*, November 9. Accessed December 12, 2015. http://www.empireonline.com/features/50-greatest-video-game-characters/default.asp?film=20fault.asp?film=20.
Above the game, a guide to getting women, raises $16,000 on Kickstarter, despite complaints. 2013. *Huffington Post*, June 21. Accessed July 5, 2013. http://www.huffingtonpost.com/2013/06/19/above-the-game-kickstarter-tofutofu_n_3466538.html.
Aldred, Jessica, and Brian Greenspan. 2011. A man chooses, a slave obeys: *BioShock* and the dystopian logic of convergence. *Games and Culture* 6 (5): 485–486. https://doi.org/10.1177/1555412011402674.
Alexander, Leigh. 2014. Gamers don't have to be your audience. "Gamers" are over. *Gamasutra*, August 28. Accessed September 3, 2014. http://www.gamasutra.com/view/news/224400/Gamers_dont_have_to_be_your_audience_Gamers_are_over.php.
Allway, Jennifer. 2014. #Gamergate trolls aren't ethics crusaders; they're a hate group. *Jezebel*, October 13. Accessed December 9, 2014. http://jezebel.com/gamergate-trolls-arent-ethics-crusaders-theyre-a-hate-1644984010.

AnonymousFan8675309. 2013. Special guest edition: The Hawkeye initiative IRL! *Tumblr*, May 15. Accessed July 2, 2013. http://thehawkeyeinitiative.com/post/50432219744/special-guest-edition-the-hawkeye-initiative-irl.

ArenaNet. 2005. *Guild Wars* [Computer Software]. Bellevue, WA: NCSOFT.

Behm-Morawitz, Elizabeth, and Dana Mastro. 2009. The effects of the sexualization of female video game characters on gender stereotyping and female self-concept. *Sex Roles* 61 (11–12): 808–823. https://doi.org/10.1007/s11199-009-9683-8.

Björkand, Staffan and Maria Åresund. 2009. The importance of being a player. *HumanIT* 10 (1): 119–143. https://humanit.hb.se/article/view/95.

Blodgett, Bridgett and Anastasia Salter. 2013. Hearing lady game creators tweet: #1ReasonWhy, women and online discourse in the game development community. *Selected Papers of Internet Research* 3.

Bungie. 2001. *Halo: Combat Evolved* [Computer Software]. Redmond, WA: Microsoft Studios.

Burgess, Melinda C.R., Steven Paul Stermer, and Stephen R. Burgess. 2007. Sex, lies, and video games: The portrayal of male and female characters on video game covers. *Sex Roles* 57 (5–6): 419–433. https://doi.org/10.1007/s11199-007-9250-0.

Callaham, John. 2010. Interview: We chat with gearbox's randy pitchford about *Duke Nukem Forever*. *Big Download*, December 28. Accessed February 2, 2013. http://news.bigdownload.com/2008/06/26/big-download-interview-gearbox-software-ceo-randy-pitchford/.

Casting call: Hollywood needs more women. 2013. *NPR All Things Considered*, June 30. Accessed August 2, 2014. http://www.npr.org/templates/transcript/transcript.php?storyId=197390707.

Consalvo, Mia. 2012. Confronting toxic gamer culture: A challenge for feminist game studies scholars. *Ada: A Journal of Gender, New Media, and Technology* 1.

Denes, Amanda. 2011. Biology as consent: Problematizing the scientific approach to seducing women's bodies. *Women's Studies International Forum* 34 (5): 411–419. https://doi.org/10.1016/j.wsif.2011.05.002.

Dill, Karen E., Brian P. Brown, and Michael A. Collins. 2008. Effects of exposure to sex-stereotyped video game characters on tolerance of sexual harassment. *Journal of Experimental Social Psychology* 44 (5): 1402–1408. https://doi.org/10.1016/j.jesp.2008.06.002.

Doom. 1993. id Software. Video game.

Duke Nukem 3D. 1996. 3D Realms. Video game.

Duke Nukem Forever. 2011. 3D Realms. Video game.

Duncan, Sean C. 2013. Well-played and well-debated: Understanding perspective in contested affinity spaces. *Well-Played: A Special Issue on Theories of Well Played*: 37–58.

EA Redwood Shores. 2008. *Dead Space* [Computer Software]. Redwood City, CA: Electronic Arts.

Epic Games. 2006. *Gears of War* [Computer Software]. Redmond, WA: Microsoft Studios.

Fox, Jesse, and Wai Yen Tang. 2014. Sexism in online video games: The role of conformity to masculine norms and social dominance orientation. *Computers in Human Behavior* 33: 314–320. https://doi.org/10.1016/j.chb.2013.07.014.

Gamasutra Salary Survey 2014. 2014. *Gamasutra*. Accessed May 2, 2015. http://www.gamasutra.com/salarysurvey2014.pdf.

Gray, Kishonna L. 2014. *Race, gender, and deviance in xbox live: Theoretical perspectives from the virtual margins*. New York: Routledge

Hawken. 2012. Meteor Entertainment. Video game.

Heretic. 1994. id Software. Video game.

Hicks, Michael. 2013. De-brogramming the history of computing [Think piece]. *Annals of the History of Computing, IEEE* 35 (1): 88. https://doi.org/10.1109/mahc.2013.3.

Hoffman, Erin. 2012. The problem with the lowest difficulty setting. *Erin Hoffman Blog*, May. Accessed October 10, 2014. http://www.erinhoffman.com/wp/?p=535.

Hudson, Laura. 2013. Hawken staff call out sexy mechanic poster with gender-swap prank. *Wired*, May 16. Accessed July 2, 2014. http://www.wired.co.uk/news/archive/2013-05/16/hawken-gender-swap.

Hudson, Soft. 1983. *Bomberman* [Computer Software]. Tokyo, Japan: Konami.

Humphreys, Sal, and Karen Orr Vered. 2013. Reflecting on gender and digital networked media. *Television & New Media* 15 (1): 3–13. https://doi.org/10.1177/1527476413502682.

Insomniac Games. 2006. *Resistance: Fall of Man* [Computer Software]. San Mateo, CA: Sony Interactive Entertainment.

Jagex. 2001. *Runescape* [Computer Software]. Cambridge, England: Jagex.

Kirkland, Ewan. 2009. Masculinity in video games: The gendered gameplay of Silent Hill. *Camera Obscura* 24, 2 71: 161–183. Doi 10.1215/02705346-2009-006

Krahulik, Mike and Jerry Holkins. 2011. One of many possible responses. *Penny Arcade*, March 23. Accessed May 5, 2014. http://www.penny-arcade.com/comic/2011/03/23.

Lee, Dave. 2014. Zoe Quinn: Gamergate must be condemned. *BBC*, October 29. http://www.bbc.com/news/technology-29821050.

Lees, M. 2016. What Gamergate should have taught us about the alt-right. *The Guardian*. December 1. Accessed March 2, 2016. https://www.theguardian.com/technology/2016/dec/01/gamergate-alt-right-hate-trump.

Leisure Suit Larry in the Land of the Lounge Lizards. 1987. Sierra On-line. Video game.

Leisure Suit Larry 6: Shape Up or Slip Out! 1993. Sierra Entertainment. Video game.

McKinney, Luke. 2013. 5 gamer comments that give straight white guys a bad name. *Cracked*, May 27. Accessed June 1, 2013. http://www.cracked.com/blog/5-gamer-comments-that-give-straight-white-guys-bad-name/.

Moll, Ellen. 2014. What's in a Nym? Gender, race, pseudonymity, and the imagining of the online persona. *M/C Journal* 17 (3). http://journal.media-culture.org.au/index.php/mcjournal/article/view/816.

Near, Christopher E. 2013. Selling gender: Associations of box art representation of female characters with sales for teen-and mature-rated video games. *Sex Roles* 68 (3–4): 252–269. https://doi.org/10.1007/s11199-012-0231-6.

N-Fusion Interactive. 2013. *Leisure Suit Larry: Reloaded* [Computer Software]. Austin, TX: Replay Games.

Poon, Tim. 2011. The hardcore gaming myth. *Kotaku*, September 23. Accessed October 4, 2014. http://kotaku.com/5843253/the-hardcore-gaming-myth.

Raimi, Sam. 1992. *Army of darkness*. Los Angeles: Universal Pictures. DVD.

Replay Games. 2012. Make Leisure Suit Larry come again! *Kickstarter*, May 2. Accessed September 3, 2014. https://www.kickstarter.com/projects/leisuresuitlarry/make-leisure-suit-larry-come-again.

Ryan, Lizardi. 2009. Repelling the invasion of the "Other": Post-apocalyptic alien shooter videogames addressing contemporary cultural attitudes. *Eludamos: Journal for Computer Game Culture* 3 (2): 295–308.

Salter, Anastasia, and Bridget Blodgett. 2012. Hypermasculinity & dickwolves: The contentious role of women in the new gaming public. *Journal of Broadcasting & Electronic Media* 56 (3): 401–416. https://doi.org/10.1080/08838151.2012.705199.

Sarkeesian, Anita. 2013. Damsel in distress: Part 1—Tropes Vs women in Video Games. *YouTube*, posted March 7. Accessed February 18, 2014. https://www.youtube.com/watch?v=X6p5AZp7r_Q.

Sarkeesian, Anita. 2014. It's game over for "gamers." *The New York Times*, October 28. Accessed December 15, 2014. http://www.nytimes.com/2014/10/29/opinion/anita-sarkeesian-on-video-games-great-future.html?_r=0.

Scalzi, John. 2012a. Straight white male: The lowest difficulty setting there is. *Whatever blog*, May 15. Accessed October 8, 2014. http://whatever.scalzi.com/2012/05/15/straight-white-male-the-lowest-difficulty-setting-there-is/.

Scalzi, John. 2012b. *Redshirts*. New York: Tor Books.

Shaw, Adrienne. 2012. Do you identify as a gamer? Gender, race, sexuality, and gamer identity. *New Media & Society* 14 (1): 28–44. https://doi.org/10.1177/1461444811410394.

Shaw, Adrienne. 2013. On not becoming gamers: Moving beyond the constructed audience. *Ada: A Journal of Gender, New Media, and Technology* 2.

Skjaldmeyja. 2012. The Hawkeye initiative. *Tumblr*. Accessed July 12, 2014. http://thehawkeyeinitiative.com/.

Spurr, Bendilin. 2012. Beat up Anita Sarkeesian. *Newgrounds*, July 5. Accessed July 6, 2012. http://www.newgrounds.com/portal/view/598591.

Stabile, Carol. 2014. 'I will own you': Accountability in massively multiplayer online games. *Television & New Media* 15 (1): 43–57. https://doi.org/10.1177/1527476413488457.

Stuart, Keith. 2014. UK gamers: more women play games than men, report finds. *The Guardian*, September 17. Accessed October 2, 2014. http://www.theguardian.com/technology/2014/sep/17/women-video-games-iab.
Taito. 1978. *Space Invaders* [Computer Software]. Chicago, IL: Midway.
Tavinor, Grant. 2009. BioShock and the art of rapture. *Philosophy and Literature* 33 (1): 91–106. https://doi.org/10.1353/phl.0.0046.
Taylor, T.L. 2006. *Play between worlds*. Cambridge, MA: The MIT Press.
The Secret of Monkey Island. 1990. Lucasfilm Games. Video game.
Totilo, Stephen. 2011. Duke Nukem draws them in with the ladies, and the chandeliers. *Kotaku*, March 11. Accessed January 12, 2012. http://kotaku.com/5781073/duke-nukem-draws-them-in-with-the-ladies-and-the-chandeliers/.
Trammell, Aaron, and Anne Gilbert. 2014. Extending play to critical media studies. *Games and Culture* 9 (6): 391–405. https://doi.org/10.1177/1555412014549301.
Turbine. 2006. *Dungeons & Dragons Online* [Computer Software]. New York, NY: Atari Interactive.
Ubi Soft Montreal. 2002. *Tom Clancy's Splinter Cell* [Computer Software]. Rennes, France: Ubi Soft Entertainment.
Valve. 1998. *Half-Life* [Computer Software]. Bellevue, WA: Valve Corporation.
Valve. 2004. *Half-Life 2* [Computer Software]. Bellevue, WA: Valve Corporation.
Vanderhoef, John. 2013. Casual threats: The feminization of casual video games. *Ada: A Journal of Gender, New Media, and Technology* 2.
Wachowski, Lana, and Lily Wachowski. 1999. *The matrix*. Los Angeles: Warner Brothers. Blu-ray.
Waddell, T. Franklin, James D. Ivory, Rommelyn Conde, Courtney Long, and Rachel McDonnell. 2014. White man's virtual world: A systematic content analysis of gender and race in massively multiplayer online games. *Journal for Virtual Worlds Research* 7 (2). https://doi.org/10.4101/jvwr.v7i2.7096.
Wagner, Kyle. 2014. The future of the culture wars is here, and it's Gamergate. *Deadspin*, October 14. Accessed October 14, 2014. http://deadspin.com/the-future-of-the-culture-wars-is-here-and-its-gamerga-1646145844.
Williams, Dmitri, Nicole Martins, Mia Consalvo, and James D. Ivory. 2009. The virtual census: Representations of gender, race and age in video games. *New Media & Society* 11 (5): 815–834. https://doi.org/10.1177/1461444809105354.
Winegarner, Tyler. 2009. Greatest game hero: Duke Nukem. *Gamespot*, September 15. Accessed October 12, 2012. http://www.gamespot.com/videos/greatest-game-hero-duke-nukem/2300-6226795/.

5

Through the Boob Window: Examining Sexualized Portrayals in Transmedia Comic Franchises

While superhero comics only account for a small portion of the varied world of comics and sequential art, they remain the foundation of the print comic book industry and for most people are the first thought when comics are mentioned. Superhero comics may bring to mind bold colors, spandex costumes, and unrealistic physical feats performed by impossible beings. Outside of comic fandom, where new stories of superheroes are pulled off the shelves of comic stores consumed through weekly or monthly installments at the steep price of several dollars for a short issue, superheroes dominate on movie screens and television sets. The dizzying story arcs, interconnected webs of lineages and reboots, and universe-spanning events demand a level of dedication from followers of comics that makes it very difficult for a new or casual reader: keeping up with even one hero's story can often involve following crossover issues, team-ups, and solo series through the hands of multiple creative teams and timelines. Many people have tried to explain the enduring appeal of superheroes, but it is a challenge akin to explaining our need for mythology and the desire for an individual's strength to seem meaningful against an otherwise insurmountable world. Even reboots (such as the much-touted "Rebirth" arc from DC Comics, which started in 2016) build upon intense archival knowledge, with only a few issues relatively accessible to the reader crossing over from other parts of the transmedia franchise (Dyce 2016).

For superhero comic fans, the rewards take the form of a complexity of interwoven arcs and mythos that is at the heart of many geek cultural franchises. For those who followed the *Star Wars* extended universe prior to its

© The Author(s) 2017
A. Salter and B. Blodgett, *Toxic Geek Masculinity in Media*,
DOI 10.1007/978-3-319-66077-6_5

reset, the availability of stories from every corner of the galaxy and era on the timeline promised years and even decades of immersion. Marvel and DC both offer stories to dwarf the *Star Wars* extended universe, and comic collectors take a completionist approach to preferred sections of their hobby. Relying on a fairly loose blend of science fiction, fantasy, and magical realism, comics are a top choice for a geek-coded pursuit. And of all geek pursuits, superhero comics themselves have proven among the most resistant to mainstreaming. Comic books are still primarily sold in specialty shops, with graphic novel compilations only making their way to the stores much later in the publication cycle. While digital comics have made individual issues and archives more accessible, digital comics still account for only 10% of comic sales (Barnett 2015). Even online distribution has not yet succeeded in putting comic book shops out of business as gathering points for local fans.

However, the space of superheroes as icons is rapidly shifting. Many dedicated fans of heroes from DC's Batman and Superman to Marvel's Iron Man, Thor, and Captain America have never picked up a comic book. The nature of comic book issue sales makes it difficult to know the gender and demographic distributions of comic readers to any level of accuracy, but the visible superhero fandom online and at conventions is decidedly diverse. This diversity has led to some of the most virulent battles over gendered participation in geek culture and spaces, with attention fixed firmly on the comic book convention as a contested zone of participation. Over the last several years, the desire of some comic book creators and fans to police their spaces against the invasion of outsider (and particularly women outsiders) has erupted into conflict (Fig. 5.1).

On November 13, 2012, comic book artist Tony Harris took to Facebook to rant about "CON-HOT" women who came to prey on "average Comic Book Fans who either RARELY speak to, or NEVER speak to girls" (Jill 2012). His lengthy and poorly punctuated rant reinforced many stereotypes about both men who create comic book geeks and the comic book fan, suggesting that geek masculinity was particularly vulnerable to attacks by women who paired their attractiveness with a faked interest in comics, managing both to criticize them for not being sexually attractive enough while also demanding they stop pretending to be sexually available to geeks. This type of misogynist rant has helped to perpetuate the "fake geek girl" meme—a concept pushed by Tara Tiger Brown (2012), a writer for *Forbes*, who suggested that credentials-checking was important to "separate the geeks from the muck" thanks to an influx of "pretentious females who have labeled themselves as a 'geek girl.'" Joe Peacock, a writer for *CNN*, chimed in a few months later suggesting condescendingly that "I find it fantastic

Tony Effing Harris
10 hours ago near Macon, GA ·

I cant remember if Ive said this before, but Im gonna say it anyway. I dont give a crap.I appreciate a pretty Gal as much as the next Hetero Male. Sometimes I even go in for some racy type stuff (keeping the comments PG for my Ladies sake) but dammit, dammit, dammit I am so sick and tired of the whole COSPLAY-Chiks. I know a few who are actually pretty cool-and BIG Shocker, love and read Comics.So as in all things, they are the exception to the rule. Heres the statement I wanna make, based on THE RULE: "Hey! Quasi-Pretty-NOT-Hot-Girl, you are more pathetic than the REAL Nerds, who YOU secretly think are REALLY PATHETIC. But we are onto you. Some of us are aware that you are ever so average on an everyday basis. But you have a couple of things going your way. You are willing to become almost completely Naked in public, and yer either skinny(Well, some or most of you, THINK you are) or you have Big Boobies. Notice I didnt say GREAT Boobies? You are what I refer to as "CON-HOT". Well not by my estimation, but according to a LOT of average Comic Book Fans who either RARELY speak to, or NEVER speak to girls. Some Virgins, ALL unconfident when it comes to girls, and the ONE thing they all have in common? The are being preyed on by YOU. You have this really awful need for attention, for people to tell you your pretty, or Hot, and the thought of guys pleasuring themselves to the memory of you hanging on them with your glossy open lips, promising them the Moon and the Stars of pleasure, just makes your head vibrate. After many years of watching this shit go down every 3 seconds around or in front of my booth or table at ANY given Con in the country, I put this together. Well not just me. We are LEGION. And here it is, THE REASON WHY ALL THAT, sickens us: BECAUSE YOU DONT KNOW SHIT ABOUT COMICS, BEYOND WHATEVER GOOGLE IMAGE SEARCH YOU DID TO GET REF ON THE MOST MAINSTREAM CHARACTER WITH THE MOST REVEALING COSTUME EVER. And also, if ANY of these guys that you hang on tried to talk to you out of that Con? You wouldnt give them the fucking time of day. Shut up you damned liar, no you would not. Lying, Liar Face. Yer not Comics. Your just the thing that all the Comic Book, AND mainstream press flock to at Cons. And the real reason for the Con, and the damned costumes yer parading around in? That would be Comic Book Artists, and Comic Book Writers who make all that shit up.

Fig. 5.1 Tony Harris's Facebook rant

that women are finally able to enjoy a culture that has predominately been male-oriented and male-driven," but "I get sick of wannabes who couldn't make it as car show eye candy slapping on a Batman shirt and strutting around comic book conventions instead … they're poachers. They're a pox on our culture" (2012).

The phrase "pox on our culture" is particularly powerful here as it demonstrates both a sense of ownership and even a desire to gatekeep the consumption of comics-related merchandise. It recalls Hebdige's (1999) discussion of the ways subcultures are recuperated and made financially profitable to the mainstream, and thus reinforces the perception that the comics artists are fans are protecting their space and identity from this type of appropriation. However, the actual power dynamics at work are precisely the opposite of the narrative advanced from the geek community: what is being protected is not a marginalized subculture, but an intensely powerful space of hegemonic masculinity. The perceived incursion being defended against is not the commercialization of geek culture—that ship has sailed, and mainstream comics artists including Tony Harris are decidedly part of it. Instead, the invaders being resisted are those marginalized by the persistence of hegemonic masculinity in a space masquerading as a subculture that in fact possesses significant control of the rules and order of the social world (ibid.). This hostility can be interpreted through the lens of geek masculinity as victimized by the presence of femininity, as Rachel Edidin (2012) noted in her critique of the fake geek girl:

> For the first time, there are visible swathes of geek culture that aren't only female-majority, but unabashedly girly—in a culture where feminization is very directly equated to deprecation of value. And all of this is happening in a community primed to respond aggressively to newcomers, and particularly to female newcomers.

It's also significant that so many of the men (and women) seeking to label "fake geek girls" focused on their physical presentation and sexual desirability.

The tension of geek-coding and sex appeal plays out both in geek icons and in geek culture, coming to a head in the "Fake Geek Girl" meme popularized by the comics community. Katrin Tiidenberg suggests that this dualistic discourse eliminates the space geek women might occupy:

> In short, women are sex objects. Geeks are not sexy. If Girl Geeks define themselves as geeks but sexy, in order to perform heteronormativity and not commit gender inauthentication, the very act of foregrounding their sexuality marks them as fakes. Within this discourse there seems to be no quarter for a girl geek. (McKnight et al. 2013)

This reinforces an impossibility for women operating within superhero fandom: the women allowed to be visible within superhero comic books are continually sexualized, but sexuality demonstrated by a "girl" fan is an immediate marker of outsider status and fakeness. The same artists who design the costumes invalidate the fans of all gender identities who might seek to occupy them. This segment of geek discourse thus positions women superheroes as objects of desire, not of aspiration or presence. Surveying comic book fandom, Suzanne Scott points out that this marginalization applies to both characters and fans, and thus:

> female comic book fans, like Sue Storm [the invisible woman, Fantastic Four], must consider the different and often paradoxical, forms of power that visibil-

ity and invisibility afford. If the goal is for female comic creators and fans to become more than an industrial niche or surplus audience, to become invisible (read: accepted) members of that culture, increased visibility will be necessary to encourage that shift. (Scott 2012)

Invisible Geek Girls

This growing communal distrust of fake geek girls coincided with the release of *The Avengers* in 2012 (Whedon), a first culmination of the growing Marvel Cinematic Universe that took several comic-book icons and brought them to the level of mainstream blockbuster hits. New levels of mainstream attention suddenly overwhelmed comic book conventions such as San Diego Comic Con, which over the past decades had already seen the growing influence of films and movies into the domain of comic books and comic fans. The attendance numbers of women at major comic conventions is on the rise: women attendance saw a 62% growth rate between 2010 and 2013 at New York ComicCon (McNally 2014) while a survey of attendance at San Diego Comic Con in 2014 found that 45% of attendees were women, with an even split of attendees among younger (under 30) con-goers (Reynolds 2015). These younger demographics suggest a change in newer attendees versus the demographics of older and previous con-goers, a demographic that may explain some of the hostility of Tony Harris and his supporters, whose vision of "our" ComicCon might look decidedly different from the demographics of the ComicCon of the near future.

Of course, making the commitment to attend some of the largest (and most expensive) comic conventions in the world is not enough to save a woman from the accusation of fake geekdom. The debates on who "qualifies" as a comic book geek have escalated at a moment when comic books can no longer be rightly seen as an alternative or geek medium, although it is notable that the success of the film adaptations has not translated directly into massive rises in sales of comic books themselves. The Marvel Cinematic Universe is not a direct mapping of comic book stories and characters, but an adaptation; likewise, the fandom for the comic books and the films overlaps but also conflicts, with results that bring debates and prejudices of geek culture into light alongside the larger misogynist challenges of mainstream cinema. The Marvel Cinematic Universe has certainly still proven to be a bastion of the male hero, as we discussed previously in our examination of *Iron Man* and the hypermasculine ideal, to such an extent that as of 2017 there has still been no woman-led movie in the franchise, and only one has been announced as forthcoming in a crowded schedule of new hero origin stories. Yet the series is just one of many changing the face of Comic Con, and others (such as *The Hunger Games* and, earlier, *Twilight*) brought with them their own influxes of women and girl fans who, even more unforgivably by the standards of Tony Harris et al., were perhaps not even comic fans. *Twilight* in particular is often cited as part of the transformation of Comic Con, with Alexander Abad-Santos (2013) commenting in an op-ed entitled "How the Nerds Lost Comic-Con" that fans coming to see *Twilight* stars sit at "the apex of Comic-Con pop culture invasion." The metaphor of invasion is crucial, as it evokes the idea of the comic convention as under siege by outsiders bringing their desires and pop culture franchises into a previously safe space.

When *Avengers* arrived in theatres with next to no merchandise featuring Black Widow, an anonymous former Marvel employee spoke out on the intentionality of the decisions in the line:

> Disney does not care about Marvel's female market, which makes us virtually invisible. I could probably populate Pluto with the amount of Princess items Disney makes. But where are Gamora and Black Widow? The exclusion of women from Marvel movie merchandise is completely purposeful. I know, I was there ... while working at Marvel post-acquisition, I saw a deck circulated by Disney's Brand Marketing team. I'm prohibited from sharing the slides, but the takeaway is that, unlike the *actual* demos, the *desired* demographics had no females in it whatsoever. (Mouse 2015)

This message from the adapted comics world comes through as clearly as Tony Harris's rant: women are not the intended consumers of comics, even when they are visible within the comics and adaptations themselves. In commentary during March of 2017, Marvel executives have stated that part of the publisher's sales slump was a result of including more women and diverse characters in their recent series (Griepp 2017). The politics of visibility continue to play out in even the most mainstream and recognized spaces of the comics industry: with the release of *Avengers: Age of Ultron* (Whedon 2015), Disney brought out sixty new items of merchandise, but only three with Black Widow—a tote bag, a single Lego set, and a men's shirt, with her absence inspiring an entire blog on Tumblr (Vincent 2015). The placement of Black Widow as the team's lone woman drew further attention when cast members Jeremy Renner and Chris Evans referred to her as a "slut" and "complete whore" in an interview, with one editorial on the incident noting "there's nothing less frivolous than fiction. You'd think the star of the mind-blowingly successful *Avengers* franchise might have realized that" (Petri 2015).

One writer on comics wrote about the problem of fan discourse after receiving several threats following her essays on hypersexualized and misogynist depictions in comic covers and art:

> I have a theory on why a small segment of men who read comics send rape threats to women who write about comics. To put it simply, they think we're destroying their masturbatory fantasies (literal or otherwise). You may laugh but it's quite possibly the source of all the hatemongering. They're under the impression comics are for men. Men only. And the characters therein, specifically the female characters, are there for them to ogle. The mere thought of that being taken away from them is frightening (even though, you know, porn and porn comics!). So frightening they will do anything to stop it. And they think silencing women with threats is the answer. (Pantozzi 2014)

This discourse in part reflects a failure of comic books both to grow up and to diversify their understood and implied audiences. Comic book companies, creators, and fans have long been typed as male. The incidents with Tony Harris and Joe Peacock reinforce a message that the comics industry has been selling for years: superhero comics are for, by, and about men. Even as the medium of the comic book has grown in artistic respect and influence, with authors and artists such as Art Spiegelman, Alison Bechdel, and Neil Gaiman winning awards and accolades outside the comics industry, superhero comics in particular have been stuck in a self-reinforcing pattern of gender dynamics and exclusion that remains foundational to the Marvel and DC mindset even as stories of men fighting evil in spandex have become the dominant blockbusters of mainstream cinema. Women creators and characters have grown in influence in comics, but much of this transformation is outside of the superhero arena. The numbers of women creators employed by Marvel and DC reflect this disparity: an examination of the percentage of credited women from 1991–2011 at both Marvel and DC demonstrates that while women have some growing presence as editors, assistant editors, and colorists, they have never broken 10% of the writers at DC or Marvel, and hover at around 10% of the overall creators, with no real improvement over the past twenty years (Hanley, Gendercrunching 2015). Likewise, while the number of women characters in superhero comics is difficult to estimate thanks to the multitude of continuities, the number of featured women characters and women with solo titles remains low.

Women creators and characters can be found on the web, where artists can find fan bases outside the traditional spaces of comic fandom. Yet even in those spaces women go unrecognized: no women creators were nominated for the Grand Prix d'Angoulême for 2015, causing several nominated artists to boycott and decline to be considered (Reisman 2016). The controversy has drawn attention to the fact only one woman has won the award since it was established in 1974 (Guzman 2016). Women are being recognized for their accomplishments in comics at the Eisners: in 2015, Shannon Watters, Grace Ellis, Noelle Stevenson, and Brooke Allen took home Best New Series for *Lumberjanes* (Okay 2015). The number of women recognized for the Eisners had been going up steadily, from 6.9% in 2004 to 19% in 2015, but there is still a long way to go and most of the recognition comes for work outside of the largest comics publishers (Shannon 2015).

Many of the women-created comics that have achieved recognition take a very different approach from the traditional superhero comic, which remains a bastion of male-dominated control. Even attempts to discuss comics as a growing art form tend to sidestep the problem of the superhero comic, encouraging readers to look elsewhere. Aaron Meskin writes on his reasons for this exclusion in his essay on comics as literature:

> I do not believe that mainstream superhero comics typically possess much in the way of substantive literary value(s). There are exceptions of course—superhero comics by Alan Moore, Neil Gaiman, and Grant Morrison among others … I suspect that it is this fact—that superhero comics (and, perhaps, daily newspaper comic strips or "funnies") do not generally possess much in the way of literary or artistic value—that underwrites much across-the-board skepticism about the art of comics. (Meskin 2009)

Despite this critique, superhero comics retain their cultural significance, to the point where "the superhero figure has developed into a lasting and vigorous presence in American and European popular culture such that recognition of the Batman or Superman, for example, by millions who have never read a Batman comic or seen a Superman film is ensured" (Bongco 2014). But while Wonder Woman has close to this level of recognition and visibility, few other women superheroes sit on this pedestal of near-universally known (if culturally derided) popularity. And even Wonder Woman herself cannot escape marginalization. In the months leading up to the release of *Wonder Woman*, an absence of marketing materials relative to her franchise counterparts sparked discussion as to the sincerity of DC's desire to see a women-led film succeed (Kane 2017). As Vivian Kane writes, "For an industry so fearful to exist outside of binaries, a female hero with the potential to appeal to a bunch of different demographics equally is bound to confuse them" (Vivian 2017).

This disparity is reflected in assumptions of audience as well as in the superhero media, despite little actual market research on the demographics of comic readers. Exit polling of audiences at *The Avengers* showed an audience of 40% women, while *Guardians of The Galaxy* broke that record with 44% (Comicbook 2014). Data on comic book readers are harder to find: DC Comics did a self-study following the launch of the New 52 in 2012, surveying about 5,000 readers and finding them to be 93% male (ICv2 2012). There were several questions about the methodology of the DC study, and notably the in-store survey (conducted through designated comic shops) reflected a different percentage than the open online survey, which was 23% women (MacDonald 2012). This might indicate a difference in demographics between the print collector who goes to a physical store to regularly purchase comics versus readers invested in various online and digital comic infrastructures, as well as those who wait for graphic novels as opposed to picking up single issues. It's also difficult to generalize about the readers of superhero comics from just a sample of the readers of the New 52, which has included some particularly misogynist and alienating content we will examine later in this chapter.

By contrast, the independently conducted study two years later by Brett Schenker (2014) used publicly available Facebook information to suggest that of those "liking" comics and specific publishers, 46.67% identified as women. This could indicate a rising presence of women fans, particularly online, and certainly Marvel in particular has made some explicit moves to attract women as an audience. However, one of the authors on the new all-women superhero team comic from Marvel, A-Force, suggested that this is not a sign of a change in readership so much as an acknowledgement of readers who have always been there:

> Women have always read comics. It's not that there are more women reading them now … but I think that historically there have not been as many safe and welcoming spaces for women to talk about comics. And Tumblr and Twitter have provided that space where fans can connect with each other. (Dockterman, Why Marvel Decided to Create an All-Female Superhero Team 2015)

The perceived gender disparity in comic readership is so familiar that it has become a pop culture trope in itself: to return to *The Big Bang Theory*, for instance, the women leads enter a comic shop in an episode advertised

Fig. 5.2 *The Big Bang Theory* promo. Screen Capture from Burlingame (2013)

with the promo caption "Where no woman has gone before" (Fig. 5.2) (Burlingame 2013). Comic books have traditionally served as intermediaries for establishing "nerd-culture": like comic book conventions, they both enable and gatekeep participation in and consumption of geek-centered media (Woo 2012). The episode and its promo inspired a lot of critique from women in comics fandom, with Kristy Pirone (2013) noting the self-reinforcing message of the show: "By perpetuating the stereotype that women aren't participating in 'geeky' activities, *The Big Bang Theory* is providing a justification for the men who like to think that it is their sacred duty to keep women out of geekdom through demeaning and insulting confrontations." This rhetoric of exclusion is one we will revisit, as the outbreak of "fake geek girl" labeling and policing within comics and comic conventions and public spaces goes hand in hand with the messages of popular culture and the roles women are offered as sexual objects and motivators within both superhero comics and comic-adapted films.

As we turn our gaze to superhero comics, we consider the superbody as an object of desire and an actor. Superbodies on the comics page can ignore human realities and limitations to occupy whatever forms an artist's mind can conjecture, and yet superbodies rarely explore liminal spaces or offer new ways to conceptualize gender or strength—instead, they often fall into predictable and stereotyped patterns of a fetishized ideal. We look at a few case studies of comics that present complex male–female relationships (from DC, *Batgirl*, and from Marvel, *Alias* and *Jessica Jones*) and offer moments of gendered struggle and opportunities to observe and critique common comic tropes. From these case studies, we demonstrate how superhero comics provide primarily an illusion of "feminine" strength, while presenting their readers with dynamics of gender that place the woman's body in a primarily instrumental role for male narratives of power and growth. Finally, we consider how the gradual mainstreaming of superheroes is pushing back against these established norms of gendered power as established by comic books.

Gendered Superbodies

It is impossible to discuss hypermasculinity within comics without considering the roles offered to women, and particularly the tensions among gender representations of superbodies (which tend with very view exceptions to be cisgendered and heteronormative). The superbody fills a particular place in the construction of fantasies that go beyond gender stereotypes: often, they take stereotype and push it into the absurd or even the surreal. Trina Robbins wrote in 2002 about the changes she had witness in the evolving depiction of men and women through the eighties and nineties:

> [T]he almost entirely male mainstream comic book artists began exaggerating certain sexual characteristics on both the male and female characters they drew. The males grew progressively more muscular, their necks thickened, while their heads grew smaller. The females, on the other hand, developed longer legs while their breasts attained incredible proportions, perfectly round in shape, and often larger than their heads. To show off these bizarrely morphed bodies, the artists clothed the women in bottom-baring thong bikinis, with as little as possible on top. (Robbins 2002)

These echo the highly sexualized avatars of computer and video games, as we discussed in Chap. 4.

Superheroes' inhuman bodies represent a particular challenge for adaptation to cinema as they tend towards an exaggerated representation that draws not on the realism of film but on a more eroticized form of exaggeration: "The superbody currently functions quite near to a pornographic polemic. Interestingly, both the female and male comic figure continue to be a site of spectacle, if not outright fetishism" (Taylor 2007, 345). Aaron Taylor suggests that this otherness holds within it a "subversive potential" that could "undermine the culturally enforced, dualistic engenderment of the body" (346). However, Taylor also acknowledges how current comics fall short of this potential, with comic artists demonstrating "almost hysterical determination to perpetuate visible sexual difference [which] indirectly reveals the artificiality of its endeavours" (353). This art style can also be quite jarring to the expectations of outside gazes, which presents another challenge for comics as a medium in breaking out of the geek cultural landscape. The superhero body also has cultural implications when situated contextually within their stories. The form of Captain America has come under scrutiny recently with a story arc focused on Steve Rogers being a member secret member of Hydra (Whitbrook 2017). Given the group's Nazi connections, Steve's body not only reads as powerful, but also emblematic of the superior race espoused by the Nazis and white superiority groups since World War 2. Many fans have raised their concerns with the publisher given the popularity of Captain America within the larger Marvel Cinematic Universe (ibid.). The hypersexual superhero body is read one way within the context of comics, but is transformed when it moves on to screen.

Sabine Lebel (2009) reminds us that these exaggerated bodies cannot even be occupied by real actors and are thus digitally enhanced to construct the perfect superhero:

> Spider-Man's body has been carefully crafted down to the minutest details. Reading these descriptions there is an insistence on the traditionally masculine aspects of the Spider-Man construct's body—namely his muscles. Even though Spider-Man is not necessarily coded as "hypermasculine," his construction as heroic figure is signified, and emphasized, through built muscles. (61)

This portrayal of muscularity is particularly interesting given that Peter Parker serves as an avatar for the male geek fan. He is commonly depicted as one of the youngest heroes of the Marvel universe and his comics often have him balancing a troubled high school love life with the need to defeat supervillains—a giant leap from the grown-up worries and bodies of the other Avengers. Yet even his masculinity must be reinforced, both in comics and film. Just as the unassuming Clark Kent can be forgiven his bumbling as long as his hypermasculine spandex super-suit waits underneath his reporter's guise, so too can Peter Parker better face the stigma of science geek outcast as long as his acrobatic spider-enhanced body waits beneath.

This hypermasculinity has been revised in newer superhero movies, which corresponds with the transition away from a niche geek and comic book fan audience to more mainstream intentions. Masani McGee (2014) examines the representation of male superheroes within the MCU, suggesting that Joss Whedon's portrayals have complicated the typical hypermasculine body thanks to the portrayals of Iron Man and Hulk:

Both he [Banner] and Stark are at odd with the types of masculinities represented by their peers. Banner complicates many of the correlations between the ideal male form and its definition through the superhero costume, as he is famously lacking any clothing other than a torn pair of pants, almost as if his physicality has moved beyond any message that may be conveyed by mere clothing. (4)

We are particularly aware of the conflation of identity and costume in superheroes with the transition from comic to film, as film makes us aware of the ridiculousness of many superhero tropes when mapped on to real human bodies. Some of these moments become infamous, such as the visible nipples on the Bat-suit worn by George Clooney or the fetish-inspired trappings of Halle Berry's portrayal of Catwoman. The impact of Clooney's Bat-suit of *Batman & Robin* (Schumacher 1997), along with the film's homoerotic subtext, was so extreme that Nick Winstead analyzed Christopher Nolan's careful choices in rebooting Batman as a "de-queering" of the character (Winstead 2015).

On the other hand, the women of these same CG-enhanced movies are left with their femininity "surprisingly 'intact.' Neither the mutation nor special effects work to visually disrupt, dismantle, or change the surface of the female form" (Lebel 2009, 65). Women heroes (with powers that tend to represent "female" powers) are left a much smaller space within which to operate: women are "contained, not just by the narrative, but also by the production process that is unable or unwilling to imagine ways in which the surfaces of the female body might shift" (66). Even within the costume design of many female characters the focus is on the constraint and selective revelation of the clothing than in how it develops the character. The female body within these films is exaggerated only in ways that do not risk detracting from the desirability of that body when viewed through a traditional masculine gaze.

This inequity of depiction of the comic book superbody has not gone without significant cultural critique. The Hawkeye Initiative draws attention to the absurdity of the representation gap by replacing women characters in illustrations with Hawkeye (and occasionally other male superheroes) in the same pose. Such images emphasize both the ludicrousness of the positioning and emphasis of anatomy as well as the difference between the standards for costumes and coverage. The images are meant to be jarring to the viewer and force them to recognize the incongruity of these poses and outfits when they are applied to male identified characters. This cognitive shakeup helps to reveal the insidious nature of the objectification that women in comics regularly face and the increasingly twisted levels it much reach to seem more than its competitors.

While the images from The Hawkeye Initiative draw attention to the positioning of bodies for the masculine gaze, covers such as this one reinforce the narrow assumption of audience that the comic book shop supports. They are unlikely to be viewed as friendly to women readers, even if the content of the story holds potential universal appeal. Even postmodern superhero texts, such as Alan Moore's *Watchmen*, rarely challenge these stereotypes. Erin Keating (2012) notes that the "revisionary" narrative of Moore's work does not extend to its women superheroes, with those characters revealing "a conservative, heterosexual framework operating as a foundation for the moral ambiguity and the displacement of traditional superhero tropes enacted by the revisionist aspects of the text" (1266). This conservative framework takes center-stage when examining the different arcs available to women and men superheroes, which, like their bodies, seem to follow two distinct sets of priorities.

Women in Refrigerators

> It comes down to sex, really. It's no big secret that, in the adolescent power fantasy which are the bread and butter of superhero comics, fight scenes are symbolic surrogates for sexual activity. You can't get up the nerve to ask the girl who sits next to you in geometry class for a date, but you can buttress your virility by vicariously beating the crap out of the Joker. At heart, superhero comics are conservative, exonerating status quo attitudes rather than undermining them, and a basic tenet of the conservative attitude in this country is that women shouldn't enjoy sex. When superheroines go out there and beat up villains, hey, those fight scenes are symbolic surrogates for sexual activity, too. They have to be punished for enjoying it, because it's just too threatening for women to enjoy power corresponding to that enjoyed by men. So heroines are de(p/fl)owered, mutilated, raped or sexually threatened, and killed. "Serves'em right for trying to do a man's job." (Grant 1999)

In 1999, Gail Simone launched a website entitled Women in Refrigerators. The site included a list of women characters in comics who, as Simone describes, "have been either depowered, raped, or cut up and stuck in the refrigerator," that last referring to the fate of Green Lantern's girlfriend in *Green Lantern 54*, the primary origin of the trope's name (Conway and Kane 1973). The list of characters on the site includes a number of minor characters as well as big names such as Black Canary, Elektra, Gwen Stacy, and even

Wonder Woman. Simone compiled many responses from professionals in the field, including the one from Steven Grant, a frequent writer for Marvel Comics, excerpted above. The term "fridging" rose in popularity to describe the condemnation of a woman character to an unpleasant fate or peril in order to motivate a male hero or advance a plot point. Such acts don't always result in the death of the character, but usually do—Gwen Stacy, as Spiderman's girlfriend, has been doomed to die at the hands of Green Goblin in comics and film adaptations since her first fatal fall (Baker-Whitelaw 2014).

While this trend was described over fifteen years ago, it remains relevant today, thanks to incidents like the recent elimination of founding Avengers member Wasp from the *Ant-Man* (Reed 2015) movie adaptation. When the news was announced, Gavia Baker-Whitelaw summed up the fan reaction:

> The founding members of the Avengers team were Iron Man, the Hulk, Thor, Ant-Man, and Janet Van Dyne as the Wasp. In other words, all of the male characters get their own movie franchises, while the Wasp is not only sidelined, but killed off to provide backstory for characters in the new *Ant-Man* movie. (2014)

The Marvel Cinematic Universe is one of the most powerful and popular cultures to cross the boundary from geek culture into mainstream media, and the enthusiasm of its geek fanbase for unlikely heroes such as Thor and Iron Man has been telling. However, no woman has yet played a primary role in one of the cinematic adaptations, and the first leading woman in a Marvel TV adaptation—Peggy Carter—started out as Captain America's girlfriend and was left behind by the film franchise when Captain America ended up trapped in ice, remaining youthful while she was left behind to die of old age. In the films she has only appeared on screen again in an *Avengers: The Age of Ultron* dream sequence as a reminder of Captain America's sacrifices rather than as part of her own story, and in *Captain America: Civil War* (Russo and Russo 2016) to die and leave behind her niece as a substitute love interest.

The use of women's suffering as motivating incidents in the stories of male superheroes has been the subject of both academic and fan discourse. Hannah Starke (2013) has examined the fate of Lois Lane in parallel to the fates of mythic women from Hera to Calypso: Lois

> does not grow; she just absorbs experiences and never changes because of them. As the some female in the series who is a permanent character, she tends to stand for women as a whole, and this image of her presents the idea that women are not truly interacting with the world around them.

Lois Lane epitomizes the roles for women offered by many superhero comics and adapted films: such characters are love interests, victims, and objects of desire, but rarely actors with agency in their own narratives.

We are a long way removed from the first publication of Women in Refrigerators (hereafter WIR). Matthew Costello (2013) looked at the trends from fourteen years post-WIR and noted that "although more women are creating comics, frequently they are still… getting fridged." As comics have moved from a perceived specialized media to major, records-breaking blockbuster franchises, the opportunities for expanding the awareness and fandoms of male characters have increased. The women portrayed within these media have not received the same benefits from the increased attention. We will focus on the role that women have played within the media narrative as plot points for advancing male characters' stories as either love interests or tragic victims. By deconstructing the narrative limitations placed upon female characters, we will dismantle the instrumentalization of women in male narratives, and subsequently better understand the relationship between these stories and the expectations of the role that women will play in their lives as expressed in geek culture fantasies.

Being Batgirl

While the concept of "fridging" often involves a non-superhero—most often a love interest of a super hero with no powers of her own—the status of a woman as a superhero is not enough to save her from this fate. Indeed, O'Reilly suggests that women superheroes regularly undergo trials that focus on their right to exist as a superhero, and "provide a narrative representation of the duality of the female superhero, an objectified character who still drives the story line… [and] may serve as a reminder of the ever-present threat of replacement" (O'Reilly 2005). Of all the superheroines who have suffered fridging or its equivalent in the name of advancing the stories of men, one of the most talked about is Batgirl. Batgirl's arc reached its pinnacle thanks to Alan Moore's 1988 arc *Batman: The Killing Joke*, which was approved in a now-infamous phone call with the DC editor:

> I asked DC if they had any problem with me crippling Barbara Gordon—who was Batgirl at the time—and if I remember, I spoke to Len Wein, who was our editor on the project, and he said, "Hold on to the phone, I'm just going to walk down the hall and I'm going to ask [former DC Executive Editorial Director] Dick Giordano if it's alright," and there was a brief period

where I was put on hold and then, as I remember it, Len got back onto the phone and said, "Yeah, okay, cripple the bitch." (Cochran 2007)

Batgirl's paralysis occurs in the space of two panels, with no opportunity for her to fight back. The attack occurs when she is not in costume, her main crime being her association with men (her father, James Gordon, and Batman himself.)

> It is perhaps the ultimate irony—perhaps the ultimate insult—that Batgirl's personal trauma was poached from her and added to Batman's memory-bank of bad experiences. Barbara Gordon's shooting and sexual assault—an event that Bruce Wayne never even witnessed—became just another reason for Batman to feel sorry for himself, to channel the guilt and sorrow into anger and use it to fuel his never-ending "war" on "crime"; his nightly patrols and the endless beatings dealt out to petty thugs and costumed clowns. (Brooker 2011)

The paralysis is not the only consequence of Joker's assault: after Batgirl is paralyzed, the Joker strips her and takes photographs (with rape and sexual assault implied, if not explicitly depicted). He then uses those photographs to make a demented funhouse for James Gordon with the goal of driving him mad. The implication of the Joker's acts is that his form of madness compels him to push others towards the same fate, and for him Barbara Gordon's suffering is simply the right tool to inflict suffering on her father.

After the attack, the Joker compares Barbara Gordon to a broken book: "there's a hole in the jacket and the spine appears to be damaged." Unlike the suffering of most comic book heroes, this damage goes unrepaired for a long time, providing the impetus for Barbara Gordon's transformation into Oracle. Given the tendency of tragedies in comics to be quickly erased (particularly for superheroes), this decision to keep Batgirl paralyzed is striking. As Pedler (2007) questions: "why is Barbara still in her wheelchair, nearly twenty years later, where Bruce's once-broken back is barely even mentioned? Why do some events resist the aura of the status quo, and others do not?" (7), Pedler's comparison of Barbara Gordon's fate to that of Batman or even the various apparent deaths of the Joker himself is a reminder of the status of the minor character—the "loved one"—a status from which even donning her own Batsuit couldn't protect Barbara Gordon.

However, Batgirl's stories post-*Killing Joke* could be viewed through a progressive lens: two writers, Kimberly Yale and John Ostrander, pulled the newly paralyzed Barbara Gordon into another DC title for a rebirth. As John Ostrander explains,

> Since the Batman office had no further plans for her at the time, we got permission to use Barbara in *Suicide Squad*… we felt that the gunshot as seen in *Killing Joke* would leave her paralyzed. We felt such an act should have repercussions. So… we took some of her other talents, as with computers, and created what was essentially an Internet superhero—Oracle. (Rogers 2011)

This move took Barbara's formerly underutilized PhD in library science and turned it into a new form of superpower, drawing attention to her mental prowess and offering a new depiction of the woman librarian. As Dough Highsmith (2003) notes, "As Oracle, Barbara Gordon is arguably the first true librarian-as-super-hero yet seen in a mainstream comic book (as opposed to super-hero who happens to be a librarian in his/her private life)." This is a sharp contrast to her librarian identity as Batgirl, which was essentially a dowdy disguise for her superhero self.

As Oracle, Barbara's sexualized body (or lack thereof) is more complicated, as Caroyln Cocca (2014) critiques:

> While her invisibility to many characters allows her to escape both the gaze at women and the stare at people with disabilities if she so chooses, she is not, however, invisible to us. In her wheelchair, she is still embedded in the habitual sexualized portrayals of women in mainstream superhero comics. But while we can and should critique sexualized portrayals, we can and should also see the disruptive potential of portraying the character as disabled and beautiful and as an agent of her own sexuality.

Such moments serve as a reminder of the intersectional complexity that must accompany our readings of geek culture, particularly when we are dealing with the layering of marginalized identities. In superhero comics, this is essential when looking at representations of disability, race, and other marginalized identities that the superbody construction is likely to fetishize or erase.

Batgirl has been propelled into the spotlight as a character at the heart of these debates through multiple incidents since then. While post-paralysis Batgirl lived on as Oracle, one of the few superheroes ever depicted in a wheelchair and the intellectual heart of a number of Gotham superhero operations, she was recently rebooted as part of DC's New 52 and regained the ability to walk. Her reboot was at the hands of Gail Simone, the original author of the WIR list, and attracted much examination. Gail Simone defended the decision to bring Batgirl out of her wheelchair with references to the ephemerality of suffering in the rest of the comic universe:

The most persuasive argument to put Babs back in the boots has always been one that I would argue against vehemently for story reasons, but that was impossible to argue with ethically. And I have heard this question a million times... why is it that virtually every single hero with a grievous injury, or even a death, gets to come back whole, except Barbara Gordon? Why? Why was Batman's back broken, and he was barely in the chair long enough to keep the seat warm, and now it's never even mentioned? Arms and legs get ripped off, and they grow back, somehow. Graves don't stay filled. But the one constant is that Barbara stays in that chair. (Pantozzi 2011)

The erasure of physical disability through magical or pseudo-scientific solutions, after all, is key to the maintenance of superbodied heroes that can last through decades of episodic drama.

The New 52, DC's most recent comic-reboot, has been found guilty of several other instances of moving portrayals of female characters backwards rather than forwards. In fact, the tendency demonstrated by DC Comics towards problematic actions inspired the founding of an online "Has DC Comics Done Something Stupid Today?" countdown clock. One clock-resetting incident occurred with Batgirl in March 2015 a cover for the Batgirl comic was released that brought Batgirl back to her status as victim. The image featured Joker holding Batgirl captive with a gun draped over her shoulder while she stares at the camera wide-eyed, tears in her eyes and a panicked expression emphasized by the lipstick smeared on her face in a parody of the Joker's grin. The cover is part of a series of variant covers featuring the Joker and disconnected from Batgirl's history would still make for a disturbing image. The cover was particularly inappropriate given the audience for the Batgirl reboot at the time, as Rob Bricken explained in his critique of the cover:

> The image also suggests this [sexual assault] by its very content—Batgirl, crying, powerless, and at the Joker's complete physical mastery, evidenced by the way he's touching her. Regardless of what it's an homage to, the tone could not be less appropriate for the current "Batgirl of Burnside" comic, which is fun and not dark and has many female readers, especially young ones. Moreover, it's incredibly sexist—I would hope even the most bitter of woman-hating male comic fans surely have to agree that a male superhero, unless he was a child, would *never* be drawn crying while held hostage by a supervillain. (Bricken 2015)

Ultimately, DC pulled the comic variant following a "#ChangeTheCover" Twitter campaign and numerous debates in media over the cover's appropriateness and offensiveness (Barnett, DC Comics pulls cover of Batgirl menaced by Joker after online protests 2015). However, the decision was too late to stop the criticism, and ultimately draws our attention to the fact that while Batgirl's creators might have deemed her physically "healed," her body is forever tied to the Joker's abuse and its aftermath in the eyes of the DC universe. Meanwhile, the Joker continues to be one of the best-loved villains in DC comics, thanks in part to Heath Ledger's portrayal in *The Dark Knight* (Nolan 2008). The Joker received continual accolades, with an article on *Forbes* recently declaring him "the best villain of all time" (Kenreck 2015).

While the Joker has thrived in popular culture, other characters whose masculinity is secondary or compromised by queer readings are subject to similar ends as women. Batman in particular has often been surrounded by men and the homosocial relationships at the center of his life. His sidekick and butler are his primary intimates, and women characters in the universe are primarily villainous. DC Comics held a poll to determine whether Batman's sidekick, Jason Todd, should live or die in 1989. The vote in favor was by a slim margin, but Todd was eliminated, and as Shyminsky (2011) notes "It is entirely possible that Jason Todd's death is indicative of a desire in some readers of Batman comic books to erase or repress the possibility of non-heteronormative sexuality by eliminating its most obvious signifier in Robin" (305).

Batman's villainous women, on the other hand, are forced into exaggerated positions of femininity:

> These women, in order to obtain and keep their power, must also use a mask of femininity to survive in a male-dominated society, forcing them to sometimes use typical female displays of sexuality and seduction to fight back. Most of Poison Ivy's appearances feature her use of poison kisses to manipulate men; her use of typically feminine symbols of beauty and gentleness, such as flowers, subverts those feminine symbols into monstrous and destructive creatures. Both Harley Quinn and Catwoman also fall into these roles, at times working against the men who control them, Batman and The Joker, by acting as love interests and exploiting the female roles that they are forced to endure. (Austin 2015)

Kilgrave and Jessica Jones

Villains such as the Joker present equal foils to superheroes and alternative definitions of masculinity that often go as celebrated as the hypermasculinity of the superheroes themselves. However, the move of superhero characters into the hands of women creators outside of comics brings with it some powerful changes to the standard villains. The *Jessica Jones* adaptation (Rosenberg 2015–), a collaboration between Marvel and Netflix, has drawn new attention to some of the standards of villainy from some of Marvel's lesser-known superhero comics. The show loosely adapts *Alias*, a twenty-eight-issue series by Brian Michael Bendis and artist Michael Gaydos released from 2001–2004. *Alias* itself represented an unusual moment for Marvel Comics: a shift to "mature audiences." With the release of *Alias*, Marvel launched a new R-rated imprint, MAX. The cover of each issue featured a large warning, "Parental Advisory: Explicit Content," and the very first word of the first issue is "FUCK!"—its first appearance in the Marvel world. It wasn't the only instance for long: the word is printed ten times in the first three pages of the issue alone. It appeared that thanks to this new imprint comic books (and superheroes themselves?) were going to grow up, if the use of swear words can be considered progress. And it seemed to be just in time—this first issue hit comic stores in November 2001, not long after September 11 changed American cultural sensibilities, and only a few years before *Batman Begins* would take cinematic superheroes to new levels of gritty realism.

Many elements of the comic and TV adaptation follow the same path: Jessica Jones is a private investigator with superpowers that didn't quite make her Avengers material. She is involved with Luke Cage (in the comics, the relationship is established, while in the series the relationship is quickly formed and almost as quickly ended.) Several moments in *Jessica Jones* make knowing nods back to the *Alias* comic series that also act as commentary on some of the problematic aspects of the comic portrayal. In the series, Jessica Jones was formerly a superhero going by the name of Jewel: her costume, a white and blue sparkly strapless suit, makes an appearance on screen (though decidedly not on Jessica) in episode five. Jones rejects both the costume and the "stripper's name" that goes with it. Other aspects of the comic book are abandoned just as readily, including an emphasis on storylines featuring other Avengers and superheroes.

However, the show is most interesting for its rethinking of Jessica Jones's enemy Kilgrave as a particularly harrowing portrait of white geek masculinity. The show cast David Tennant, well-loved geek icon best known from *Doctor Who*, as Kilgrave, a man who emits pheromones that allow him to control people's actions with a simple command. The character of Kilgrave has been part of the Marvel comic world since *Daredevil #4,* where he was announced as "Killgrave, the Unbelievable Purple Man!"—the TV adaptation dropped both the second "l" in Killgrave and his purpleness, but kept his nightmarish power. In the comics, Killgrave's purple skin is the result of an unfortunate encounter with nerve gas; thankfully, this is dropped here to allow Kilgrave to be more unnerving (if occasionally clad in purple). In his original encounter with Daredevil, only Daredevil could resist Killgrave's powers: in the world of *Jessica Jones*, she is the only one able to resist, and that only after having time to adapt.

When comparing the two versions, Jacob Hall notes this difference in Kilgrave as a significant change:

> While the on-paper of this version is terrifying and has been the subject of more than his fair share of great comic storylines, David Tennant transforms him into something far more pathetic and compelling. Kilgrave's obsession with Jessica is less that of a bad guy wanting to hurt a good guy, and more that of jilted ex-boyfriend refusing to move on after a bad break-up. (Hall 2015)

This transforms Kilgrave into a stalker and persistent figure in Jones's life, continually present even when off-screen in the show, while in the comic his arc was mostly confined to a big reveal in the final eight issues of the cyle. Arthur Chu (2015) captured the compelling intersections of Jessica Jones and Gamergate in his review of the series, observing:

> Kilgrave's power is an analog, low-tech, "meatspace" version of a power that some men in the Gamergate crowd seem to dream of having: the power to be anyone, be anywhere, and do anything without social repercussions. It's a power that, in our world, can be acquired by any determined troll with basic computer skills and an Internet connection.

This association of a villain with a geek power fantasy is important and groundbreaking for Marvel. In both the comics and cinematic universe, most of the villains have been more associated with traditional masculinity than geek values: Iron Man battles with businessmen and advocates of the military-industrial complex, Captain America fights against Nazi-influenced spies and government agents, and Hulk has his own carnival-mirror solider turned monster to defeat. Only Thor has brought forth a surprisingly compelling villain in Loki, whose mythological roots make him both canonically queer and more likely to triumph with wits and magic than strength (Baker-Whitelaw, Tumblr's favorite Marvel villain, comes out as bisexual 2014).

Some of Loki's powers are reminiscent of Kilgrave: his ability to overwrite minds and possess victims such as Hawkeye to do his bidding is particularly notable. And as with Kilgrave, there is a gendered violent streak that particularly comes through in Loki's threats to Black Widow: "I won't touch Barton. Not until I make him kill you! Slowly, intimately, in every way he knows you fear! And then he'll wake just long enough to see his good work, and when he screams, I'll split his skull! This is MY bargain, you mewling quim!" (Whedon 2012). Yet these threats never come to fruition, and the closest the cinematic universe comes to dealing with the aftermath of the mental violations Loki specializes in is in the fate of Erik Selvig. In *Thor: The Dark World* (Taylor 2013), we see Erik Selvig recovering from the aftermath of having a god in his head. We see Erik apparently going mad, conducting experiments at Stonehenge while nude and ending up confined to a mental institution. Much of his madness is played for laughs and the resolution of his insanity comes with apparent ease after a sighting of birds traveling through a dimensional portal convinces him to throw away his medication and embrace the chaos. This is very different from how the aftermath of mental and physical violations are handled in *Alias* and *Jessica Jones*, and in *Jessica Jones* the traumatic aftermath is thoroughly explored to demonstrate a superhero in a recovery that is very different from Batgirl's.

Superheroes in the Mainstream Gaze

The mainstreaming of superheroes seems to be an unstoppable force. In 2015, CBS debuted *Supergirl* (Adler, Berlanti, and Kreisberg), bringing another woman superhero to broadcast TV and causing avid debates on its depiction of women and feminism, or lack thereof (Lane 2015). Meanwhile, the Marvel Cinematic Universe is powering forward, while DC is working on a competing series of films setting up for a Justice League team-up. Netflix is already planning for more *Daredevil* and *Jessica Jones* and a *Luke Cage* solo series was released in 2016 (Coker), while *Gotham* (Cannon 2014–) continues to air a pre-Batman view of the DC Comics metropolis. Superheroes are everywhere, and the slow movement towards greater diversity is attracting pushback from within the community.

Cinema fans have found their box offices taken over by superheroes, and yet note that comic book fans still act like their medium is under siege. As AO Scott and Manohla Dargis (2012) write, "comic book fans need to feel perpetually beleaguered and disenfranchised, marginalized by phantom elites who want to confiscate their hard-won pleasures. And this resentment—which I have a feeling I'm provoking more of here—finds its way into the stories themselves, expressed either as glowering self-pity or bullying machismo." Nowhere is this more evident than in the current cycle of DC Comics films, with the machismo stand-off of Batman versus Superman taking center stage. Meanwhile, there is no avoiding the sexist, heteronormative, white standard still imposed on superhero bodies, as Manohla Dargis laments:

> For all the technological innovations, the groovy new Bat cycles and codpieces, superhero movies just recycle variations on gender stereotypes that were in circulation back in the late 1930s… the movie superhero remains stuck in a pre-feminist, pre-civil rights logic that dictates that a bunch of white dudes, as in *The Avengers*, will save the world for the grateful multiracial, multicultural multitudes. (ibid.)

Comic book fandom has proven remarkably resistant to change, as demonstrated from both the treatment of women within the community and on the pages of popular titles. But with shows like *Agent Carter* (D'Esposito 2014–2015), *Jessica Jones*, and even *Supergirl* demonstrating new possibilities for women superheroes on screen and women creators in the writer's and director's chairs, there is hope for transformative forces in the community. With this shifting gaze, new attention must necessarily fall on how masculinity is captured and heralded in these different superbodies, particularly as the geek community is offered reflections of themselves in forms that are villainous as often as they are heroic.

References

Abad-Santos, Alexander. 2013. How the nerds lost Comic-Con. *The Wire*, July 19. Accessed August 5, 2015. http://www.thewire.com/entertainment/2013/07/how-nerds-lost-comic-con/67304/.

Austin, Shannon. 2015. Batman's female foes: The gender war in Gotham city. *The Journal of Popular Culture* 48 (2): 285–295. https://doi.org/10.1111/jpcu.12257.

Baker-Whitelaw, Gavia. 2014. Marvel unceremoniously snuffs out female founding member of Avengers. *Daily Dot*, July 30. Accessed February 12, 2015. http://www.dailydot.com/geek/ant-man-janet-van-dyne/.

Baker-Whitelaw, Gavia. 2014. Tumblr's favorite marvel villain comes out as bisexual. *Daily Dot*, October 24. Accessed January 14, 2016. http://www.dailydot.com/fandom/loki-marvel-lgbt-bisexual-tumblr.

Barnett, David. 2015. Comics capture digital readers—and grab more print fans. *The Guardian*, July 3. Accessed January 20, 2016. https://www.theguardian.com/books/2015/jul/03/comics-capture-digital-readers-and-grab-more-print-fans.

Barnett, David. 2015. DC Comics pulls cover of Batgirl menaced by Joker after online protests. *The Guardian*, March 12. Accessed January 18, 2016. http://www.theguardian.com/books/2015/mar/17/dc-comics-pull-batgirl-joker-cover-after-protests.

Bongco, Mila. 2014. *Reading comics: Language, culture, and the concept of the Superhero in comic books*. New York: Routledge.

Bricken, Rob. 2015. The real problem with the Batman cover. *i09*, March 18. Accessed August 1, 2015. http://io9.gizmodo.com/the-real-problems-with-this-controversial-batgirl-cove-1692184909.

Brooker, Will. 2011. From Killer Moth to Killing Joke: Batgirl, a life in pictures. *Mindless Ones*, November 9. Accessed April 23, 2015. http://mindlessones.com/2011/11/09/from-killer-moth-to-killing-joke-batgirl-a-life-in-pictures/.

Brown, Tara Tiger. 2012. Dear fake geek girls: Please go away. *Forbes*, March 26. Accessed March 2, 2015.

Burlingame, Ross. 2013. *The Big Bang Theory* controversy: Girls in a comic shop. *ComicBook.com*, January 8. Accessed April 12, 2014. http://comicbook.com/blog/2013/01/08/the-big-bang-theory-controversy-girls-in-a-comic-shop/.

Chu, Arthur. 2015. How Jessica Jones absorbed the anxieties of Gamergate. *Slate*, November 24. Accessed January 5, 2016. http://www.slate.com/articles/arts/television/2015/11/marvel_s_jessica_jones_and_Gamergate_how_the_netflix_series_absorbed_the.single.html.

Cocca, Carolyn. 2014. Negotiating the third wave of feminism in Wonder Woman. *PS. Political Science & Politics* 47 (1): 98–103.

Cochran, Shannon. 2007. The cold shoulder: Saving superheroines from comic-book violence. *Bitch Media*, February 28. Accessed April 12, 2016. http://bitchmagazine.org/article/comics-cold-shoulder.

Comicbook, Joe. 2014. Guardians of the Galaxy had highest percentage of female viewers of any Marvel Studios movie. *ComicBook.com*, August 4. Accessed February 4, 2015. http://comicbook.com/blog/2014/08/04/guardians-of-the-galaxy-had-highest-percentage-of-female-viewers/.

Conway, Gerry and Gil Kane. 1973. *The Amazing Spiderman #121*. Marvel Comics.

Costello, Matthew J. 2013. The super politics of comic book fandom. *Transformative Works and Cultures* 13. http://dx.doi.org/10.3983/twc.2013.0528.

Dargis, Manohla and AO Scott. 2012. Super-dreams of an alternate world order. *The New York Times*, June 27. Accessed January 4, 2015. http://www.nytimes.com/2012/07/01/movies/the-amazing-spider-man-and-the-modern-comic-book-movie.html?pagewanted=all.

Dockterman, Eliana. 2015. Why Marvel decided to create an all-female superhero team. *Time*, February 6. Accessed March 12, 2015. http://time.com/3699450/marvel-aforce-secret-wars-superhero-female/.

Dyce, Andrew. 2016. DC Comics rebirth: A complete guide for new readers. *Screen Rant*, May 25. Accessed April 13, 2017. http://screenrant.com/dc-comics-rebirth-preview-guide/?view=all.

Edidin, Rachel. 2012. The myth of the fake geek girl. *io9*, November 15. Accessed May 12, 2015. https://io9.gizmodo.com/im-not-claiming-that-a-isnt-a-geek-because-they-dont-m-268724129.

Grant, Steven. 1999. Steven Grant responds. *Women in Refrigerators*, March. Accessed April 26, 2015. http://www.lby3.com/wir/c-sgrant.html.

Griepp, Milton. 2017. Marvel's David Gabriel on the 2016 market shift. *ICV2*, March 31. Accessed May 1, 2017. https://icv2.com/articles/news/view/37152/marvels-david-gabriel-2016-market-shift.

Guzman, Jennifer de. 2016. Thirty names, without one woman: Comic book creators withdraw from nomination for the Angouleme Grand Prix in protest. *Comics Alliance*, January 6. Accessed January 22, 2016. http://comicsalliance.com/angouleme-grand-prix-2016-protest/.

Hall, Jacob. 2015. "Jessica Jones" vs "Alias": How Marvel's new Netflix series compares to the comic that inspired it. *Slashfilm*, November 23. Accessed January 1, 2016. http://www.slashfilm.com/jessica-jones-vs-alias/.

Hanley, Tim. 2015. Gendercrunching. *Bleeding Cool*, May 29. Accessed February 2, 2016. http://www.bleedingcool.com/2015/05/29/gendercrunching-march-2015-variant-covers-drive-marvel-and-a-blast-from-the-past/.

Hebdige, Dick. 1999. The function of subculture. In *The cultural studies reader*, ed. Simon During, 441–450. New York: Routledge.

Highsmith, Dough. 2003. The long, strange trip of Barbara Gordon: Images of librarians in comic books. *The Reference Librarian* 37 (78): 61–68.

ICv2. 2012. "New 52" appealed to avid fans & lapsed readers. *ICv2*, February 9. Accessed March 15, 2014. http://icv2.com/articles/comics/view/22113/new-52-appealed-avid-fans-lapsed-readers.

Jill. 2012. Wow I'm never buying anything Tony Harris does. *Tumblr*, November 13. Accessed March 2, 2015. http://thenerdybird.tumblr.com/post/35636753452/wow-im-never-buying-anything-tony-harris-does.

Kane, Vivian. 2017. Are you wondering where the Wonder Woman marketing is? Yeah, us too. *The Mary Sue*, April 28. https://www.themarysue.com/where-is-wonder-woman/.

Keating, Erin M. 2012. The female link: Citation and continuity in Watchmen. *The Journal of Popular Culture* 45 (6): 1266–1288. https://doi.org/10.1111/j.1540-5931.2011.00808.x.

Kenreck, Todd. 2015. Why Joker is the best villain of all time. *Forbes*, August 3. Accessed December 13, 2015. http://www.forbes.com/sites/toddkenreck/2015/08/03/why-the-joker-is-the-best-villain-of-all-time/#20b4ca34507b.

Lane, Carly. 2015. We don't need Supergirl OR Jessica Jones: We need both. *The Mary Sue*, November 25. Accessed January 20, 2016. http://www.themarysue.com/supergirl-vs-jessica-jones/.

Lebel, Sabine. 2009. "Tone down the boobs, please!" Reading the special effect body in superhero movies. *CineAction* 77: 56–67. https://www.questia.com/library/journal/1G1-200253754/tone-down-the-boobs-please-reading-the-special.

MacDonald, Heidi. 2012. DC's rood breaks down reader survey. *Publishers Weekly*, February 14. Accessed October 12, 2014. http://www.publishersweekly.com/pw/

by-topic/industry-news/comics/article/50633-dc-s-rood-breaks-down-reader-survey.html.

McGee, Masani. 2014. Big men in spangly outfits: Spectacle and masculinity in Joss Whedon's *The Avengers*. *Slayage: The Journal of the Whedon Studies Association* 11 (12.1): 1–14. http://www.whedonstudies.tv/uploads/2/6/2/8/26288593/mcgee_slayage_11.2-12.1.pdf.

McKnight, John Carter, Katrin Tiidenberg, Michael Burnam-Fink, and Cindy Tekkobe. 2013. Navigating boundaries and taboos in the digital frontier. *Selected Papers of Internet Research* 3. http://spir.aoir.org/index.php/spir/article/view/892.

McNally, Victoria. 2014. Female NYCC attendees. *The Mary Sue*, July 9. Accessed Februay 8, 2015. http://k8monstrscloset.com/2014/07/24/gender-parity-and-harrassment-at-sdcc-and-beyond/.

Meskin, Aaron. 2009. Comics as literature? *The British Journal of Aesthetics* 49 (3): 219–239. https://doi.org/10.1093/aesthj/ayp025.

Mouse, Annie N. 2015. Invisible women: Why Marvel's Gamora & Black Widow were missing from merchandise, and what we can do about it. *The Mary Sue*, April 7. Accessed April 8, 2015. https://www.themarysue.com/invisible-women/.

Nolan, Christoher. 2008. *The Dark Knight*. Warner Bros. DVD.

Okay, Arpad. 2015. Women rule the Eisner Awards. Observation Deck, July 11. Accessed January 15, 2016. http://observationdeck.kinja.com/women-rule-the-eisner-awards-1717184001.

O'Reilly, Julie D. 2005. The Wonder Woman precedent: Female (super) heroism on trial. *The Journal of American Culture* 28 (3): 273–283. https://doi.org/10.1111/j.1542-734x.2005.00211.x.

Pantozzi, Jill. 2011. Gail, Jill and Babs: A conversation about BATGIRL & ORACLE. *Newsarama*, June 9. Accessed June 14, 2015. http://www.newsarama.com/7777-gail-jill-and-babs-a-conversation-about-batgirl-oracle.html.

Pantozzi, Jill. 2014. Sorry to burst your masturbatory comic bubble (no, I'm not). *The Mary Sue*, April 17. Accessed April 12, 2015. https://www.themarysue.com/misogyny-in-comic-book-community/.

Peacock, Joe. 2012. Booth babes need not apply. *CNN*, July 24. Accessed May 4, 2015. http://geekout.blogs.cnn.com/2012/07/24/booth-babes-need-not-apply/.

Pedler, Martyn. 2007. Suffering and seriality: Memory, continuity and trauma in monthly superhero adventures. *MiT5 Media in Transition: Creativity, Ownership and Collaboration in the Digital Age Conference*, Cambridge, April 27.

Petri, Alexandra. 2015. What Jeremy Renner really got wrong about Black Widow. *The Washington Post*, April 24. https://www.washingtonpost.com/blogs/compost/wp/2015/04/24/what-jeremy-renner-really-got-wrong-about-black-widow/.

Pirone, Kristy. 2013. Why geek girls are tired of "Big Bang" bullshit. *FemInspire*, July 5. Accessed September 16, 2014. http://feminspire.com/why-the-big-bang-theory-makes-me-cringe/.

Reed, Peyton. 2015. *Ant-Man*. Burbank, CA: Marvel Studios. DVD.

Reisman, Abrahan. 2016. Comics stars boycott international prize because no women were nominated. *Vulture*, January 7. Accessed January 22, 2016. http://www.vulture.com/2016/01/comics-boycott-angouleme.html.

Reynolds, Kate. 2015. Gender parity and harassment at San Diego Comic Con and beyond. July 24. Accessed August 2, 2014. http://k8monstrscloset.com/2014/07/24/gender-parity-and-harassment-at-sdcc-and-beyond/.

Robbins, Trina. 2002. Gender differences in comics. *Image and Narrative* 4. http://www.imageandnarrative.be/inarchive/gender/trinarobbins.htm.

Rogers, Vaneta. 2011. Why they endure(d): ORACLE remebered by creators, advocates. *Newsarama*, September 7. Accessed June 14, 2015. http://www.news-arama.com/8317-why-they-endure-d-oracle-remembered-by-creators-advocates.html.

Rosenberg, Melissa. 2015. *Jessica Jones* (TV series). Created by Melissa Rosenberg. Neflix.

Russo, Joe and Anthony Russo. 2016. *Captain America: The Winter Soldier*. Burbank, CA: Marvel Studios. DVD.

Scheckner, Brett. 2014. Market research says 46.67% of comic fans are female. *Comics Beat*, February 5. Accessed September 21, 2015. http://www.comicsbeat.com/market-research-says-46-female-comic-fans/.

Schumacker, Joel. 1997. *Batman & Robin*. Burbank, CA: Warner Brothers. DVD.

Scott, Suzanne. 2012. Fangirls in refrigerators: The politics of (in)visibility in comic book culture. *Transformative Works and Cultures* 13. 10.3983/twc.2013.0460.

Shannon, Hannah Means. 2015. Gendercrunching February 2015 including the Eisners—more women everywhere. *BleedingCool*, May 1. Accessed January 4, 2016. http://www.bleedingcool.com/2015/05/01/gendercrunching-february-2015-including-the-eisners-more-womeneverywhere-but-wait/.

Shyminsky, Neil. 2011. "Gay" sidekicks: Queer anxiety and the narrative straightening of the superhero. *Men and Masculinities* 14 (3): 288–308. https://doi.org/10.1177/1097184x10368787.

Starke, Hannah. 2013. The degradation of women to plot points in Superman and classical epics. In *Examining Lois Lane: The scoop on Superman's sweetheart*, ed. Nadine Farghaly, 113–127. Lanham, MD: Scarecrow Press.

Taylor, Aaron. 2007. 'He's gotta be strong, and he's gotta be fast, and he's gotta be larger than life': Investigating the engendered superhero body. *Journal of Popular Culture* 40 (2): 344–360. https://doi.org/10.1111/j.1540-5931.2007.00382.x.

Taylor, Alan. 2013. *Thor: The Dark World*. Directed by Alan Taylor. Marvel Studios. DVD.

Vincent, Alice. 2015. Is Disney ignoring Marvel's female fans? *Telegraph*, April 24. http://www.telegraph.co.uk/culture/disney/11552960/Are-Disney-ignoring-Marvels-female-fans.html.

Whedon, Joss. 2012. *The Avengers*. Burbank, CA: Marvel Studios. DVD.

Whedon, Joss. 2015. *Avengers: Age of Ultron*. Directed by Joss Whedon. Marvel Studios. DVD.

Whitbrook, James. 2017. Is Captain American currently a Nazi? The answer is complicated. *Kotaku*, April 13. Accessed May 1, 2017. https://www.kotaku.com.au/2017/04/is-captain-america-currently-a-nazi-the-answer-is-complicated/.

Winstead, Nick. 2015. "As a symbol I can be incorruptible": How Christopher Nolan de-queered the Batman of Joel Schumacher. *The Journal of Popular Culture* 48 (3): 572–585. https://doi.org/10.1111/jpcu.12228.

Woo, Benjamin. 2012. Alpha nerds: Cultural intermedias in a subcultural scene. *European Journal of Cultural Studies* 15 (5): 659–676. https://doi.org/10.1177/1367549412445758.

6

Bronies on the Iron Throne: Perceptions of Prosocial Behaviors and Success

Fantastical narratives where women serve as rewards for gallant behavior are certainly, to quote Disney's *Beauty and the Beast*, "a tale as old as time" (Trousdale and Wise 1991). In *The Bard's Tale*, a video game that satirizes and plays with this trope, a woman even describes herself to the player character as a reward to keep him motivated in his quest. While the game does include the traditional theme of good versus evil, the structure of the narration helps to undermine the concept that the player is making serious moral decisions. The game ends in a final choice between good or evil, as so many quest narratives do. However, the player's choices don't impact one underlying message of the text: in the game's logic, The Bard deserved all of his rewards (riches, power, and Caleigh herself). Thus, when the player chooses a path where the rewards are forfeited, the implication is that The Bard chose to abandon his rewards, rather than that his actions make him undeserving of them. But the unintended twist is that in all three endings the narration follows the idea that The Bard deserved all of the items that Caleigh was offering him, even in the endings where he does not end up with the woman, riches, and power the narration implies that The Bard chose to forgo his deserved rewards. The game may be mocking the quest trope that has carried through video games from Sir Graham's quests for kingship and wife in the *King's Quest* series (Sierra 1984–1998) onwards, but in the end the assumptions of just rewards for heroism are left unchallenged, and women are still relegated to instrumental status in the narrative. Heroes throughout Western culture and history have sought to save the damsel in distress, and usually succeeded: only occasionally is this stereotype subverted, as with Shrek's rescue of Princess Fiona in the iconic 2001 animated film as a means not for getting the girl but for getting his swamp back (Adamson and Jenson 2001). Even in the case of Shrek, this parody is ultimately again subverted, as Shrek does get the girl—and his swamp—as his ultimate reward for becoming a hero. The idea of a damsel in distress as the motivation for heroism is such a powerful cliché that when Anita Sarkeesian kicked off her *Tropes vs. Women* series on video games (discussed in Chap. 4, and at the center of the gendered "Gamergate" conflict within the game fan community), she opened with a segment on gaming's many women in distress. As Sarkeesian (2013) points out within the first video of the series, the concept of a woman as reward works well because it provides easy reference for the protagonist's motivation within the story and provides a clear trajectory to move the plot forward. Given the construction of the male geek as a socially challenged outsider, rejected by those in power and found unsuitable as a potential partner, the idea of women as a reward can be particularly compelling in geek spaces.

Geek culture is full of stories in which heroes receive their due reward, often embodied in the form of a woman alongside property, status, and wealth. These narratives are often translated into a perception of action and reward within communities: just as in the transmedia giant *Game of Thrones* (Martin 1996–) Jaime Lannister is expected to be rewarded for his rescue of Brienne or Littlefinger for his "rescue" of Sansa Stark, so too do geek men expect to be rewarded for their "white knighting." White knights, or men to the rescue, are a common form of advocate in both the media and geek communities. The very concept of white knighting is tied to rewards and spoils and is often used in contradictory ways within social groups. This chapter will trace how the belief that men should be rewarded for their "good behavior" is often a point of internal conflict within masculine geek groups when issues dealing with women or marginalized identities arise. For many the just rewards should be delivered to the dominant group simply because they are the good guys, and geek masculinity has offered many self-defensive tropes (such as protests that women don't appreciate "nice guys" or the concept of the "friend zone") to explain when women don't appropriately respond to their qualities. But when conflict arises and some men splinter to support women they are seen as acting against the good of the group, or selfishly hogging the anticipated rewards of attention and female flesh for themselves in an inherently hypocritical move. These expectations go hand in hand with the power dynamics of geek culture, even as male fans occupy a privileged position and can act as the saviors of fandoms and causes that, left to women, would fall to ridicule or obscurity.

Women as Rewards

There's a reason that popular images of fantasy narratives involve swashbuckling knights and questionably clad women: many iconic franchises in geek culture draw upon pseudo-medieval source material (Chaytor 2004). Legends and myths, particularly of Western origin, act as the foundation for modern tales of heroes, drawing on some of the same themes which the troubadours of the Middle Ages explored in their ballads and poems (Houghton 2005; Phelpstead 2006). Many of these stories were filtered through pulp fiction, comic books, and decades of retellings but kept some of their core assumptions of power and culture. Many of the quests of heroes such as King Arthur and Sir Lancelot are driven in part by the legal mandates of coverture, marital power, or chattel marriage (Schroeder 1905; Ahern 2004). These laws are found throughout Western Europe from the fall of the Roman Empire to the modern twentieth century (Herlihy 1962; Schroeder 1905). Most of the laws placed a woman and children under the control of the most notable male relative in their lives, usually the husband or father (ibid.). A wedding under these laws was a legal transfer of property from one man to another, often with additional treaty-like bargaining for actual property (Herlihy 1962). To pursue a woman who was stolen from you was similar to retrieving any of the valuable property which could have been taken—a mindset that still exists today in some spaces, and not just in stories.

Ballads, poems, and stories of medieval times drew upon this idea of proving oneself worthy of very valuable property, often despite humble or lowly origins. Knights would rove the countryside looking for deeds to perform to increase their standing, and eventually their physical property and power. Women were often part of this bargain, being the ultimate prize to be won, since they not only counted towards a knight's property but also showed that the individual was respected by those in power. JRR Tolkien, one of the founders of modern geek canon, was familiar with the problems that arose from incorporating the ideals of previous romantic ages within current literature (Holmes 2004; Seaman 2006). Tolkien took issue with the uncritical use of the ideals of chivalric love by previous art movements as being harmful and dangerous to people's understandings of modern relationships (ibid.). As he commented in a letter to his son:

> It takes, or at any rate has in the past taken, the young man's eye off women as they are, as companions in shipwreck not guiding stars. (One result is for

observation of the actual to make the young man turn cynical.) To forget their desires, needs and temptations. (2014)

Tolkien's words suggest that he viewed the concept of chivalric love as harmful to the ability of men to form attachments to women as something other than objects. It is thus only appropriate that we can read Tolkien's epic sagas in part as breaking down the trope of masculinity as expressed primarily through the actions of the heroic knight that stands alone to save the day. Many other scholars have noted Tolkien's ability to show the differences between the solitary hero that dominates much romantic literature, represented by Boromir in the *Lord of the Rings* trilogy, and the more community and people-centric hero which Tolkien prefers, Aragorn and Faramir within the books (Madil 2008; Smol 2004; McBride 2007).

Tolkien's views on gender roles are an issue of debate within academic communities where compelling arguments from multiple viewpoints have been put forward. For many, Tolkien's construction of masculinity and femininity remains an interesting and engaging point of analysis (ibid.). But one thing that many of these deconstructions is missing is an analysis of the relationships between the genders within Tolkien's work. Tolkien can be progressive in his deconstruction of masculinity while still reinforcing the traditional poise of women as representative objects of power that show the communal bonds between men. In particular, when the relationships between the love triangle of Aragorn, Arwen, and Eowyn are examined some beliefs about the roles of women in relationship to men of power become apparent (Enright 2008; Wollock 2011). Arwen and Eowyn represent two of the three primary female characters within Tolkien's *Lord of the Rings* trilogy. Both roles are most defined by the character's relationship to a male lead, Aragorn (Wollock 2011). This relationship is shown to lead to tension between the female characters and a significant male figure in their lives, their fathers Elrond, Lord of Rivendell and Theoden, King of Rohan (Enright 2008; Wollok 2011). It is significant that these women are both daughters of rulers who have not yet chosen to fully support Aragorn and the fight against Sauron. Through winning the love and following of both women and proving himself through other heroic feats Aragorn is shown to win the support of their fathers as well. The relationships between the two women and Aragorn is only a retelling of a courtly love story which Tolkien despised. But elements from within the same political structures and ideologies can be seen when the women themselves represent the power of the kingdoms or fathers within the story. Women are seen as useful for the symbolic importance of the relationships they choose to have as well as for the physical necessity of the armies/resources their families have available. To win the woman not only grants a love but also access and free use of everything their fathers have.

This continued dehumanization of women, not just as heavenly beings for a knight to chase after, but also as pawns within a political game has serious implications for how modern media and consumers conceptualize interpersonal relationships. Within the text *Courtly Seduction, Modern Subjections* Fajardo-Acosta (2010) examines the impact that the ideas inspired by the troubadours and passed along within modern media may have upon us:

> we cannot transcend medievality and challenge unjust, arbitrary, and predatory social structures because we are unwilling to give up our cherished dream, the heart of our secret identity, our desire to be the lord who in turn possesses the symbolic lady who is power (55–56).

This desire to be lord and possess the symbolic lady shows up in a range of geek canonic texts. One of the more popular media enterprises of the last decade has been George RR Martin's *A Song of Ice and Fire*, better known to many through the *Game of Thrones* HBO series. The series features a more realistic and gritty style that appears more naturalistic to many consumers than the flowery prose of older fantasy writers like Tolkien. Within the series the main plot thread follows the desires of multiple characters to rule the fictional land of the Seven Kingdoms. Martin uses this plot to explore the relationships between the people of power in medieval-like settings and to take the concept of women as political pawn to its brutal and logical conclusion.

Within *Game of Thrones* the female characters often face the harsh realities of the world in which they live. From Daenerys Targaryen being sold into a marriage at age 13 by her brother in return for the support of the Dothraki army, to Cersei Lannister, the Queen Regnant of Westeros, forced into two political marriages by her father, the women within *Game of Thrones* understand their roles within their society, even as they struggle to survive and flourish. One interesting inversion that Martin indulges in is the self-awareness that many of the female characters have about their status within the world of Westeros. In particular, the relationship between Cersei Lannister and Sansa Stark takes on overtones of both mentorship and control when the subject of women's roles arises:

> So now you are a woman. Do you have the least idea of what that means?
>
> "It means that I am now fit to be wedded and bedded," said Sansa, "and to bear children for the king."
>
> The queen gave a wry smile. "A prospect that no longer entices you as it once did, I can see. I will not fault you for that. Joffrey has always been difficult. Even his birth … I labored a day and a half to bring him forth. You cannot imagine the pain, Sansa. I screamed so loudly that I fancied Robert might hear me in the kingswood. (114, 1999)

Cersei does not spare Sansa's feelings throughout their discussions. She states what she sees as the blunt truth to Sansa, attempting to put some fear and realism into a young girl who she sees as being too idealistic. Within this exchange Cersei acknowledges her own worth and the concept that her services as a mother as simply a prize for the king to collect. Much like a skilled hunter has trophy prizes, a good queen and mother has male heirs they may present to their spouse.

Cersei sees her own fate, and the fate of any royal woman, as being inescapable. Her experience has made her bitter through her years as she has found the role of being queen limiting. She tries repeatedly to show Sansa that lessons that she has learned about the role and power that women have within their society but often comes across as off putting instead of helpful:

Cersei: "When we were young Jamie and I looked so much alike that even our father couldn't tell us apart. We could never understand why they treated us so differently. Jamie was taught to fight with sword and lance and mace. And I was taught to smile and sing and please. He was heir to Casterly Rock and I was sold to some stranger like a horse to be ridden whenever he desired."
Sansa: "You were Robert's Queen."
Cersei: "And you will be Joffrey's. Enjoy." (Marshall 2012)

The dehumanization that Cersei feels is clearly expressed within this passage. She knows that her role is little more than that of an animal that is useful to the king. Any power that she has now is derived through her relationships to powerful men and that when her utility or ability to acquiesce to their demands had decreased, even her little control will be gone, as is shown graphically in the later books when she is forced to walk naked through the city while the populace hurls insults and rotten food.

Olenna Tyrell, a character introduced recently in both the books and series, is often outspoken and clear about understanding how the power relationships within the kingdom works. She uses this to her, and her family's, advantage throughout her interactions. Her knowledge that a woman's real power is in her utility as a bearer of children is put to play in the following discussion.

Olenna: "Impossible. My grandson is the pride of Highgarden, the most desirable bachelor in all seven kingdoms. Your daughter ..."
Tywin: "Is rich, the most beautiful woman in all seven kingdoms. And the mother of the king."
Olenna: "Oooold."
Tywin: "Old?"
Olenna: "Old. I'm something of an expert on the subject. Her change will be upon her before long. I'll spare you the details of what'll happen then. You men may have a stomach for bloodshed and slaughter but this is another matter entirely." (Sakharov 2013)

Olenna acknowledges that while there is much that Cersei has to offer her family, a marriage between the older Cersei, who will shortly be menopausal, and the young Loras Tyrell is unlikely to result in children, male heirs in particular. Since Sir Loras is the last male of the Tyrell line it is important to the family that he be able to have children. Binding him in marriage to a woman who is unable to perform her basic function within the relationship would doom the entire family. Loras, identified in the show's text as homosexual, notably has as little say in this arranged marriage as Cersei, and both characters are subject to in-text censorship for their deviance from expected heterosexual norms later in the show and book series.

Beyond their utility as brood mothers, the women of the *Game of Thrones* acknowledge their symbolic utility in another way. During one of the more dramatic scenes within the series, Cersei and the ladies of the court, including Sansa Stark, wait out a siege and battle outside the city walls. Sansa has a dislike for Sir Illyn, the executioner, who is standing in the room with the women throughout the duration and asks Cersei why he is present. As things in the battle go poorly, and Cersei drinks more heavily, she tells Sansa the truth about the knight's presence:

Cersei: "When I told you about Sir Illyn earlier I lied. Do you want to know the truth? Why he is really here? He is here for us. Stannis may take the city. He may take the throne but he will not take us alive." (Marshall 2012)

Cersei understands that the women would not only be facing the horrific reality of rape but that their bodies and presence are a symbolic victory for Stannis. To allow him to claim them put their side to a relative disadvantage. These women represent many noble houses and ransoming their safety would be a strategic advantage for Lord Stannis who could use it to force his own victory. The women are a tool and spoil of war and Cersei is determined to not allow the other side the chance to gain that power, even if denial means killing all of the court ladies in the process.

While the pseudo-medieval setting of *Game of Thrones* lends itself to a discussion of chivalry and all it entails, such interpretations are not confined to historical settings. Although much modern media ignores or rewrites the more explicit statements of women as chattel, many of the concepts that arose from this connection are freely employed. In *Scott Pilgrim Vs. the World* (Wright 2010), a movie and comic series powered by geek-referential humor and the building of constant parallels to classic arcade games in scenes of conflict, the main protagonist, Scott Pilgrim, must fight and defeat the evil ex-partners of his would-be girlfriend, Ramona Flowers. Throughout most of the story the narrative focuses on the fact that Scott must prove himself to be worthy of attaining Ramona's love and distancing himself from the shady and harmful characters within her past.

Scott Pilgrim:	"Wait! We're fighting over Ramona?"
Matthew Patel:	"Didn't you get my email explaining the situation?"
Scott Pilgrim:	"I skimmed it."
Wallace Wells:	[shaking head] "Mm-mm."
Matthew Patel:	"You will pay for your insolence!"

Throughout the narrative Ramona is treated as an object to be fought over but not necessarily protected since most of the exes don't care about how she feels regarding their interventions. The basic mentality behind the entire plot line draws from the idea of "If I can't have her no one can" with the evil exes attempting to keep anyone from being with Ramona if they can't do so. The moment when Scott proves himself better than any individual ex is conveyed through a metaphor drawn from defeating bosses in video games, as each ex falls into pieces and leaves behind only coins and a point value. As Scott draws closer to winning Ramona, he also literally gains a higher "score" (see Fig. 6.1), a metaphor the film version takes to its full on-screen videogame extremes.

Fig. 6.1 Scott "leveling up" in his pursuit of Ramona

Ramona's own position with regards to her would-be suitor is not entirely as prize for battle: the narrative reminds us she is not "won" through Scott's victory over her ultimate evil ex, but through Scott's growth and self-development. However, she has no development arc of her own, and the dynamics of their relationship reinforce the norms of courtly love. As Ryan Lyzardi's (2013) analysis of the Scott Pilgrim graphic novels notes, the apparently transgressive potential of the series falters and "ends up reaffirming dominant hegemonic gender roles and a dangerous brand of heteronormativity." To return to Tolkien's letter (2014):

> It inculcates exaggerated notions of "true love," as a fire from without, a permanent exaltation, unrelated to age, childbearing, and plain life, and unrelated to will and purpose. (One result of that is to make young folk look for a "love" that will keep them always nice and warm in a cold world, without any effort of theirs; and the incurably romantic go on looking even in the squalor of the divorce courts.)

Tolkien's criticism of the outcomes of courtly love is reflected in modern discourse across geek media. Within other productions, in particular Japanese anime, there is a strong rhetoric of a submissive or perfect woman who understands her place as servant to the important man in her life. Asian wives/housemaids/school girls often lauded on Internet and anime message boards plays back to this original idea. One popular show recently, *Puella Magi Madoka Magica* (Shaft 2011–2013), takes this idea to a logical conclusion where the young girls in the show are punished with pain and death for having independent wants and desires, and acting in their own self-agency, to attempt to achieve their own goals. As Kumiko Saito (2014) analyzes the show, "the magical girl's true task is to fight against her own adult form called 'witch,'" as "the magical girl's power can be considered as power only so far as her entry into the adult world of 'real' power is precluded" (161). In other Anime shows, such as *Fruits Basket*, the heroine Toru is rewarded for subsuming their own desires in order to better help and serve the men in their lives. The heroine of *Fruits Basket* similarly retains her innocence: as Kukhee Choo (2008) discusses, "even though Toru works amongst older women at a tough night job, she is not jaded by the harshness of her reality and maintains her 'cute' attitude" (285). This innocence is maintained even as she is "subject to violence and enforced sexualization," making her "dependent on the mercy of male characters" in a way that undermines her supposed power (288). In these narratives, the magical "girl" is an object of male desire, while the adult woman is a threat even to the magical girl's desirability.

While such narratives are prevalent in works of fiction, similar attitudes play out in what Peter Glick and Susan Fiske (1996) refer to as "benevolent sexism," which manifests primarily as paternalism and the desire to protect some presumed quality of women, not unlike the innocence of the magical girl. Benevolent sexism is benevolent in name only, and can play out violently, as Evan Anderson (2014) notes in his bleak analysis "I Used to be Elliot Rodger":

> We do not know much about Elliot Rodger's life or his interactions with society and women aside from what he has left in word documents and rants in YouTube videos, but absent some other potential explanation for his declaration of having "suffered" at the "hands" of women, we can deduce that his anger stems from his oft-repeated perception that women "denied" him sex while "rewarding" other, less-deserving and inferior men with just that. In other words, his anger is a result of being denied that which he believes he is entitled to.

Rodgers also had ties to pick up artists, who likewise put forth "the idea that men should go out and 'get' sex, that 'women' are not so much people as obstacles to prevent men from achieving self-actualization through the loss of virginity-or, with virginity-loss accomplished, just through having lots of sex" (Dean 2014).

The attitudes of benevolent sexism and entitlement at the core of these attitudes would not be out of place in geek misogynist movements such as Gamergate. As we discussed in Chap. 4, Gamergate as a movement arose out of possessive sexism: the ex-boyfriend of independent game developer Zoe Quinn posted about Quinn's sex life in elaborate detail, suggesting that she had cheated on him with several men who worked in the games industry, and as Jay Hathaway (2014) summarizes:

> a conspiracy immediately took root: Quinn had definitely fucked those five guys, gamers decided (they even turned it into a joke about the burger chain) and she'd done it to get publicity for her games. Quinn's address and phone number were made public shortly afterward, and the threats against her became so intense that she left her house and started couch-surfing.

The rhetoric of Gamergate, and particularly the feeling of ownership that not only Zoe Quinn's vindictive ex but other men in the Gamergate movement have taken over Quinn's body and sexuality, suggests that a similar sense of entitlement and frustration over women who "deny" or "reward" sex is at root in both movements.

Playing the White Knight

The concept of the white knight arises from tales of the dark and middle ages where brave knights errant would roam the land looking for those distressed to aid or defend. Just as concepts of chivalric love, medieval heroics, and seeking a damsel in distress are very familiar to the geek canon, so too is the trope of the white knight as a questing hero. Since there are few actual dragons left to slay or ladies in towers today, the concept has evolved to be more encompassing of the types of struggles that could be considered heroic today. The core assumptions recall the same benevolent sexism that fuels the flames of the more aggressive, violent sexism of Gamergate, Rodgers, and pick-up artists. Smaller heroic deeds are often considered important to the modern white knight, such as opening the door, paying for a meal, giving compliments or time spent listening to a woman—all of which, when placed in the context of chivalry for reward, carry with them a condescension towards women as a protected class in need of such support. Even though these heroics lack the action and excitement of a daring rescue, they are encoded in structures that suggest they should be rewarded. This conflation has led to the development of what some call White Knight Syndrome. The concept of "White Knight Syndrome" (related to, yet distinct from, the psychological definition of the term) is described by self-proclaimed Dr. Nerdlove (2012) as a tendency to try to rescue women, and in doing so "by trying to come to her 'rescue', the White Knight is essentially denying that women have agency of their own and have to wait for someone else—the self-declared hero, in this case—to come to her 'rescue' and 'save' her from all of her trouble." This assumption allows the same behaviors that play out in geek canonical texts to be brought into fan communities and gender relations between geeks.

The portrayal of the white knight of mentality plays out in two ways. The first is that which primarily concerns the Dr. Nerdlove article, men exposing themselves to potential risks in a relationship. The concern here is itself twofold. First, men may open themselves up to abusive partners under the idea that they could somehow get the person to change, but end up being abused and taken advantage of. Secondly, is that the man may become abusive or controlling in an attempt to fix their partner from whatever has been identified as the hurtful item, drugs or mental illness being two common ones. These attitudes can play into rape culture, as a disturbing study by G. Tendayi Viki and Dominic Abrams (2002) found in studying victim blame in acquaintance rape: benevolent sexists in the study were much more likely to blame the victim of acquaintance rape who was described as a married woman than the one whose marital status was unknown, suggesting "that individuals high in BS [benevolent sexism] are more likely to react negatively to rape victims who can be viewed as violating social norms concerning appropriate conduct for women" (289). That is, a woman who may be construed as cheating on her male partner is less human than one who is not. The root issue stems from the white knight's inability to truly see and value their partner as a person with flaws and not a damsel that needs rescuing and should provide expected rewards. This entitlement can result in feelings of frustration, anger, and aggression against the group or individual who seems to be thwarting the knight's entitlement.

In many cases today, the appellation of the White Knight is a pejorative rather than a claimed title. It is used in forum wars, discussions, and memes to paint a man who has chosen to defend women as an outcast from the brotherhood of the geek. For these identity gatekeepers a white knight is not someone who is the righteous defender of the weak and imperiled as painted by older tales. Instead, a White Knight is someone who has gone seeking their own self-interest in a cowardly move to ingratiate themselves with those with the power to deny and reward sex.

Left Head: "Halt! Who art thou?"
Minstrel: [sings] "He is brave Sir Robin, brave Sir Robin, who …"
Sir Robin: "Shut up! Nobody really, just passing through."

Left Head:	"What do you want?"
Minstrel:	[sings] "To fight and …"
Sir Robin:	"Shut up! Uh, n-n-nothing, really. J-j-just passing, uhm, just passing through."(Gilliam and Jones 1975/2006)

To those who use the title of White Knight against others within the geek community, white knights are subject to derision, fearful of demanding their full rights and respect when it comes time to defend their identity. Much like Sir Robin, they would rather attempt to hide their identity and act as a false hero for feminists against the real geeks. While Sir Robin is attempting to avoid a fight, and keep himself in one piece, the white knights are attempting to curry favor in the hopes of receiving the just rewards that "regular" geeks are so often denied given their outsider/undesirable status (Rosewarne 2016).

When it comes to geek self-identity and gender or sexual interpersonal relations, the community and media love to paint geeks as outcasts from the sphere of normalcy (Rosewarne 2016). While in geek media the portrayal is often painted more as a spirited underdog, such as within movies like *Weird Science*, *Superbad*, *Ghostbusters*, and *Spider-Man*, they are shown as being a long shot, but ultimately the better choice in partner. In stark contrast, if one listens to discussions among geek circles shows a self-image more like that of Gollum than Frodo. Geeks often self-paint their identity as being repulsive to the opposite sex. Much of the media that shows geeks as getting the girl could be seen as wish fulfillment for this group. Interestingly, unlike the media targeted at teenage girls, another group heavily invested in wish fulfillment romances, the geek media strongly urges the main characters to remain true to their identity. It is their natural nerdiness and awkward interests that make them attractive in the end. This helps to push the message that by acting out on their natural behavioral patterns they will be rewarded with the things they desire most. Since this is the major theme in many of the geek as protagonist media avenues the application of white knight as a derogatory term begins to make sense. Those who have chosen to side with the "enemies" of geekdom are failing the primary test, selling out their true identity, for a short-term reward. It is assumed that women's attention is owed to the group either way. It is simply seen that the waiting and being true to yourself is the preferable route. Just like Shrek is rewarded for being true to his onion-like ogre nature with the true love of Fiona, a geek must pass the test of the misogyny within their identity to win genuine female attention and love. A person who fails this important test and changes the presentation of who they are, and any deviance from the centralized identity is seen as a failure, must be like the characters who show themselves to be too cowardly or weak willed to wait for the inevitable reward. Like the coward character Beni in *The Mummy*, their greed and weakness are seen as being their eventual downfall to the real heroes of the story.

The notable part is that the white knights are not fully seen as outsiders. Their motivations are painted as understandable, in line with the motivations of other men. For those bandying about the white knight label, the application isn't so much othering the person they are applying it to as it is providing a warning about the wrong path. Much like the many examples of the geek getting the girl in the end, media is heavily invested in the redemption arc for villains or anti-heroes. Those being labelled as white knights are seen as still being capable of understanding and accepting the offered help to return to the righteous path. This leaves open a shared bond and connection between the two groups. By using the title white knight as an offering it forms a bond of kinship or shared experiences that allows the geek to connect with their supposed opponent. White knights are humanized within the narrative. They are making a mistake but they still have a chance to turn their ways around and realize their mistake, joining the ranks of the heroes in the process. This is an important tool because it keeps a shared connection between the two groups, still allowing the cultural narratives of the insider men and outsider women to be upheld. Instead of forcing the gatekeeper to examine their own interests and prejudices, the white knight label keeps the boundaries they are invested in patrolling remain. Instead, there are some people who have switched to the enemy's side. This helps to reinforce the need to secure the borders and more strongly limit potential contamination by the outside group. The white knight serves as a rallying cry, not only for more people to come forward but also for the group to more carefully patrol their own identity for imposters or heretics that could expose them to weakness from their opposing group.

Women as People

Subverting the expectations of the White Knight and the space afforded to women within the geek canon is difficult, and often accomplished superficially through relying upon the "strong female character" to demonstrate that women can now rescue themselves. Often the strong woman character is allowed to possess attributes associated with masculinity, such as the ability to out-fight, out-drink, out-swear and ultimately "out-man" the man, particularly on a first encounter. Women in this archetype run the gamut from Fiona in *Shrek*, who gets to know kung-fu and fight even after waiting patiently in a tower for her rescuer, to Black Widow in the Marvel movieverse, who opens *Avengers* (2012) by taking a phone call during a fight in which, apparently captured and about to be tortured as a spy, she turns out to have the entire situation under control. However, the "strong female character" trope has serious limitations, as Sophia McDougall (2013) editorializes:

> Is Sherlock Holmes strong? It's not just that the answer is "of course," it's that it's the wrong question. What happens when one tries to fit other iconic male heroes into an imaginary "Strong Male Character" box? A few fit reasonably well, but many look cramped and bewildered in there. They're not used to this kind of confinement, poor things. They're used to being interesting across more than one axis and in more than two dimensions.

While male characters invite us to consider them as dimensional characters, as our previous discussion of icons ranging from Sherlock Holmes to Doctor Who and Iron Man in Chap. 3 noted, the strong woman wears her power as a way to distract us from how she essentially occupies the same role as the courtly damsel in the narrative's progression. Ultimately, it is difficult for the woman reader to become immersed in such characterizations or see them as role models, as their narratives continually break immersion by reminding the reader that these women have no personhood: they are designed for the masculine gaze and built (often literally) for sexualized consumption.

Comic book characters are particularly infamous for this design and the obviousness of their sexualized portrayals. When DC comics introduced their most recent reboot, the New 52, in 2011 there was a great deal of discussion about the ways DC had chosen to reinterpret their characters and storylines. (We discuss several in Chap. 5.) Two that have gotten the most criticism from media scholars and fans include the redesign of Starfire in *Red Hood and the Outlaws* and the first re-appearance of Catwoman. In both instances the woman are primarily presented within the narrative as an object for the gaze of the male viewer. The women both break character and historic interpretations of their personalities to provide the comic readers with a chance to view them chasing after random men for meaningless sex or putting their sex on display, on a roof in the case of Catwoman. Criticisms of these two issues not only revolved around the appearance of the women and the multiple panels focused on gratuitous sexy shots that added nothing to the narrative or plot development but also targeted the defense that these were "modern, sexually free" women. In particular, criticism focused on the fact that both women are characters, not real people, and could not make personal decisions about how to appear. Instead, they are constructed by the largely male comics industry and authors have chosen to portray them in a way that is both demeaning and detrimental to their development. These depictions go hand in hand with editorial decisions that deny women characters the right to humanity. Most notably, the reboot of Batwoman drew attention repeatedly: first for featuring a lesbian superhero in a meaningful relationship, and soon after for succumbing to the trope of punishing lesbian sexuality (TVTropes documents it as "dead lesbian syndrome") by first forbidding her marriage and later for placing her in a situation where she is hypnotized into having sex with a vampire ("Bury Your Gays" 2015). The original creative team, J.H. Williams III and W. Haden Blackman, left after the marriage plotline was vetoed by DC: in the hands of the new creative team, she both breaks up with her fiancée and ends up in a forced relationship (Kistler 2014). While one or two extreme examples are not out of place, when these portrayals are painted against the background irrelevance of female characters in comics they show how geek media and comics views the role of women.

This view of women as other than people, defined by their sexual desirability and relationship with male protectors or spectators, plays out in the fan community itself. The gendering of fans and fan behaviors is essential to how they are interpreted and the lens with which they are viewed. While the term "fanboy" might not be the most loving or generous, it is a definitive term in fan communities, and owners of geek franchises are often expected to cater to their "fanboys" or perish. Suzanne Scott (2013) argues that this is not only thanks to the visibility of the male fan but also to their perceived value, and particularly their role as the financial sustainers of a franchise: "it has long been the case that male audiences are more valued and courted, but as media producers shape their definition of an ideal fandom, it is increasingly one that is defined as fanboy specific, or one that teaches its users to consume and create in a fanboyish manner by acknowledging some genres of fan production and obscuring others." On the other hand, the fangirl audience is easy to dismiss. When asked about the gender of viewers for his children's television program one TV show executive declared: "They're all for the boys, we do not want the girls! I mean, I've heard executives say this, you know, not where I am but at other places, saying like, 'We do not want girls watching these shows … They don't buy toys. The girls buy different toys'" (Pantozzi 2013). These attitudes often mean ignoring women, particularly in some of the most powerful geek fandom spaces. Even discussions of the growing visibility of women as creators and readers in comics tend to focus on independent comics while letting the monolith of superhero comics remain uncontestably masculine territory. As Trina Robbins wrote in 2002,

> Meanwhile, in American mainstream superhero comics, women readers are rare and working women artists can be counted on the fingers of one hand. Too bad for the mainstream artists, who may have to leave their studios and comic stores if they want to look at real women! And until that day happens, mainstream superhero artists will continue to expose their personal sex fantasies on paper.

As Suzanne Scott (2012) notes, "I don't mean to suggest that the comic book industry treats female fans as brutally as it occasionally treats its female heroes, but rather that female fans of comic books have long felt 'fridged,' an audience segment kept on ice and out of view." A woman in a comic book or video game store is assumed to be either out of place or present as an accessory to a male partner, a micro aggression that is self-reinforcing as such attitudes make women less likely to venture into these spaces. This phenomenon is satirized on *The Big Bang Theory*: when Penny accompanies the male geeks to the comic book store, she notes "Everybody is staring at me," only to be reassured by Leonard: "Don't worry. They're more scared of you than you are of them." Penny's response, "Unlikely," is particularly appropriate given the shaming and hostility towards women at comic conventions and similar geek-coded venues (Cendrowski 2009).

The idea that the male audience is the prime movers and shakers of culture is deeply grounded within the geek identity. Just like the world of the video game or story exists to challenge and reward the dutiful heroes, modern geek media is intended to cater to the interests and tastes of the male geek identity. McRobbie and Garber (1994) suggest that our reading of subcultures is always centered on men: "a subculture as encoded and defined by the media is likely to be one which emphasizes the male membership, male 'focal concerns,' and masculine values" (212). Given these lenses, it is not surprising that it takes the presence of men to make a fan culture visible. The *My Little Pony* franchise was developed by Hasbro in 1983 and centered on plastic ponies with brushable manes, glittery "cutie marks," and animated movies and television shows featuring their exploits. The original show and merchandise were marketed along gender lines in a very conventional fashion and sold well to collectors and girls until a revamp of the show and line in 2010. The 2010 show still featured young female ponies, unicorns, and pegasi, with lessons about "friendship" in each episode. The show would perhaps have gone mostly unremarked except it attracted an unanticipated audience: young and adult men.

Once these men gathered through 4chan, a powerful geek fandom was born: in a history of the fandom, Una LaMarche chronicles how fans first gathered on the /co/(comics) and /b/(random) boards on 4chan until it exploded. LaMarche (2011) quotes one fan "We were going to make fun of it, but instead everybody got hooked. And then the first pony threads exploded." The group was attacked on 4chan (ponies, in fact, were banned from mention for a time), adding to the sense that this group of fans was marginalized. And now, Bronies are the defining face of *My Little Pony* fandom, taking what would have been a "pink ghetto" show and making it both masculine and cool. Andrew Silverstein (2013) examined the discourse surrounding Bronycon and the Equestria Daily forums and suggested that while bronies appear to be engaging in a rejection of traditional masculinity, they still frequently use gender-specific discourse and a rhetoric of dominance. Venetia Laura Delano Robertson (2013) suggests that "the Brony community, through their consumption of 'girly' anthropomorphic animal media, engage in a playful re/construction of the largely masculine category of the geek" (23), despite the very obvious association of My Little Pony with young female audiences since the show's emergence in 1981. The term "Brony" is sometimes used for women fans, but it is inherently gender exclusive, and thus the secondary identifier "Pegasister" has arisen in some sections of the community. The resulting message is clear: it takes a real man (geek) to appreciate My Little Pony.

Nowhere is suspicion and hatred of the female fan as an audience as clear in the rejection of *Twilight*, one of the few visibly geek-encoded franchises dominated by women audiences. Even other women-led franchises such as *Hunger Games* and *Divergent* are always discussed in terms of their ability to both men and women, while *Twilight*—and by extension, the *Fifty Shades of Grey* movies based on a *Twilight* fanfic turned novel—has stayed firmly women-oriented. The term "Twi-hard" is used derisively for the fanbase, and even geek women often work to distance themselves from both the works and the fandom, making unnecessarily vicious attacks on the work. The refusal of Twilight to meet the needs of a masculine audience makes it remain one of the most mocked and attacked franchises on the web: the Urban Dictionary defines a Twihard as "stupid obsessive people (mostly teenage girls) who are in love with fictional characters and wouldn't know a good book if it punched them in the face" (2015). Note the dimensions to the hatred of the young female fan: she is mocked both for being unable to appreciate "good" books, that is, books men like, and for desiring fictional characters. This goes hand in hand with our previous discussion of benevolent sexism: desire on the part of women does not fit with the woman as innocent vessel awaiting male protection or conquest, and it is rarely welcome in geek spaces.

Disgust with female desire can be channeled into outright fear of the female gaze, as the portrayal of the fangirl as monster in Supernatural reveals. Supernatural chronicles the struggles of two brothers who are demon hunters battling monsters in a world where all kinds of mythological and supernatural creatures are real. Over ten seasons as of 2014, the show has branched out from its early *Buffy the Vampire Slayer* meets *X-Files* roots to include its own metaverse, including a series of *Supernatural* books within the television show's universe, and a corresponding fandom that the brothers interact with. The first acknowledgement of the *Supernatural* fandom occurs in Season 4 with "The Monster at the End of This Book," which reveals the existence within the show's universe of *Supernatural* comic books as well as their author and fans (Rohl 2009). The episode depicts cult fans, but also reinforces the godlike power of the author, as Laura E. Felschow (2010) critiques:

> The acknowledgment of fan behavior within this episode is not an overt invitation to participate, but a demonstration that the producers/writers of the program are aware of exactly what their fandom is doing without an invitation. Whatever the producers' stated intentions, whether their die-hard fans view this as an inclusive or exclusive act, a compliment or an insult, the end result is the same. The cult fan is reminded that s/he cannot decide what is to be included and excluded, who can be complimented or insulted. Fans may feel a certain way in response to the episode, but they cannot change it.

The cult fan is primarily embodied in Becky Rosen, who is introduced in Season 5 after she is sent to the Wincester brothers with a message. Becky serves as an outright parody of online fans of *Supernatural* itself: her online handle is "samlicker81" and she is a fanfiction writer.

When Becky appears again, it is as the organizer of a *Supernatural* convention in the episode "The Real Ghostbusters": however, most of the fandom depicted in the episode are men, almost all cosplaying in the iconic wardrobe of Sam and Dean (Conway 2009). The brothers are at first both disturbed and unimpressed with their fans: when they encounter two male fans dresses as them, Dean threatens them with a gun, calling them "freakin' annoying" (ibid.). During the episode, the brothers are forced to team up with the two fans in investigating a haunting, and in doing so confront a parody of themselves. The episode ends with a reveal that the two fans are partners, which Darren Elliott-Smith (2011) notes "highlights the gay men's possession of an essential masculinity to a mere performance of it through role play," notably role-play of the hypermasculine Sam and Dean (115). Lorrie Palmer (2011) notes that the episode's mention of a talk on "the homoeotic subtext of *Supernatural*" suggests "awareness on the part of the series' writers of both the onscreen chemistry between Ackles and Padalecki as well as the real-world production of 'Wincest' fan fiction" (86). That same awareness is reflected in Becky: while she is depicted as personally desiring the character of Sam, she also writes "Wincest" fanfiction that explores the possibilities of a sexual relationship between the brothers.

Judith May Fathalllah (2010) suggests that Becky can only be unthreatening to a female viewer who is privileged enough to accept the show's rejection of her as a desiring agent:

> For Becky is available for appropriation; but to appropriate her without fear, the female viewer must already be in a relatively privileged position. She must have the internal and external resources to assert her nonofficial desire. Internally, she must be secure in the conviction that hegemonic stories of female passivity and traditional heterosexual unions are not the only legitimate ones, which implies a degree of education in feminist and gender studies. Externally, she cannot be practically dependent on those hegemonic narratives, which implies a degree of financial security.

Becky's own agency, on the other hand, is portrayed negatively. In season 7s "Time for a Wedding," Becky reappears as a villain: she drugs Sam with a love potion to make him marry her (see Fig. 6.2). At this stage, her fandom crosses a line, hinting towards rape, and Charlotte Howell (2013) suggest that Becky:

> represents a caricature of female fandom that has persisted despite the growth of nerd culture and influence of fandom studies. Becky may be a textual poacher, but she's also a character who gropes a stranger merely because she thinks she knows him through devotion to a text… she even ties Sam up in a bed in her remote cabin, a scene that evokes one of the strongest images of the "pathological fan": Kathy Bates in Misery. (26)

The act of typing Sam up is particularly suggestive of the destructive impact the creators of the show associate to the gaze of the female fan. As KT Torrey (2012) states, "the threat that Becky poses to Sam, to *Supernatural*, lies in her status as a woman and as a fan writer, as a figure who can upend the

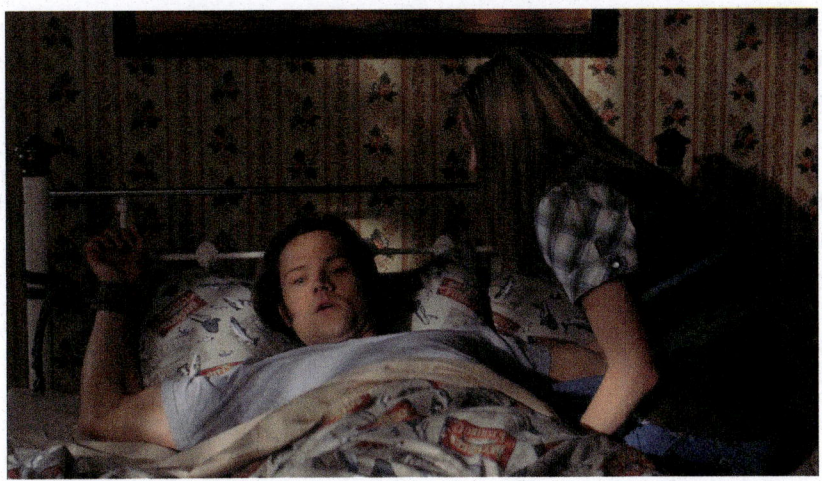

Fig. 6.2 Becky as predator in "Time for a Wedding"

central narrative by affixing the masculine to her 'rightful' place as the signifier of meaning while claiming the role of producer for herself"—it is the threat of a woman to a hypermasculine narrative in which women have been repeatedly marginalized (and, when that doesn't work, typically killed off). The suggestion is that the female gaze and desire represented by the production of fanfiction is in fact a predatory act, as Torrey analyzes:

> A primary effect of this visual sequence, then, is that it puts female fans in the position of questioning their own pleasure, of consciously reconsidering the liberties that they take with Sam and Dean's bodies within their own texts. As fan crowleyshouseplant huffs on her tumblr site: "[B]elieve me, I am the antithesis of thrilled with the rape analogy in its meta context." Indeed, recasting Becky in this way suggests that the producers believe that female slashers are taking similar advantage of Sam and Dean; that when they produce or consume slash fiction—or even play with the boys within the privacy of their own minds, for their own pleasure—fans are performing the imaginative equivalent of tying Sam and Dean to a bed and fucking them against their will.

Becky Rosen is untrustworthy for having desires of ownership not unlike that of the White Knight, and, given that in Season 5 she reveals essential information to the Winchesters that save their mission, it could even be argued that by old standards of chivalry she earned her reward. Cait Coker and Candace Benefiel (2014) suggest that the relationship of *Supernatural* with its fans echoes predator and prey—"Whether the *Supernatural* writers are laughing with or at the fans, there seems to be a basic distrust of the fan's motives. Even more, as fans appropriate the characters, mythology, and style of the series for their own fanworks, they edge into the more threatening realm of the predator, and this attitude seems to appear thematically across multiple seasons of the show." However, male and female fans are presented as threats in very different ways centered on their relationship with Dean and Sam as objects of desire: the gay fan couple wants to be the Winchesters, while the female fans want to possess the Winchesters.

Conclusion

The concept of white knight serves mostly to enforce new types of gatekeeping behaviors within the geek community. It helps those within the community to believe that their desires are well deserved and their actions justified as being inherently good in nature. Although cast as being good in nature the actions of the white knight serve to limit and bound the community of geeks by preventing women from being able to participate as real people. Combined, the narratives of the fan boy and the white knight contribute to placing women fans in a position where they are denied agency and visibility. While fan boys (and the fan boy as auteur) hold a privileged role thanks to the perception that they are essential to the success of a media franchise, women and "fangirls" are objects of suspicion and desire, often serving narratives as possessions rather than actors. This places women and fangirls in the space allotted to them by narratives of chivalry and courtly love, reducing the agency and voice of women in the process.

The fate of My Little Pony as an adult fandom should, on its surface, be similar to *Twilight*. My Little Pony begun ignominiously as the counterpart to GI Joe: in gendered Happy Meal toys of the 1980s and 1990s, boys would get soldiers while girls would be handed the pink and pastel ponies. The reboot doesn't change the franchise's focus on young girl ponies in a magical anthropomorphized world, and the update at first appeared to be superficial. However, *My Little Pony* did not end up in the "pink ghetto" of girls' shows thanks to the intervention of the Bronies, who formed as a fandom around the idea that *My Little Pony* could be a show for masculine viewers to enjoy and rally around. This seems harmless enough: just as the well-intentioned actions of "White Knights" jumping into protect women geeks seems, well, mostly harmless. But both the rise of the Bronies and the actions of White Knights have a similar impact in silencing the very groups they apparently are supporting. The attention on "Bronies" has pushed women in fandom (including women who have been part of the fandom since the earlier versions of the franchise) to the sidelines, with a huge amount of media attention and fascination instead directed towards the Bronies. The fanboy image is dominant: the fangirl, even when part of the "original" demographic of the show, is marginalized in her own space. And while *Supernatural* has changed its portrayals of the woman fan over time (as we will examine in the next chapter), their willingness to use Becky Rosen as monster suggest that whatever power the woman fan enjoys to project her own desire and gaze on the show can always be pushed back by the larger forces of male authorship and the male creative community. The male fans can thus be cast as the "White Knights" constructing media franchises and their corresponding attention to fan communities, just as they are the desired audience. Their gaze, when cast to a woman-aligned text with desire or empathy, can elevate it to geek cult status: likewise, their disapproving gaze can cast the *Twilight*s of the world into the convention hall's pink ghetto. And of course, once the "White Knight" rescues a fan, fandom, or franchise, they expect their reward.

References

Adamson, Andrew and Vicky Jenson. 2001. *Shrek*. Dreamworks. DVD.
Ahern, Stephen. 2004. Listening to Guinevere: Female agency and the politics of chivalry in Tennyson's "Idylls." *Studies in Philology* 101, no. 1: 88–112. https://doi.org/10.1353/sip.2004.0002.
Anderson, Evan. 2014. I used to be Elliot Rodger. *Medium*, July 29. Accessed February 9, 2015. https://medium.com/@tw0headedb0y/i-used-to-be-elliot-rodger-34eb4070091c.
Bury your Gays. 2015. TV|tropes, last edited October 15. Accessed October 6, 2015. http://tvtropes.org/pmwiki/pmwiki.php/Main/BuryYourGays?from=Main.DeadLesbia nSyndrome.
Cendrowski, Mark. 2009. The Hofstadter Isotope. *The Big Bang Theory*. Season 2, episode 20. CBS, April 13.
Chaytor, HJ. 1912. *The Troubadours*. Reprint, eBook, 2004. http://www.gutenberg.org/files/12456/12456-h/12456-h.htm.
Choo, Kukhee. 2008. Girls return home: Portrayal of femininity in popular Japanese girls' manga and anime texts during the 1990s in Hana yori Dango and Fruits Basket. *Women: A Cultural Review* 19, no. 3: 275–296. https://doi.org/10.1080/09574040802137243.
Coker, Cait, and Candace Benefiel. 2014. The hunter hunted: The portrayal of the fan as predator in Supernatural. In *Supernatural, humanity, and the soul: On the Highway to Hell and Back*, ed. Susan A. George and Regina M. Hansen, 97–110. New York: Palgrave Macmillan.

Conway, James. 2009. The Real Ghostbusters. *Supernatural*. Season 5, episode 9. CW, November 12.

Dean, Michelle. 2014. Why is it so hard for people to get that Elliot Rodger hated women? *Gawker*, May 27. Accessed March 15, 2015. http://gawker.com/why-is-it-so-hard-for-people-to-get-that-elliott-rodger-1582030975.

Dr. Nerdlove. 2012. Do you have White Knight Syndrome? *Paging Dr. Nerdlove*, January 16. Accessed April 3, 2015. http://www.doctornerdlove.com/2012/01/white-knight-syndrome/all/1/.

Elliott-Smith, Darren. 2011. "Go be gay for that poor, dead intern": Conversion fantasies and gay anxieties in Supernatural. In *TV goes to Hell: An unofficial road map to Supernatural*, ed. Stacey Abbott and David Lavery, 105–117. Toronto: ECW Press.

Enright, Nancy. 2008. Tolkien's females and the defining of power. In *Bloom's modern critical interpretations: The lord of the rings—New edition*, ed. Harold Bloom, 171–186. New York: Infobase Publishing.

Fajardo-Acosta. 2010. Fidel courtly seductions, modern subjections: Troubadour literature and the medieval construction of the modern world. *Medieval and Renaissance Texts and Studies* 376. Tempe, AZ: Arizona Center for Medieval and Renaissance Studies.

Fathallah, Judith May. 2010. Becky is my hero: The power of laughter and disruption in Supernatural. *Transformative Works and Cultures* 5. http://journal.transformativeworks.com/index.php/twc/article/view/220/173.

Felschow, Laura E. 2010. "Hey, check it out, there's actually fans": (Dis)empowerment and (mis)representation of cult fandom in supernatural. *Transformative Works and Cultures* 4. http://journal.transformativeworks.org/index.php/twc/article/view/134.

Fredrick, Candice and Same McBride. 2007. Battling the woman warrior: females and combat in Tolkien and Lewis. *Mythlore* 25, no. 3–4. https://www.questia.com/library/journal/1G1-163972501/battling-the-woman-warrior-females-and-combat-in.

Glick, Peter and Susan T. Fiske. 1996. The ambivalent sexism inventory: Differentiating hostile and benevolent sexism. *Journal of Personality and Social Psychology* 70, no. 3: 491–512. doi:https://doi.org/10.1037/0022-3514.70.3.491.

Hathaway, Jay. 2014. What is Gamergate, and why? An explainer for non-geeks. *Gawker*, October 10. Accessed October 12, 2014. http://gawker.com/what-is-gamergate-and-why-an-explainer-for-non-geeks-1642909080.

Herlihy, David. 1962. Land, family, and women in continental Europe, 701–1200. *Traditio* 18: 89–120. https://doi.org/10.9783/9780812207675.13.

Holmes, John. 2004. Oaths and oath breaking: Analogues of Old English Comitatus in Tolkien's myth. In *Tolkien and the invention of Myth: A reader*, ed. Jane Chance, 249–262. Lexington, Kentucky: University Press of Kentucky.

Houghton, John William. 2005. Maldo, Gettysburg and the Somme: Tolkien's homecoming and the idea of chivalry. *Scientia Scholar* 3, no. 1.

Howell, Charlotte E. 2013. The gospel of the Winchesters (and their fans): Neoreligious fan practices and narrative in Supernatural. *Kinephanos: Media, Fans, and the Sacred* 4, no. 1: 17–31. http://www.kinephanos.ca/Revue_files/2013-howell.pdf.
Kistler, Alan. 2014. Why is rape in Batwoman more interesting than marriage to DC Comics? *The Mary Sue*, December 3. Accessed December 5, 2014. http://www.themarysue.com/dc-comics-batwoman-rape/.
LaMarche, Una. 2011. Pony up haters: How 4chan gave birth to the Bronies. *Observer*, August 3. Accessed February 9, 2015. http://betabeat.com/2011/08/pony-up-haters-how-4chan-gave-birth-to-the-bronies/.
Lizardi, Ryan. 2013. Scott Pilgrim vs. hegemony: Nostalgia, remediation, and heteronormativity. *Journal of Graphic Novels and Comics* 4, no. 2: 245–256. https://doi.org/10.1080/21504857.2012.747974.
McDougall, Sophia. 2013. I hate strong female characters. *New Statesman*, August 15. Accessed December 4, 2014. http://www.newstatesman.com/culture/2013/08/i-hate-strong-female-characters.
McRobbie, Angela, and Jenny Garber. 1994. Girls and subcultures: an exploration. In *Resistance through rituals: youth subcultures in post-war Britain*, ed. Stuart Hall and Tony Jefferson, 209–222. New York: Routledge.
Madil, Leanne. 2008. Gendered identities explored: The Lord of the Rings as a text of alternative ways of being. *The ALAN Review* 35, no. 2. https://doi.org/10.21061/alan.v35i2.a.6.
Marshall, Neil. 2012. Blackwater. *Game of Thrones*. Directed by Neil Marshall. Season 2, episode 9. HBO, May 27.
Gilliam, Terry, and Terry Jones. 1975. *Monty Python and the Holy Grail*. DVD: Sony Pictures Home Entertainment.
Palmer, Lorrie. 2011. Rural masculinity in supernatural: Abbott, Stacey and David Lavery. *TV Goes to Hell: An Unofficial Road Map to Supernatural*, ed. Stacey Abbot and David Lavery, 105–118. Toronto: ECW Press.
Pantozzi, Jill. 2013. Warner Bros. Animation takes issue with girls watching their programs. The Mary Sue, December 20. Accessed January 8, 2015. http://www.themarysue.com/warner-bros-animation-girl-market/.
Phelpstead, Carl. 2006. On translating Beowulf. In *J.R.R. Tolkien Encylopedia: Scholarship and Critical Assessment*, ed. Michael DC Drout, 482–483. New York: Routledge.
Robbins, Trina. 2002. Gender differences in comics. *Image & Narrative* 4, September 4. http://www.imageandnarrative.be/inarchive/gender/trinarobbins.htm.
Robertson, Venetia Laura Delano. 2013. Of ponies and men: My Little Pony—friendship is magic and the Brony fandom. *International Journal of Cultural Studies* 17, no. 1: 21–37.https://doi.org/10.1177/1367877912464368.
Rohl, Mike. 2009. The monster at the end of this book. *Supernatural*. CW, April 2.

Rosewarne, Lauren. 2016. *Cyberbullies, cyberactivists, cyberpredators: Film, TV, and internet stereotypes*. Santa Barbara, CA: Praeger.

Saito, Kumiko. 2014. Magic, Shōjo, and Matamorphosis: Magical girl anime and the challenges of changing gender identities in Japanese society. *The Journal of Asian Studies* 73, no. 01: 143–164. https://doi.org/10.1017/s0021911813001708.

Sakharov, Alik. 2013. The Climb. *Game of Thrones*. Directed by Alik Sakharov. Season 3, episode 15. HBO, May 5.

Sarkeesian, Anita. 2013. Damsel in distress: Part 1 – Tropes vs women in video games. *YouTube*, March 7. Accessed February 18, 2014. https://www.youtube.com/watch?v=X6p5AZp7r_Q.

Schroeder, Theodore. 1905. *The evolution of marriage ideals*. New York: Walker.

Scott, Suzanne. 2012. Fangirls in refrigerators: The politics of (in)visibility in comicbook culture. In Appropriating, interpreting, and transforming comic books, ed. Matthew J. Costello, special issue, *Transformative Works and Cultures* 13.10.3983/twc.2013.0460.

Scott, Suzanne. 2013. Who's Steering the Mothership? The Role of the Fanboy Auteur in Transmedia Storytelling. In *The Participatory Cultures Handbook*, ed. Aaron Delwiche and Jennifer Jacobs Henderson, 43–52. New York and London: Routledge.

Seaman, Gerald. 2006. Arthurian literature. In *J.R.R. Tolkien Encyclopedia: Scholarship and Critical Assessment*, ed. Michael DC Drout, 32–34. New York: Routledge.

Silverstein, Andrew. 2013. My little Brony: Connecting gender blurring and discursive formations. *Colloquy* 9: 98–117. http://www.calstatela.edu/sites/default/files/users/u2276/silverstein_essay6.pdf.

Smol, Anna. 2004. 'Oh … oh … Frodo!': Readings of male intimacy in *The Lord of the Rings*. *Modern Fiction Studies* 50, no. 4: 949–979. https://doi.org/10.1353/mfs.2005.0010.

Tendayi, Vicki, and Dominic Abrams. 2002. But she was unfaithful: Benevolent sexism and reactions to rape victims who violate traditional gender role expectations. *Sex Roles* 47 (5–6): 289. https://doi.org/10.1023/A:1021342912248.

Tolkien, J.R.R. 2014. *The letters of JRR Tolkien*. New York: Houghton Mifflin Harcourt.

Torrey, K.T. 2012. He's best when he's bound and gagged. *PCA/ACA National Conference*, April 11–14, 2013, Boston: The Boston Marriott Copley Place. Accessed March 3, 2015. http://www.kttorrey.com/research/hes-best-when-hes-bound-and-gagged/.

Trousdale, Gary, and Kirk Wise. 1991. *Beauty and the beast*. DVD: Disney.

Twihard. Urban Dictionary. n.d. Accessed February 3, 2015. http://www.urbandictionary.com/define.php?term=Twihard.

Wollock, Jennifer. 2011. *Rethinking chivalry and courtly love*. Santa Barbara, California: Praeger.

Wright, Edgar. 2010. *Scott Pilgrim Vs. the World*. Los Angeles: Universal DVD.

7

One of Us, One of Us!: Representations and Dialogues with "Fanboys" and "Fangirls"

The 1932 horror film *Freaks* has had a lasting influence, thanks in part to its unique qualities: it focused on a group of circus performers ostracized for physical traits and abnormalities, and painted a picture of their community. The movie centers on Cleopatra, a "normal" (read: traditionally attractive) outsider trapeze artist who seeks to marry one of the "freaks" for his inherited wealth. At the wedding, Cleopatra poisons her new husband's wine even as she is accepted into the community of freaks with the chant "One of us, one of us" (Browning 1932). The movie then takes an even darker turn when Cleopatra's betrayal is discovered after she rejects her acceptance by the community, and the freaks determine to "make" her one of them. Cleopatra is next seen as on display as a duck woman. The narrative plays out as a confirmation of every suspicion associated with the interest of an attractive woman. References to *Freaks* abound in popular culture, but one of the most unusual occurs in an episode of *The Big Bang Theory*, a show whose problematic depictions of gender and geek identity have already been thoroughly discussed here. The reference to *Freaks* occurs in an early episode in Season 2, "The Panty Piñata Polarization." The episode marks a full inclusion of Penny into the social circle, as acknowledged by Sheldon when he decides to hold her to the same rules of behavior he expects from the male geeks. After Sheldon declares Penny's acceptance, Leonard confirms it, saying "You're officially one of us" (Cendrowski 2008). Howard echoes the phrase with a sarcasm and menace recognizable from the use of the same chant in *Freaks*.

The moment has many connotations, as the woman welcomed in *Freaks*, Cleopatra, was a "desirable" normal woman in the same way Penny is marked as an outsider by her appearance among the men of *Big Bang Theory*. The episode opens with the men gathered around a game of Klingon Boggle, emphasizing their participation in an extreme level of fan culture. She puts *America's Next Top Model* on TV, distracting them from the game with images of traditionally attractive women. Notably, after Penny's induction, she is immediately banished from the apartment for the violation of Sheldon's rules—she responds by likewise banishing Sheldon from the Cheesecake Factory. While the episode does not lead in the same dark direction as *Freaks*, the episode does end uncomfortably, with Howard and Raj hacking satellites to determine the location of the *America's Next Top Model* house, then sneaking in "disguised" as cable repairmen. It closes on the two following a model further into the house, leaving the consequences to the viewer's imagination, in a scene that bears a clear resemblance to the oft-parodied clichés of pornography. When tied back to Penny's own "invasion" of the geek space at the beginning of the episode, these two moments suggest a clear double standard: the geek men are expected to make the rules and hold power in any environment, while Penny's presence and designation as "one of us" is subject to male authority and her acceptance of the rules under which she is admitted. The conditional acceptance Penny experiences as a girl marked as other by her appearance and experiences within the close-knit and structured community of geeks is not unlike the positioning of fan girls as construed more broadly. The chant "One of Us!" has more recently been adopted to describe famous people who are also nerds, such as Vin Diesel, and has become a way to claim another fan or geek as kin (TV Tropes 2015). The phrase has thus become synonymous with an identification in the apparently marginalized identity of fan culture. A study of the social behaviors of fans within several groups (including one of the most mocked, furries) confirms the strong influence of fandom on identity: "fan groups, far from being an individualistic mindless consumption of media, can have a potentially deep and meaningful impact on our values, identity, and potentially our behavior" (Plante et al. 2014). This intertwined relationship of identity and fandom has a number of consequences, particularly as the question of inclusion and control rises within geek and fan culture at large.

In this chapter, we examine the ways in which certain canonical geek texts both invite women in as "one of us" while simultaneously distancing themselves from the desires of women and the "fan girl gaze." Even as franchises are defined by and empowered by their fan boys (as our previous discussion of bronies noted), fan girls maintain an uneasy relationship with geek culture, and are often accused of reading into a text when they suggest the possibilities within relationships that go unrealized within the show's canon. This absence of the female gaze in much of geek culture, where the masculine gaze is continually catered to in everything from the style of comic book drawings to the filming of action scenes, relegates the female gaze to a secondary role in crafting what is often referred to as "fanon." And, most importantly, these fan girls actively participate in the reconstruction and redefinition of masculinity through their subversive writing, drawing responses from the wider fan community and the attention of show creators.

Fan Girls on the Margins

While male authors are disproportionately represented in the geek canonical texts (in literature, J.R.R. Tolkien and George R.R. Martin; in film, Joss Whedon, J.J. Abrams, and George Lucas; in television, Steven Moffat and Eric Krike, and so on), women are dominant as authors and producers of geek texts in alternative spaces. "Fan girls" are disproportionately represented among fan fiction writers, as a survey of users of Archive of Our Own, the dominant archive of fan fiction on the web, revealed in 2013. In that self-survey users could select multiple boxes from options including male, female, genderqueer, trans*, and agender: 60% of users self-identified as female, 25.6% as male, and 56.7% identified as genderqueer (Lulu 2013). The statistic of genderqueer is particularly significant, as that identification resonates with an additional marginalization within the fan community. Queer identity more broadly can be defined in many ways, and the term has been employed in many contexts. Annamarie Jagose offers one of the most cited explanations:

> broadly speaking, queer describes those gestures or analytical models which dramatise incoherencies in the allegedly stable relations between chromosomal sex, gender and sexual desire. Resisting that model of stability—which claims heterosexuality as its origin, when it is more properly its effect—queer focuses on mismatches between sex, gender and desire. (Jagose 1996)

In the context of fandom, this identification as queer can be linked to a number of practices, including participation in one of the dominant discourses we'll analyze here: slash fanfiction.

The practice of slash fanfiction involves writing transformative works centered characters (usually men, sometimes real people) engaged in queer relationships, typically involving romantic or sexual partnerships with persons of the same gender. While the term slash is often associated with the "/" symbol that is placed between two names in a fanfiction listing to indicate that they are a pairing, it is only used to describe queer or homosexual pairings—heterosexual-centered pairings are referred to as "het" (Fanlore 2015). Slash fanfiction is one of the most studied forms of fan production around, thanks perhaps to a combination of popularity and subversive qualities that demand discourse. Toastystats analyze the popularity of different relationships in fanfiction archived on Archive of Our Own, and determined that slash fanfiction is indeed dominant, with some of the most written-about (and tagged) relationships pairing men from popular geek franchises: Sherlock Holmes and John Watson of BBC's *Sherlock*, Castiel and Dean Winchester of *Supernatural*, Derek Hales and Stiles Stilinski of *Teen Wolf*, and Dean Winchester and Sam Winchester made the top four pairings by significant margins, with nearly 20,000 "Johnlock" stories and nearly 15,000 for "Destiel" (Toastystats 2013). These stats are most accurate for very recent fandoms, as Archive of Our Own has only become the most popular fanfiction site in recent years, but it does demonstrate the relative rarity of "het" pairings. Much of the fascination with slash fanfiction comes from outsiders trying to understand the popularity of these pairings, and often coming up with answers that oversimplify the phenomenon as the erotic fantasies of heterosexual women (not unlike the popularity of lesbian pornography produced with the masculine heterosexual gaze in mind). Certainly, the gaze of the heterosexual woman is part of slash, and many of the most popular pairings (such as *Supernatural*'s Destiel) feature undeniably conventionally attractive men who have correspondingly large women fan bases. But writing slash fanfiction is not the same as tacking a poster of *Buffy: The Vampire Slayer*'s Angel in one's locker, or even using photos of a favorite actor's magazine appearances as desktop wallpaper.

However, the image of the heterosexual woman as "fan girl" writing fantasies with male characters as her props must be challenged and complicated. After the AO3 census data was released, Luce posted an analysis of the data focused on dissecting the popularity of slash:

> The general assumption, as we know, is that the average slash fan is a heterosexual female fan. However, centrumlumina's results suggest that perhaps the combination of "heterosexual" and "female" ought to be questioned. About 90% of survey respondents were fans of M/M, but only 30% identified as both female and heterosexual. (If you're confused, consider that respondents could check as many boxes as they felt represented them—i.e., both female

and transgender under "gender," both heterosexual and pansexual under "sexuality." For this 30% figure, centrumlumina counted only the respondents who chose only female under gender and only heterosexual under sexuality.) Indeed, while most respondents were female, the majority of respondents were QUILTBAG-identifying people. (Porluciernagas 2013)

While characterizing this group more broadly under the rubric "queer" can cause problematic erasure of identities, these findings do resonate with the idea that fanfiction writers represent a queer audience, and correspondingly are targeted by show writers through a practice described as "queer baiting." Queer baiting is the term used primarily by fans to critique mainstream media's tendency towards creating characters with implied or subtextual queer identity that is never explicitly acknowledged or acted on.

While the practice of queer baiting might sound harmless in theory, it is often viewed as a way that mainstream media can avoid more nuanced representation and the inclusion of diverse identities. Writing on Tumblr, Lan offers a powerful explanation of the consequences of queer baiting:

> when queer people say, "I identified with this character as a queer person," or "I think this character could have been queer," the heteronormative parts of the audience are encouraged to tell queer people that they should not be saying that. The heteronormative parts of the audience are encouraged to tell queer people, "stop projecting," and "stop dragging respectable heteronormative characters into your weird issues." Queer people are told that they should be ashamed of themselves for thinking that the character was being portrayed as queer. Queer-baiting is even more painful than erasure, because it dangles fair and equal representation in front of your eyes, and then snatches it away. And then it tells you that the whole thing was in your imagination all along. (Lan 2012)

Following this argument, it could be argued that slash fanfiction must exist as long as mainstream media is decidedly heteronormative and un-nuanced in its binary portrayal of masculinity and femininity, as many fan practices could be viewed as responses to "queer baiting" that take subtext and realize them as text. However, that would also risk oversimplification, as slash fanfiction can involve characters who are canonically in a queer relationship (such as Kurt and Blaine in *Glee*), and it can likewise involve characters with no implied subtext at all drawn from totally different franchises and integrated into stories that fulfill the imagination of the fan author.

Although queer identities have often been disregarded by popular geek media there are occasional productions catered towards acknowledging these audiences. This chapter will look at several media productions geared towards marginalized audiences within the geek communities and will deconstruct the larger geek response to these narratives in light of the dominant hypermasculine geek identity. The perceived value of the female gaze, queer relationships and "shipper-friendly" narration is traced through geek productions across several media platforms and used to deconstruct both the cultural and capitalistic assumptions made about appealing to wider audiences' tastes. In these spaces, the female gaze is undermined even as it is apparently catered to, often with disclaimers from male creators as to having any intention to ever invite such subtextual interpretation. Most infamously, we will highlight a number of series that invite queer readings of leading men (primarily *Sherlock* and *Supernatural*) while simultaneously refusing to canonize any such interpretation. While a media franchise's use of practices identified as queer baiting is thus not necessarily the primary indicator of a slash fanfiction community, it is no coincidence that these two shows that rose to the top of the Archive of Our Own slash pairings are also frequently accused of queer baiting. *Sherlock* and *Supernatural* are both centered on pairs of male characters with strong relationships. We will examine each of these shows and their surrounding communities in turn, particularly considering the evidence of queer baiting within the franchise and the show's subsequent relationship with fan girls who create and participate within slash pairings. The depiction of masculinity and femininity within these show's canons and, by extension, their fanon, is particularly valuable to our understanding of gender in broader geek discourse.

Johnlock in Sherlock

It will come as no surprise to most viewers of BBC's *Sherlock* that "Johnlock," the romantic and/or sexual pairing of Sherlock Holmes and John Watson, is by far the dominant slash pairing within the *Sherlock* fandom. BBC's *Sherlock*, starring Benedict Cumberbatch as Sherlock Holmes and Martin Freeman as John Watson, is a concentrated modern retelling of Sherlock Holmes. The tension between the two actors as partners co-habiting and solving crimes creates an undeniably rich premise for slash fanfiction, and the attractiveness of the actors and their characters further fuels the fandom. The show itself is a work of fanfiction, falling into the category of what fanfiction writers would term an AU or alternate universe fanfic. AU fanfiction is characterized by taking familiar characters and placing them out of their context—in this case, the writers of BBC's *Sherlock* take Holmes,

Watson, and the rest of Sir Arthur Conan Doyle's characters and transport them to modern London, but in an alternate universe where those writings don't exist and thus cannot be explicitly referenced. This is in spite of some internal uses of the canonical setting within the show itself, which was represented in the show's 2016 Christmas special "The Abominable Bride" (Mackinnon 2016). Despite this status as fanfiction, the show has become its own "canon," inspiring its own incredible range of transformative works even as the show's creators remain firm on having the final say in interpretations of the lives of "their" Holmes and Watson.

The Sherlock Holmes story has always been driven by the friendship between Sherlock Holmes and John Watson, and several modern adaptations have used that intimacy as part of their marketing and appeal. Robert Downey Jr.'s Sherlock Holmes and Jude Law's John Watson are part of what Benjamin Poore notes as the contemporary turn towards "bromance": "Holmes and Watson in these versions are both relatively young men, well-dressed and groomed, with a keen eye for fashion, even if their style is artfully distressed, like Downey Junior's Holmes; in other words, they fit the template of the 'metrosexual male' rather than the good-natured Colonel Blimp figure that Watson has often been cast as" (Poore 2012). The creators of these modern adaptations are aware of the lens through which these relationships are viewed, and that consciousness is part of the subtext explicitly addressed in the very first episode of BBC's *Sherlock*.

The episode introduces John Watson to Sherlock Holmes through a mutual acquaintance who knows both are in search of a flatmate. When Watson goes to view the flat, the landlady, Mrs. Hudson, shows them around and remarks on the circumstances immediately:

Hudson: There's another bedroom upstairs if you'll be needing two bedrooms.
Watson: Of course we'll be needing two.
Hudson: Oh don't worry, there's all sorts round here. (McGuigan 2010a)

The episode references the potential for a relationship between the two explicitly on multiple occasions. Sherlock Holmes's brother Mycroft observes on his first meeting with Watson: "And since yesterday you've moved in with him and now you're solving crimes together. Are we to expect a happy announcement by the end of the week?" (McGuigan 2010a). Even Watson and Holmes themselves discuss the prospect after Watson inquires if Holmes has a girlfriend only to get the response "Girlfriend? No, not really my area." Watson then inquires if he has a boyfriend, eliciting the more succinct response "No." Holmes then explicitly rejects Watson's inquiry as a demonstration of interest: "John, erm ... I think you should know that I consider myself married to my work, and while I'm flattered by your interest, I'm really not looking for any ..." (McGuigan 2010a). These opening exchanges set the stage for the show's reputation for constant queer baiting (Rosie 2012).

The references to their relationship continue, from a restaurant owner who provides a candle for the table, saying "it's more romantic," to lingering shots of the two alone in intimate settings. This creation of romantic subtext that invites the reading of the pair as an "OTP," or one true pairing, to use the fandom term, becomes most problematic when placed in tandem with comments by show creator Steven Moffat: "There's no indication in the original stories that he was asexual or gay. He actually says he declines the attention of women because he doesn't want the distraction. What does that tell you about him? Straightforward deduction. He wouldn't be living with a man if he thought men were interesting" (Jeffries 2012). Moffat thus engages in mockery of the interpretations audiences—particularly the "fan girl" authors of transformative works—bring to his version of Sherlock, even as he includes continual references within the show's text to incite their interest and fuel such speculation. In the second episode of the first season, for instance, the parallels between Watson and Sherlock's relationship and Watson's attempts to date are mocked:

Sherlock: I need to get some air. We're going out tonight.
Watson: Actually I've got a date.
Sherlock: What?
Watson: It's where two people who like each other go out and have fun.
Sherlock: That's what I was suggesting.
Watson: No it wasn't. At least I hope not. (Lyn 2010)

In the same episode, the kidnapping of John Watson is used to motivate Sherlock Holmes to action, a plot device common to romance novels and particularly familiar to us from the discussion of the "damsel in distress" trope in both video games and comics (see Fig. 7.1). This moment is complicated by the fact that Watson's girlfriend is similarly kidnapped with him, and becomes the actual damsel in distress to get information from Watson. Ultimately, Holmes serves as rescuer and white knight: his reward is in this case only implied.

The legitimacy of Johnlock as a ship is further reinforced by the show's uncomfortable relationship with women characters. "The Abominable

Fig. 7.1 Watson held hostage by Moriarty in "The Great Game" (McGuigan 2010b)

Bride" (BBC *Sherlock* 2016) includes several exchanges that center on the near-invisibility of women characters in the canonical Holmes: Mrs. Hudson criticizes Watson, the show's in-text author, for never giving her any lines: "I never say anything do I? According to you, I just show people up the stairs and serve you breakfast." She even says outright "I'm your landlady, not a plot device," drawing attention to the fact that in the episode (as in most BBC *Sherlock* episodes) she functions precisely as that. The narrative escalates to reveal that a series of murders blamed on a ghost is in fact being conducted by an "invisible army"—women. As Sherlock explains when he uncovers the secret organization:

> Every great cause has martyrs. Every war has suicide missions and make no mistake, this is war. One half of the human race at war with the other. The invisible army hovering at our elbow, tending to our homes, raising our children. Ignored, patronised, disregarded. Not allowed so much as a vote. But an army nonetheless, ready to rise up in the best of causes. To put right an injustice as old as humanity itself. So you see, Watson, Mycroft was right. This is a war we must lose. (Mackinnon 2016)

Yet even as these sequences clumsily place gender politics at the forefront, the episode serves only as a reminder of how ignored, patronized, and disregarded most of the women characters are with relationship to Sherlock himself. As Allyson Johnson wrote in her review of the episode: "The fact that it ends up being the suffragette movement that orchestrated the main death that starts the plot demonstrates Moffat's belief that he understands the well-earned criticism the show has gotten for its female characters while also completely missing the point" (Johnson 2016). It is unsurprising that the most compelling ships to emerge in Sherlock fandom center on the men, and indeed the show itself provides plenty of evidence to suggest that Sherlock's disdain for heterosexual relationships extends to a disdain for women in general.

Johnlock is, of course, not the only pairing popular within the fan community: others include Sherlock and Moriarty, Sherlock's gay-coded nemesis, and Sherlock and Mycroft, his brother and sometimes-rival. Many of these pairings fall into paradigms popular not only in slash but also in genres with primarily female-identified readership more broadly, as Catherine Tosenberger observes: "The buddyslash, enemyslash, and powerslash models will be familiar to readers of heterosexual genre romance novels" (Tosenberger, Homosexuality at the online Hogwarts: Harry Potter slash fanfiction 2008). This is no surprise, as Catherine Driscoll argues that "the most consistent conventions of [fanfiction] remain that of formulaic romance" (Driscoll 2006). While the term "formulaic" can sound dismissive, it is worth noting that the writers of transformative works often apply such categorizations themselves, in part to help other fans find stories that appeal to their interests. As of April 16, 2017, there were 102,266 stories archived under Sherlock Holmes & Related fandoms on Archive of Our Own: within that set, the most popular ten tags for content included: Fluff, Angst, Alternate Universe, Post-Reichenbach, Romance, Hurt/Comfort, Humor, Established Relationship, First Kiss, and Crossover. Tags on particular stories offer even more detail, with popular choices including Angst, Happy Ending, Slow Burn, Drama, Fix-it, Unrequired Love, and Grief/Mourning. Similarly, fanfiction including sexual content is usually tagged as such, with specific tags added to indicate the type of content. Such tags are a way that fanfiction within the community is in dialogue both with the works of fellow fan writers and with a number of conventions that have emerged from the community.

The explicit focus on emotional content in many of these fanfiction tags is particularly important when we consider the impact the writers of transformative works can have on reconstructing the identity of a character. The "Hurt/Comfort" category, often abbreviated as "H/C" is particularly focused on demonstrations of emotion by the characters: Moonbeam's reference of fanfiction terms defines H/C as "the presence of emotional or physical angst of one character followed by emotional or physical comfort by another. A proper H/C story contains enough 'comfort'" to equal or out-weigh the amount of 'hurt' experienced; if not, then the story qualifies as angst more so than H/C" (Moonbeam 2015). This category of slash fanfiction is tied to the reconstruction of masculinity, as it often involves characters expressing feelings in ways that are not restricted to the hypermasculine modalities of their construction: "As both fans and academics agree, slash represents a way of rethinking and rewriting traditional masculinity. Sarah argued that slash's appeal lies in its placing 'emotional responsibility' on men for sustaining relationships while in reality men frequently dodge such responsibility" (Green, Jenkins and Jenkins 1998).

As fanfiction writers themselves, Moffat's team at BBC Sherlock likewise engages in moments that might be categorized through these emotional lenses, although they never progress to the full relationships that they would build in slash. One such moment comes at the end of Sherlock's first season, when Watson is kidnapped by Moriarty and strapped into a bomb jacket and makes an effort to save Sherlock by sacrificing himself. After Moriarty leaves, the scene unfolds:

Holmes frantically ripping the jacket off of Watson: Alright? Are you all right?!
Watson: Yeah, I'm fine. Sherlock—Sherlock! Are you okay?
Sherlock: Me? Yeah. Fine. Fine. That, ah—thing that you did. That you, um, you offered to do. That was, um … good.
Watson: I'm glad no one saw that.
Sherlock: Hm?
Watson: You ripping my clothes off in a darkened swimming pool. People might talk.
Sherlock: People do little else. (McGuigan 2010b)

In a later season, Watson's relationship to Sherlock Holmes as motivator is even made explicit: "But look how you care about John Watson. Your damsel in distress" (Hurran 2014). After Sherlock fakes his own death at the end of season 2 and returns to London after years of being in hiding, his first thought is of returning to John. When he discusses Watson's situation with Mycroft, Mycroft observes "He's got on with his life," and Holmes retorts "What life? I've been away" (Lovering 2014). Such indicators are in keeping with Moffat's own reading of the Johnlock relationship:

> why is sex so important? And has it always been this important to ever previous era of humanity? I bet it isn't. I think we're obsessed with it, to the point where I know a lot of people are saying 'Well, John and Sherlock clearly love

each other, they must be having sex.' But you can love someone without fancying them. If you're not wired to fancy someone, you just won't. But what's that got to do with it? Really, what's that got to do with the important relationships? (Rosenberg 2012)

Moffat's words emphasize his role as auteur and have been viewed by fans (particularly the women who write fanfiction) as a rebuke against the very concept of slash. Moffat also dismisses readings of Sherlock as queer that would undermine his notion of Sherlock's masculinity, as one interviewer reports: "Moffat is not saying that Sherlock, like Austin Powers, misplaced his mojo. 'It's the choice of a monk, not the choice of an asexual. If he was asexual, there would be no tension in that, no fun in that—it's someone who abstains who's interesting. There's no guarantee that he'll stay that way in the end—maybe he marries Mrs Hudson. I don't know!'" (Jeffries 2012). There are several problems with this statement (including the dismissiveness towards asexuality, which is already one of the least recognized queer identities), but perhaps the greatest is Moffat's claim that he doesn't "know" the outcome of Sherlock's love life, a narrative which is canonically under his control.

The depth of Sherlock's relationship with Watson becomes the obsessive focus of the series 4 finale, "The Final Problem," in which Sherlock is revealed to have a sister, Eurus, who has been the unseen villain of the season (ibid.). Positioned as an intellectual equivalent or even superior to Mycroft and Sherlock, Eurus's late addition to the Holmes family is explained away in terms of intense mental illness, psychopathic tendencies, and even an apparent ability to control minds. When she captures Sherlock, Mycroft, and John Watson, she pits them together in a series of twisted and violent tests conducted in the same asylum where she has been confined. She is presented as Sherlock's ultimate fangirl: her obsession is so great that she knows all the worst ways to torment him and his companions, from trying to force them to murder their cellmate to demanding quick crime-solving with lives on the line. She even stages an excruciating attack on Molly Hooper, the woman presented as suffering from unrequited love with Sherlock, instructing him to force her to tell him "I love you" with a threat on her life. The scene is excruciating to watch, and ends with Sherlock violently punching a coffin (see Fig. 7.2) after Eurus reveals that Molly was never in any danger, but is definitely suffering from the call. The focus is moved to his unusual display of rage (clear in his facial expression in Fig. 7.2) as validation of the moment's significance.

Fig. 7.2 Sherlock's emotional display in "The Final Problem" (Caron 2017)

However, that is the end of Molly's presence in an episode that may well serve as the series finale. Steven Moffat addressed the omission of closure to her scene by calling for the viewer to focus on Sherlock's pain rather than Molly's in an interview:

> She forgives him, of course, and our newly grown-up Sherlock is more careful with her feelings in the future. In the end of that scene, she's a bit wounded by it all, but he's absolutely devastated. He smashes up the coffin, he's in pieces, he's more upset than she is, and that's a huge step in Sherlock's development. The question is: Did Sherlock survive that scene? She probably had a drink and went and shagged someone, I dunno. Molly was fine. (Hibberd 2017)

Molly's grief (and personhood) is an aftermath, and the love life Moffat is apparently more interested in resolving is Sherlock's relationship with Watson. In one tense and climatic scene, Sherlock is told to choose one of his two companions to kill, pitting brotherly love against apparent bromance. Mycroft apparently tries to convince Sherlock to shoot Watson, insulting him repeatedly for his slow reaction:

> Make it swift. No need to prolong his agony. Get it over with, and we can get to work. God! I should have expected this. Pathetic. You always were the slow one. The idiot. That's why I always despised you. You shame us all. You shame the family name. Now, for once for your life, do the right thing. Put this stupid little man out of all our misery. Shoot him. (Caron 2017)

Watson demonstrates self-sacrificing masculinity, but Sherlock deflects the conclusion: "Ignore everything he just said, he's being kind. He's trying to make it easy for me to kill him. Which is why this is going to be so much harder" (ibid.). The scene (and the mad rush to save John Watson's life that follows) centers the finale squarely on Sherlock's relationships, with women existing primarily to be obsessed with, and impacted by, their pain and conflict.

Crazy Fan Girls, Fan Boy Auteurs

Yet in the case of Sherlock, the subtext is so explicit that it is not difficult to imagine "Johnlock" as canon. One fan analyzed the show's depiction as a romance, suggesting it was not queerbaiting but "heterobaiting" that "serves the slow-burn narrative of how Sherlock Holmes and John Watson finally end up in a relationship" (Fangirl 2014). This view has been supported by a detailed analysis of the creation of the show, including statements from show writer Mark Gattis: "I think when the day comes that you have a big detective show where the first half hour was this man at work, and he's a maverick, and all the usual things … and then we went home and his boyfriend says, 'Are you alright?', [and] it was just a thing … then something would have genuinely changed. I think the problem still is, [being gay] becomes the issue. I think the thing with gay characters is that it has to be an issue, as opposed to being part of everyday life" (Subtext 2014). Such analysis is even echoed in the canonical text, as in an encounter between Irene and Watson in which Watson protests "We're not a couple" to Irene Adler's immediate retort: "Yes you are" (McGuigan, A Scandal in Belgravia 2012).

Just as Moffat and Gattis cannot resist engaging with the fan girl audience and the prevalence of "Johnlock" slash in interviews, so too do they engage in portrayals and criticism of that same audience within the show's canon. Such explicit engagement with fans and the theories of fans is inherently unbalanced in its power dynamic. The critique can be even harsher when put into the voice of a favorite character, as with Sherlock's encounter with an apparent fan girl:

Sherlock Holmes:	There are two types of fans.
Kitty Reilly:	Oh?
Sherlock Holmes:	Catch me before I kill again. Type A.
Kitty Reilly:	Uh-huh. What's type B?
Sherlock Holmes:	Your bedroom's just a taxi ride away. (Haynes 2012)

The "fan girl" in this episode turns out to be a writer, in this case an investigative journalist. However, the questions she asks seem to be an expression of questions rising directly from fandom's speculations: "You and John Watson, just platonic? Can we put down for a 'no' there as well?" (Haynes 2012). The scene ends with Sherlock saying "You repel me," a message that could be taken as a criticism of tabloid journalism, but could also be seen as a rebuke at fans invested in the personal lives and identity of these characters.

This message of disgust at the speculations of fans and fan girls in particular echo through several episodes of *Sherlock*. The show's creators again place fans on-screen as characters subject to critique and ridicule in the opening of the first episode following Sherlock's apparent death. It opens with one fan presenting his theory for how Sherlock might have survived, which is interrupted by the criticism "Do you honestly believe if you have enough stupid theories it's going to change what really happened?" (Lovering 2014). This rebuke is relatively mild compared to the response provoked by a later fan theory, which involves enemy slash between Sherlock and Moriarty. The theory ends with Sherlock and Moriarty kissing after Sherlock drops a dummy off the roof to distract John. This theory is notably advanced by a woman, and the man listening to her interrupts with "What? Are you out of your mind?" suggesting that she is not taking this "seriously" and drawing attention to the fact that she is one of the few women in the room of "likeminded" folks assembled (Lovering 2014).

When fans took exception to this portrayal of themselves on screen, Steven Moffat responded by suggesting that the fans were projecting: "They're seeing themselves in the show," Moffat said when asked if the *Sherlock* team was engaging in a conversation with their fanbase to some degree. "We don't look. We can't look. I'm running two shows that have got very large and very vocal fandoms. I wouldn't admit it to myself if I had to look at it. No, the meta feel comes from the original Sherlock Holmes, the original stories" (Cornet 2014). This response likewise drew criticism from fans, as Megan Farnel succinctly observes: "Does he truly think he's fooling anyone by saying that an episode involving a scene that so clearly mocks slash-fiction writers, calling them 'out of their mind' and arguing they are not 'serious' enough, comes to us from the ACD canon?" (Farnel 2014).

The desire of members of the show to separate themselves from slash fanfiction doesn't end with Moffat. In one notable and regrettable incident, Sherlock Holmes actor Benedict Cumberbatch was asked to read aloud from slash fanfiction, and gave his opinion in (ironically) an interview with *Out* magazine:

'It's always, like, one of them is tired, one comes back from work, the other is horny, a lump appears in his trousers, and then they're at it,' he says. 'It's usually me getting it—I'm biting Watson's dog tags.' Perhaps, I suggest, making Holmes and Watson gay is a way to remove other women from the picture. 'Yes, yes,' he replies enthusiastically. 'I think it's about burgeoning sexuality in adolescence, because you don't necessarily know how to operate that. And I think it's a way of neutralising the threat, so this person is sort of removed from them as somebody who could break their heart.' (Hicklin 2014)

Cumberbatch not only echoed the cliché of fanfiction writers as adolescent women but further suggests that fanfiction writers are using slash fanfiction as an outlet for making their own desires less threatening, a reading that is particularly disempowering to the fan girl as author.

The politics of power at work in this type of dismissal and mockery of slash fanfiction as the work of fan girls who are, to invoke the male fan voice in Sherlock, "out of their minds," are further a reminder of the dichotomy between fan boys and fan girls. Steven Moffat explicitly invokes the importance of his fan boy status in describing his work on Sherlock: "Our own fan boyness about Sherlock Holmes means that there are absolute limits to what we do. Ours is an authentic version of Sherlock Holmes" (Jeffries 2012). This, perhaps, defines the most explicit barrier between the "fan boy" and the "fan girl" turned auteur. The fan boy is allowed to construct "authentic" and canonical texts, thanks in part to the fact that those texts already represent him and his desires. The fan girl, on the other hand, is absent from those texts, and her attempts to transform them are rejected as breaking with the "authentic" and reading in desires in a way that repels the fan boy auteur and his on-screen proxies. Yet the fan girl author persists, and the popularity of Johnlock is undiminished by Watson's now canonical marriage.

Supernatural and the Fan Girl's Gaze

The relationship between a show and its fan boys is often productively understood in commercial terms: the complaints of fan boys are taken seriously where casting or new directions on a show are concerned, and it is understood that the consumption of fan boys sustains much of the merchandise surrounding a property. Fan girls, on the other hand, have a less clear relationship with a show and its creators. Television is the perfect space for examining the construction of the fan girl gaze as active, and likewise to view the depiction of the fan girl through the eyes of the show's creator. As we discussed in Chap. 6, the fan girl is notoriously depicted as an obsessed caricature. Several films take the obsessed fan girl to the next level and characterize her as a dangerous stalker in the style of *Fatal Attraction* (1987) or *Swimfan* (2002). We have already discussed the depiction of the fan girl in *Supernatural*. As of April 2017, *Supernatural* is renewed for season 13, and is finding new fodder for its stories in the political crisis surrounding American and British masculinity. In one particularly telling moment, an earnest demon sets Lucifer free, and when asked what he wants in return declares his desire to "Make Hell Great Again" (Lopez-Corrado 2017). Throughout this season, the impact of a feminine presence on the brothers and their relationships is continually being explored thanks to the presence of Mary Winchester, the resurrected mother.

In earlier seasons of *Supernatural*, women were less visibly centered, and rarely long-term travelers in Baby. The character of Becky was handled very similarly to her counterparts in *Sherlock*, and likewise was clearly associated within the show's canon with the writing of slash fanfiction. As Sam's "fan girl" Becky is likewise taken to extremes, particularly when she engages in kidnapping Sam and holding him hostage after drugging him with a love potion. Such depictions ask fans in viewing the show either to accept the creator's critique of their fandom or to other themselves from the depictions, suggesting that there is a level at which a fan girl is acceptable, and that the show's creators have a say in dictating what that acceptable behavior might be.

If we fast forward five seasons, the depiction of *Supernatural* fans and their relationship to the text has changed, and with it some of the gendered aspect of the fandom. This transformation is best embodied in the 200th episode of *Supernatural*, a musical episode entitled "Fan Fiction" (Sgriccia 2014). The announcement of the episode was met with some trepidation from the community, as previous mentions of fanfiction (particularly Dean's reaction to the notion of "Wincest") had been negative and dismissive of fans as producers. However, the episode proved to be the most positive and fan-aware meta-episode the show has produced. Fan and columnist Aja Romano noted that the episode marked a moment of validation for women in the fandom that had been ten years in the making:

> In Supernatural's case, the evolution has been—dare we say it?—a progressive one, a steadily shifting narrative that seems to be ever-so-slowly moving away from the many years of geek-shaming and repudiation of its mostly female fandom. We might even be moved to call it a feminist evolution. Chalk it up

Fig. 7.3 The fan actress versions of Sam and Dean in "Fan Fiction" (Sgriccia 2014)

to SPN's musical episode. We like singing and dancing. But even more, we like fan girls, fandom, and the celebration of fanwork. (Romano 2014)

The episode opens with two young actresses emerging on to a stage with wigs and costumes that immediately invoke Sam and Dean (actresses shown in Fig. 7.3). It is quickly revealed that they are starring in a musical being directed by another young woman, Marie. The "real" Sam and Dean come to investigate the disappearance of a teacher and walk in on the first song of the musical, an interpretation of the traditional pre-credits sequence *Supernatural* uses to recap story plots: "The Road So Far." The clear relationship between the two and their teenaged female doppelgangers is parodied when the two flash their fake FBI badges at the same time as the actresses. The reaction of the two at first recalls their previous encounters with fans or the even less friendly depiction of fans as authors on *Sherlock*. While previous episodes have only depicted fan women as predators (literally, in the case of Becky's use of a spell to ensnare Sam as her husband) and otherwise as a minority within the *Supernatural* fan community, the 200th episode thus placed teenage girls front and center as fans and producers. Marie is even given the opportunity to call the canonical events of the show since the book series theoretically ended with season 5 "the worst fanfiction ever," and she defends her own work as "transformative fiction":

Dean Winchester: There is no space in *Supernatural*.
Marie: Well, not canonically, no, but this is transformative fiction.
Dean Winchester: You mean fan fiction.
Marie: Call it whatever you like, okay? It's inspired by Carver Edlund's books … with a few embellishments. (Sgriccia 2014)

However, Dean is less than thrilled with Marie's interpretation of his life, particularly when Marie explains a moment with a veiled reference to Wincest, a popular pairing in slash that they previously encountered through Becky's writing:

Dean: What are they doing?
Marie: Oh, uh, they are rehearsing the B.M. scene.
Dean: The bowel-movement scene?
Marie: No. The boy melodrama scene. You know, the scene where the boys get together and they're—they're driving or leaning against Baby, drinking a beer, sharing their feelings. The two of them—alone but together. Bonded, united. The power of their pain …
Dean: Why are they standing so close together?
Marie: Uh … reasons.
Dean: You know they're brothers, right?
Marie: Well, duh. But … subtext. (Sgriccia 2014)

The two young actresses parody the closeness between brothers that is central to such scenes on the show (see Fig. 7.3). The "Wincest" pairing is one of the more popular examples of an incestuous pairing in fandom, but it is far from the only example. Incest has rarely been a barrier to fanfiction writers. "Twincest" is a rare but still represented pairing among Harry Potter fanfiction writers, primarily featuring the Weasley twins, as Vera Cuntz-leng examines:

> It is crucial that the first six movies feature no sequence where only one of the twin brothers appears; moreover, they are together in the same frame most of the time throughout all films … the high level of intimacy between the characters is the source text that may facilitate the "one true pairing" trope that is at the heart of romance novels and essential to many fandoms. (Cuntz-Leng 2014)

Marie's work highlights the same use of intimacy in the portrayal of the Wincester brothers.

Wincest, however, is not the pairing that brings Supernatural into the master league of queer baiting on television. That honor belongs to Destiel, or the pairing of Dean and Castiel. This pairing is the next we view through Dean's eyes, portrayed by the young actresses:

Dean Winchester:	What are they doing?
Marie:	Ummm. Kids these days call it hugging.
Dean Winchester:	Is that in the show?
Marie:	Oh. No. Siobhan and Kristen are a couple in real life. Although we do explore the nature of Destiel in act two.
Dean Winchester:	Sorry. What?
Marie:	Oh, it's just subtext. But then again, you know, you can't spell subtext without S-E-X. (Sgriccia 2014)

This moment is notable in many ways: Dean's reaction to the concept is distinct from his reaction to Wincest in previous episodes, more shock than anything else. Castiel's love song "I'll just wait here then" is presented in the episode as a reframing of a canonical moment, using a line from Castiel's own dialogue when he waited on the side of a road while Dean slept. And of course, both Dean and Castiel are being "played" in the musical by young women, who Marie notes as the "couple in real life"—an interesting parallel to the gay couple Dean and Sam encountered cosplaying them in "The Real Ghostbusters" (Conway 2009). Lothian, Busse, and Reid examine the construction of slash communities as a "queer female space," which describes "not only the queerness of women's sexual fantasies but also how these queer fantasy acts often lay the groundwork for nonvirtual queer acts and lives" (Lothian, Busse, and Reid 2007). This nuance of representation is rare in depictions of fan girls on screen, and the presence of lesbian couples acknowledged without a dramatic reaction likewise remains rare.

If Becky is *Supernatural*'s version of the dangerous and unacceptable fan girl, then Marie, the central "fan girl" in the 200th episode, is perhaps the show's apology for previous wrongs. Marie is active in all of the most controversial fan practices, including that of writing slash fanfiction. She is presented in the meta-context as a director with her own vision, one which the characters that are her subjects initially reject but eventually, if not embrace, then at least acknowledge as valid. That validation is a rare outcome of the depiction of a fan girl, as a comparison to more infamous moments of fan critique (such as Moffat and Sherlock, as previously discussed) demonstrates.

The episode even includes a moment of acknowledgement by Dean that fanfiction writers should keep working: as Claudine Hummel writes in her review of the episode, "Dean tells Marie-and therefore fans everywhere—to keep writing because 'I have my version and you have yours'" (Hummel 2014).

The ending of the episode takes This Endorsement To A Next Level, as Lynn Zubernis describes in her recap:

> And then we're back at the play. The publisher that Marie invited has shown up, and she's ecstatic.
> 'Go fan girl!' says Maeve, which is pretty much the theme of the entire episode.
> Marie runs up the aisle, excitedly asking the publisher 'What did you think?'
> And then we see who it is. It's Chuck, of course it is. Symbolically, it's Kripke himself, Supernatural's version of God. And what does the creator think of the fannish creation?
> 'Not bad,' he smiles.
> The creator of canon blesses the interpretation—the fanfiction, and the fans. (Zubernis and Larsen 2014)

Lynn Zubernis further suggests that this blessing can be read as a sign that the show's creators see the fans, and acknowledge their work as important:

> We see you, in all your infinite diversity and variety, with all your amazing and shocking and inspiring creativity. In all your boundless loyalty, in the depth and breadth of your passion for this Show that we've created. We may not all be the same—the script that we write and the words that we say and the direction that we perform may not be the same as the story you hear, or the story you tell—but both interpretations are important. (Zubernis and Larsen 2014)

In many such recaps across the web, the episode was read as a love letter to its fandom, and the fans responded with equal expressions of enthusiasm. One group of fans expressed their appreciation by organizing "SPN 10 Gift Basket," a collection drive for gifts and baskets for the cast as well as all the crew of the show.

However, not everyone felt the episode was entirely unproblematic in its depiction, as one commenter, BL, observed in a comment on Lynn Zubernis and Katherine Larsen's post:

> by making it a high school show it felt like the producers were patting fans on the head and saying, "There, there children. See what we did for you?" Granted

some of that might be my internalized fan-shame looking for the mockery, but something about making the writer/director/producer/star/fan someone without any real life experience or, for lack of a better term, "anything better to do," makes it feel a little patronizing. (Zubernis and Larsen 2014)

This characterization of the writers of fanfiction as adolescent girls is not unlike the stereotype that has often been applied to the entire fanfiction writing community, and its use here contrasts with the slightly older (and thus more sexually and personally threatening) fan girl portrayal of Becky.

The episode was also not without its own version of the destructive and dangerous fan girl, this time embodied by the episode's villain, Calliope. A Greek muse of storytelling, Calliope is attracted to stories, and this time she has fixated on Supernatural: The Musical: "*Supernatural* has everything. Life, death, resurrection, redemption—but above all, family. All set to music you can really tap your toe to. It isn't some meandering piece of genre dreck, it's … epic" (Sgriccia 2014). However, Calliope expresses her "appreciation" by planning to consume the show's author and the inspiring characters Sam and Dean, suggesting that the moment Calliope fixed her "fan girl" gaze on the show her goal was the type of ownership that could only come through destroying the original. Calliope's fixation is also notable as she is an adult woman and a monster who has to be defeated.

Later in the same season, in an episode entitled "Don't Call Me Shurley," the episode's meaning was retroactively changed by the revelation that the long-held fan theory was correct: Chuck is in fact God, and over the millennia he's gone from frustrated author of the Bible to *Supernatural* novel writer to a writer working on his autobiography. The moment includes some further reference to fan theories, including explicit acknowledgement by Chuck of his bisexuality: "Chuck: I did some great stuff as Chuck … I traveled, a lot, you know. And, uh, I dated. Yeah, I had some girlfriends. Had a few boyfriends. Oh! And I learned how to play guitar" (Singer 2016). The episode thus both reinforces the fan girl gaze (and responds to some of the ongoing accusations of queerbaiting on the show with the introduction of a significant, if fairly temporary, bisexual character) while reinforcing the white male author's position as deity.

Fan Girls as "Auteur"

Marie is a rare example of the fan girl author in the spotlight. When fan girls enter the spotlight as authors in geek culture more broadly, they often invite criticism and retaliation from the community. One of the most infamous cases of fanfiction by a woman author repackaged into a mainstream franchise is the recent case of *Fifty Shades of Grey* by E.L. James (2011). This franchise has been catapulted into the public eye thanks to the release of the *Fifty Shades of Grey* movie released for Valentine's Day in 2015. The series is well known to be a repackaging of a *Twilight* fanfiction, and takes its primary characters, Anastasia Steele and Christian Grey, from *Twilight*'s Bella and Edward. Jane Little took a copy of the original *Twilight* fanfiction work, *Master of the Universe*, analyzed it in comparison to the published text, and found an 89% overlap with moments like this one:

> I have survived Day Two Post Edward, and my first day at work. It has been a welcome distraction. The time has flown by in a haze of new faces, work to do and Mr. James Smith. He smiles down at me, his dark blue eyes twinkling, as he leans against my desk. "Excellent work, Bella. I think we're going to make a great team." He beams at me, knowingly. (Jane 2012)

Master of the Universe was published on Fanfiction.net in this version long before it was repackaged for self-publishing and eventually picked up to become a bestseller. Bethan Jones notes that this bestseller status is particularly troubling to some members of the fanfiction community thanks to the position *Fifty Shades of Grey* now holds as emblematic of transformative work (Jones 2014).

The work's popularity has been so polarizing that it led to the rise of what Sarah Harman and Bethan Jones characterize as a type of "snark fandom," with anti-fans reveling in disavowing and parodying the text (2013, 951). This type of anti-fandom exists in many contexts, but there are particularly virulent strains surrounding not only *Fifty Shades* but also its initial inspiration, *Twilight*. *Twilight* is an incredibly successful franchise focused on supernatural romance by a woman author with a primarily female fandom, but these fans have been termed by others as "Twi-hards" and disowned by geek culture. The Urban Dictionary definition sums up the derision such fans are held in: "Twihard—Stupid obsessive people (mostly teenage girls) who are in love with fictional characters and wouldn't know a good book if it punched them in the face." Note the implied desire towards violence and the characterization of *Twilight* fans as teenage girls, an assumption that holds echoes of the characterization of the entire community of fanfiction writers.

EL James emerged from this derided community to produce a work that, if it is possible, has attracted even more criticism from both within and outside geek culture. The significance of *Twilight* as source material for an erotic work cannot be over-emphasized, as the original story features an abstinence-driven romance where sex is prohibited until after marriage. This formula is something that many fanfiction writers rewrite, as Sara K Day observes in her examination of "smutty" *Twilight* fanfiction as an outlet for fans to explore what the series mostly implies (Day 2014, 30). In a study of the fandom, Hope Jensen Schau and Margo Buchanan-Oliver further complicates this reading by pointing out that "*Twilight* opens the discursive space for girls and women actively to negotiate femininity and normative gender roles through the *Twilight* saga. The brand serves as a vehicle to contemplate women's potential and place in the world" (Schau and Buchanan-Oliver 2013, 58). While arguments over whether the brand is "feminist" in this potential or not could last for decades, it cannot be denied that *Twilight* is fairly unique in geek culture in providing a space where fangirls are the most visible force, and the criticism it receives seems to be a direct result of the dominance of the female gaze within the franchise.

While *Fifty Shades of Grey* is now several steps removed from its positioning in this discourse, it is best understood as part of the larger queer space of fanfiction, offering its own alternative models of sexuality that have attracted attention and criticism. One of the most notable critiques of the franchise has been its modeling of a relationship that is based on BDSM (bondage, dominance, and sadomasochism) with questionable consent. The film has particularly attracted this negative attention, complete with many reviews noting that the movie depicts the grooming of women for abuse (Chu 2015). The *Fifty Shades of Grey* film has met with additional criticism for its failure to embrace its core audience: as K.T. Torrey describes in her response to the film:

> given that the book is told from Ana's first person POV, I assumed that the film would take a similar, female- gaze centered perspective: that there would be lingering looks at the gorgeous Dornan at every turn, or even some open-mouthed object porn staring at his extravagant apartment, his playroom, etc. But no. Instead, the focus was awkwardly on elements of Dakota Johnson-as-Ana's body. (Torrey 2015)

However, these interpretations are in part problematic thanks to the removal of the narrative from its initial context (as part of *Twilight* fanfiction) and the impact of remediation, which removes much of the active female gaze from the narrative.

Supernatural narratives have always lent themselves to an exploration of sexuality outside social norms, as Virginia Keft-Kennedy explores in her discussion of vampires as a tool for exploring masculinity: "in slash fiction the fantasy of homosexual sex generally, and of aggressive homosexual sex specifically, is exemplified by the figure of the vampire, a figure which, in a number of ways, traditionally operates outside hegemonic discourse of sexuality, offering a vehicle through which to encode subversive pleasures of sexuality and desire" (Keft-Kennedy 2008, 50). It is not surprising that this reference to Buffyverse slash bears with it patterns familiar from *Fifty Shades of Grey*, which of course originated in its use of BDSM and "dangerous" sexuality with the figure of the vampire and the power-charged dynamic of Bella and Edward's human/vampire love story. Both *Fifty Shades of Grey* and the Buffyverse slash Keft-Kennedy analyzes include depictions of rape, but Keft-Kennedy notes that "what is being represented in many slash rape and non-con [non-consensual] narratives is not a depiction of the actual rape of the character but a seductively aestheticised fantasy of it—a fantasy moreover, that is discursively constructed through the literary tropes of the vampire" (2008, 60). The discomfort with *Fifty Shades of Grey* suggests that fandom doesn't really have room for women authors and fans: a fantasy constructed in response to a space where discussion of women as desiring is practically forbidden must be deconstructed and criticized. Yet when placed into the larger context of "non-con" as a trope in fanfiction, particularly in supernatural texts, *Fifty Shades of Grey* appears to be if anything mild—its popularity even inspired fan critic Aja Romano to publish a guide to finding the "good" fanfiction porn (Romano 2012).

The fan girl turned auteur remains an easy figure of disdain: the success of Anna Todd in securing a book deal thanks to the popularity of her fanfiction series "After" has been similarly ridiculed. It doesn't help matters that her fanfiction was written about the singers in One Direction, and thus constitutes "Real Person Fic," which Anne Jamison describes as the easy target for a number of biases:

> One of the biggest issues is the perception that people who write fic about a boy band are only interested in writing out their own fantasies, scripting interactions between their idols and characters who serve as stand-ins for themselves. There's also the notion that the writers must be young teens—

despite the fact that data shows that most 1D fanfic readers/writers were over 16, and two-thirds of readers said they weren't interested in stories that were mere wish-fulfillment for their authors. (Rothman 2014)

Criticizing the authors of such fanfiction is like attacking Furries or "Twihards:" the marginalization of these members of the fan community makes them easy targets.

Relatively few fanfiction authors move their work into the mainstream spotlight, in part because such publication is not necessarily even a goal or desire of most fanfiction authors, but also because most fanfiction serves a different purpose than published work. Catherine Tosenberger has pointed out that the best fanfiction is in fact unpublishable: "it draws its aesthetic power from both its freedom from the constraints of the publishing industry and its embeddedness within a community of readers and writers: fanfiction, unlike published literature for young people, relies upon a presumption of readers' knowledge, rather than their ignorance" (Tosenberger 2014: 23). Most fanfiction writers operate within the relatively anonymous world of fanfiction communities, where there is an apparent meritocracy within an attention economy. Of course, that meritocracy is an illusion, and participation in fanfiction as a subculture does reflect privilege: "In a pseudonymous online culture, participants are judged on textual contributions alone, although it is important to remember that—just as the apparently democratic nature of the Internet is constrained by economic barriers to access—cultural capital evident in these texts unavoidably conditions our perceptions" (Lothian, Busse, and Reid 2007, 104–105).

However, the pseudonymous culture offers a great deal of freedom—freedom that fan girls do not as easily possess in other spaces in geek culture. It is that freedom that one fan, Kim Bannister, summarized as the greatest appeal of fanfiction:

> What I love about fandom is the freedom we have allowed ourselves to create and recreate our characters over and over again. Fanfic rarely sits still. It's like a living, evolving thing, taking on its own life, one story building on another, each writer's reality bouncing off another's and maybe even melding together to form a whole new creation, (Green, Jenkins, and Jenkins 1998, 86)

It is precisely that freedom that is potentially compromised by the attention of show creators who place the spotlight on practices such as the writing of slash without consideration for the context, drawing criticism and even attracting the attention of homophobic media and others determined to label such writers as deviant.

This rhetoric of freedom and safety within a community recalls our opening metaphor, the "freaks" of the circus, from whom fandom has borrowed the phrase "one of us" with all its promise and potential for darkness. The fan girl is not so easily embraced into a community, particularly as an active creator, but slash fanfiction offers one queer space in which the female gaze is the norm rather than the exception. When the lens of the fan boy as author turns on that space, it is often with suspicion and derision, perhaps in part because when men write "fan fiction" it is often instead part of canon. The examples of *Sherlock* and *Supernatural* demonstrate the tenuous relationship of mainstream geek media franchises and the fan girl audience, and these participants are brought in as "one of us"—but only as long as they fit into approved spaces and offer no threat to the dominant narrative.

References

Caron, Benjamin. 2017. The final problem. *Sherlock*. Season 4, episode 3. BBC, January 15.

Cendrowski, Mark. 2008. *The panty pinata polarization*, 10. CBS, November: The Big Bang Theory.

Chu, Arthur. 2015. Fifty shades of gilded cages: The luxury branding of domestic abuse. *The Daily Beast*, February 16. Accessed March 12, 2016. http://www.thedailybeast.com/articles/2015/02/16/fifty-shades-of-gilded-cages-the-luxury-branding-of-domestic-abuse.html.

Conway, James L. 2009. The real ghostbusters. *Supernatural*. Season 5, episode 9. CW, November 12.

Cornet, Ruth. 2014. *Sherlock*: Steven Moffat on the fake death, if the series has gone meta, character vs. mystery driven stories, Doctor Who crossover. IGN, January 26. Accessed May 17, 2015. http://www.ign.com/articles/2014/01/26/sherlock-steven-moffat-on-the-fake-death-if-the-series-has-gone-meta-character-vs-mystery-driven-stories-doctor-who-crossover.

Cuntz-Leng, Vera. 2014. Twinship, incest, and twincest in the Harry Potter universe. *Transformative Works and Cultures* 17. http://journal.transformativeworks.org/index.php/twc/article/view/576.

Day, Sara K. 2014. Pure passion: The Twilight saga, "abstinence porn", and adolescent women's fan fiction. *Children's Literature Association Quarterly* 39 (1): 28–48. doi:10.1353/chq.2014.0014.

Driscoll, Catherine. 2006. One true pairing: The romance of pornography and the pornography of romance. In *Fan fiction and Fan communities in the age of the internet*, ed. Karen Hellekson, and Kristina Busse, 79–96. Jefferson, NC: McFarland & Company.

Fangirl, Mad. 2014. It's not queerbaiting, it's storytelling: BBC's *Sherlock*. Now real life has no appeal, July 20. Accessed January 19, 2015. https://nowreallifehasnoappeal.wordpress.com/2014/07/20/its-not-queerbaiting-its-storytelling-bbcs-sherlock.

Fanlore. 2015. Slash. Fanlore, August 5. Accessed August 5, 2015. http://fanlore.org/wiki/Slash.

Farnel, Megan. 2014. Case study: On *Sherlock*, fandom, and Steven Moffat. *HASTAC*, April 16. Accessed October 12, 2015. http://www.hastac.org/blogs/mfarnel/2014/04/16/case-study-sherlock-fandom-and-steven-moffat.

Freaks. 1932. Directed by Tod Browning. Metro-Goldwyn-Mayer. DVD.

Green, Shoshanna, Cynthia Jenkins, and Henry Jenkins. 1998. Normal female interest in men bonking: Selections from "The Terra Nostra Underground" and "Strange Bedfellows". In *Theorizing fandom: Fans, subculture and identity*, ed. Cheryl Harris, and Alison Alexander, 9–38. Creskill, NJ: Hampton Press.

Harman, Sarah, and Bethan Jones. 2013. Fifty shades of ghey: Snark fandom and the figure of the anti-fan. *Sexualities* 16 (8): 951–968. doi:10.1177/1363460713508887.

Haynes, Toby. 2012. The Reichenbach Fall. *Sherlock*. Season 2, episode 3. BBC, May 20.

Hibberd, James. 2017. Sherlock showrunner explains that intense (and conclusive?) finale. *Entertainment Weekly*, January 16. http://ew.com/tv/2017/01/16/sherlock-showrunner-season-4-finale/.

Hicklin, Aaron. 2014. The gospel according to Benedict. *Out Magazine*, October 14. http://www.out.com/out-exclusives/2014/10/14/poised-make-alan-turing-his-own-sherlock-star-benedict-cumberbatch-no-stranger-sexual-politics-and-bullying.

Hummel, Claudine. 2014. Supernatural 200th episode review. *Fan Front*, November 15. Accessed November 20, 2015. http://www.fan-front.com/supernatural-200th-episode-review/.

Hurran, Nick. 2014. His last vow. *Sherlock*. Season 3, episode 3. BBC, February 2.

Jagose, Annamarie. 1996. Queer theory. *Australian Humanities Review*, December. http://www.australianhumanitiesreview.org/archive/Issue-Dec-1996/jagose.html.

James, E.L. 2011. *Fifty Shades of Grey*. New York, NY: Vintage Books.

Jane. 2012. Master of the Universe versus fifty shades by E.L. James comparison. Dear Author, March 13. Accessed December 5, 2014. http://dearauthor.com/features/industry-news/master-of-the-universe-versus-fifty-shades-by-e-l-james-comparison/.

Jeffries, Stuart. 2012. 'There is a clue everybody's missed': Sherlock writer Steven Moffat interviewed. *The Guardian*, January 20. Accessed October 20, 2014. http://www.theguardian.com/tv-and-radio/2012/jan/20/steven-moffat-sherlock-doctor-who.

Johnson, Allyson. 2016. Review: The good and bad of *Sherlock*: The Abominable Bride. *The Mary Sue*, January 18. Accessed January 22, 2016. http://www.themarysue.com/review-the-good-and-bad-of-sherlock-the-abominable-bride/.

Jones, Bethan. 2014. Fifty shades of exploitation: Fan labor and *Fifty Shades of Grey*. *Transformative Works and Cultures* 15. doi:http://dx.doi.org/10.3983/twc.2014.0501.

Keft-Kennedy, Virginia. 2008. Fantasising masculinity in Buffyverse slash fiction: Sexuality, violence and the vampire. *Nordic Journal of English Studies* 7 (1): 49–80. https://gupea.ub.gu.se/bitstream/2077/10206/1/Vol7No1%20-%20KeftKennedy.pdf.

Lan. 2012. An explanation of queer-baiting and why it's a problem. *ActualAnimeVillain Tumblr*, November 28. Accessed December 5, 2014. http://actualanimevillain.tumblr.com/post/36720884625/an-explanation-of-queer-baiting-and-why-its-a.

Lopez-Corrado, N. (Director). 2017. *Somewhere Between Heaven and Hell* [Television Series episode] in Singer, R., and Dabb, A.'s, Supernatural. Burbank, CA: the CW.

Lothian, Alexis, Kristina Busse, and Robin Anne Reid. 2007. Yearning void and infinite potential: Online slash fandom as queer female space. *English Language Notes* 45 (2): 103–111. http://www.colorado.edu/english-language-notes/issues/45-2.

Lovering, Jeremy. 2014. The empty hearse. *Sherlock*. Season 3, episode 1. BBC, January 19.

Lulu. 2013. Gender: AO3 census data. *The Slow Dance of the Infinite*, October 1. Accessed December 4, 2015. http://centrumlumina.tumblr.com/post/62816996032/gender.

Lyn, Euros. 2010. The Blind Banker. *Sherlock*. Season 1, episode 2. BBC, October 31.

Mackinnon, Doug. 2016. *The abominable bride*, 1. BBC, January: Sherlock. Special issue.

McGuigan, Paul. 2012. A Scandal in Belgravia. *Sherlock*. Season 2, episode 1. BBC, May 6.

McGuigan, Paul. 2010a. A Study in Pink. *Sherlock*. Season 1, episode 1. BBC, October 24.

McGuigan, Paul. 2010b. The Great Game. *Sherlock*. Season 1, episode 3. BBC, November 7.

Moonbeam. 2015. Fanfiction terminology. *Moonbeam*, February 9. Accessed February 9, 2015. http://www.angelfire.com/falcon/moonbeam/terms.html#H/C.

Plante, Courtney N., Sharon E. Roberts, Stephen Reysen, and Kathleen C. Gerbasic. 2014. One of us: Engagement with fandoms and global citizenship identification. *Psychology of Popular Media Culture* 3 (1): 49–64. doi:10.1037/ppm0000008.

Poore, Benjamin. 2012. Sherlock Holmes and the leap of faith: The forces of fandom and convergence in adaptations of the Holmes and Watson stories. *Adaptation* 6 (2): 158–171. doi:10.1093/adaptation/aps024.

Porluciernagas. 2013. Why is there so much slash fic?: Some analysis of the AO3 census. *LadyGeekGirl*, November 12. Accessed August 5, 2015. https://ladygeekgirl.wordpress.com/2013/11/12/why-is-there-so-much-slash-fic-some-analysis-of-the-ao3-census/.

Romano, Aja. 2012. Where to find the good (fanfiction) porn. *Daily Dot*, August 17. Accessed December 5, 2014. http://www.dailydot.com/culture/where-to-find-good-fanfic-porn/.

Romano, Aja. 2014. *Supernatural*'s 200th episode is a fiffing tribute to its fangirls. *Daily Dot*, November 13. Accessed June 8, 2015. http://www.dailydot.com/geek/supernatural-episode-200-fan-fiction-takes-on-fan girls/.

Rosenberg, Alyssa. 2012. Steven Moffat on Sherlock's return, the Holmes–Watson love story, and updating the first supervillain. *Think Progress*, May 7. Accessed March 13, 2015. http://thinkprogress.org/alyssa/2012/05/07/479306/steven-moffat-on-sherlocks-return-the-holmes-watson-love-story-and-updating-the-first-supervillain/.

Rosie. 2012. Sherlock is the grossest example of queerbaiting. *Fandoms and Feminism Tumblr*, December 3. Accessed October 12, 2014. http://fandomsandfeminism.tumblr.com/post/37116303807/sherlock-is-the-grossest-example-of-queerbaiting.

Rothman, Lily. 2014. One direction fanfiction writer gets book deal, but not much respect. *Time*, June 4. Accessed August 9, 2015. http://time.com/2822591/one-direction-fanfiction-writer-gets-book-deal-but-not-much-respect/.

Schau, Hope Jensen and Margo Buchanan-Oliver. 2013. The creation of inspired lives: Female fan engagement with the Twilight saga. In *Gender, Culture, and Consumer Behavior*, ed. Cele C. Otnes and Linda Tuncay Zayer, 33–60. New York: Routledge.

Sgriccia, Philip. 2014. Fan fiction. *Supernatural*. Season 10, episode 5. CW, November 11.

Singer, Robert. 2016. Don't call me Shurley. *Supernatural*. Season 11, episode 20. CW, May 4.

Subtext, Loudest. 2014. Softly, softly: The BBC's 2009 LGB Research Commision and The Johnlock Conspiracy. *Tumblr*, June 19. Accessed August 20, 2015. http://loudest-subtext-in-television.tumblr.com/post/88272799479/softly-softly-the-bbcs-2009-lgb-research.

Toastystats. 2013. [Fandom stats] Which are the biggest ships on AO3? Archive of our own, November 1. Accessed June 16, 2015. http://archiveofourown.org/works/1026780.

Torrey, K.T. 2015. Whose gaze is it anyways? *Cute Girl Discount*, February 14. Accessed April 12, 2015. https://cutegirldiscount.wordpress.com/2015/02/14/whose-gaze-is-it-anyway/.

Tosenberger, Catherine. 2008. Homosexuality at the online Hogwarts: Harry Potter slash fanfiction. *Children's Literature* 36 (1): 185–207. doi:10.1353/chl.0.0017.

Tosenberger, Catherine. 2014. Mature poets steal: Children's literature and the unpublishability of fanfiction. *Children's Literature Association Quarterly* 39 (1): 4–27. doi:10.1353/chq.2014.0010.

TV Tropes. 2015. One of us. TV Tropes, August 20. Accessed November 20, 2015. http://tvtropes.org/pmwiki/pmwiki.php/Main/OneOfUs.

Zubernis, Lynn and Katherine Larsen. 2014. Now that's how you do a 200th episode! Supernatural's fan fiction. *Fangasm!*, November 13. Accessed November 16, 2014. https://fangasmthebook.wordpress.com/2014/11/13/now-thats-how-you-do-a-200th-episode-supernaturals-fan-fiction/.

8

Conclusion: That's Not How Geek Masculinity Works!

From approximately 2013 until 2017, the time of writing, the Hugo Awards have played host to an internal struggle. The Hugos are the World Science Fiction Society's awards, and since 1953 they have been recognizing novels, short stories, movies, television, and even fan work in science fiction and fantasy. Many geek icons, Robert Heinlein, Philip K. Dick, Orson Scott Card, and Neil Gaiman, among many others, have been recognized and heralded at this bastion of genre fiction. Unlike similar awards in other genres, the Hugo Awards do not restrict voting to those working in the field. Anyone who pays the membership fee to be part of the voting block can have his or her voice represented, although historically the number of voters each year has not been very high, making a Hugo more of a fan-based award than those of the more industry-centric Nebula. This system seemed to work well for many decades, but has been the subject of attention thanks to a few factions looking to use the Hugo Awards as a platform to address what they view as a great inequity within science fiction as a genre.

Those two factions are the "Sad Puppies" and the "Rabid Puppies," two group names that spring, appropriately, right out of web culture. The Sad Puppies take their name from a Sarah McLachlan ad against cruelty to animals, as Correia explains: "We did a joke based on that: That the leading cause of puppy-related sadness was boring message-fic winning awards" (quoted in Wallace 2015). The derisive term "message-fic" holds echoes of the language of Gamergate: we have heard the same railing against so-called politically correct content across geek media. The Sad Puppies have evolved over the years: as writer Jim C. Hines compiled in his timeline of the movement,

© The Author(s) 2017
A. Salter and B. Blodgett, *Toxic Geek Masculinity in Media*,
DOI 10.1007/978-3-319-66077-6_8

the first iteration in 2013 was more of a self-nomination push than an organized political statement, while the second iteration was more explicit about pushing "pulp stories" over the political favorites of the "literati." Both of those iterations were organized by author Larry Correia. The campaign took on a more intensely political feel with the third iteration in 2015, when Brad Torgersen, author of what he calls "blue collar speculative fic," took over (Torgersen 2015a). He offered his take on how encountering social themes is ruining what science fiction and fantasy should "really" be about:

> The book has a spaceship on the cover, but is it *really* going to be a story about space exploration and pioneering derring-do? Or is the story merely about racial prejudice and exploitation, with interplanetary or interstellar trappings? There's a sword-swinger on the cover, but is it *really* about knights battling dragons? Or are the dragons suddenly the good guys, and the sword-swingers are the oppressive colonizers of Dragon Land?
> A planet, framed by a galactic backdrop. Could it be an actual bona fide space opera? Heroes and princesses and laser blasters? No, wait. It's about sexism and the oppression of women.

The reductive language used by Torgersen and his allies to discuss what they see as unwanted changes in science fiction is telling: "heroes and princesses" are desirable; stories questioning those power structures are not. And, of course, the "knights" should be the good guys, and a narrative that suggests otherwise is unwelcome. The organizer of the Rabid Puppies, Castalia House lead editor Theodore Beale, better known as Vox Day (Day 2015c), criticized modern science fiction and fantasy using similar logic: "we value excellence in actual science fiction and fantasy, rather than excellence in intersectional equalitarianism, racial and gender inclusion, literary pyrotechnics, or professional rabbitology." Vox Day is also the author of *SJWs Always Lie: Taking Down the Thought Police*, a book from his own editorial house that includes a guide for "When SJWs attack" (Day 2015a). Vox Day uses almost laughably over-the-top rhetoric in response to what he views as his persecution by social justice warriors, and in the description of his book declares himself "Supreme Dark Lord of the Evil Legion of Evil" (ibid.). His Twitter page[1] displays a shortened version of the honorific "Supreme Dark Lord" with an accompanying handle picture of a mask against a red and orange sky. The book was published on August 27, 2015—what

---

[1] See: https://twitter.com/voxday.

Vox declared as the "first anniversary" of Gamergate, the same day Adam Baldwin first posted a tweet with the hashtag (Day 2015b).

The distinction between Sad and Rabid Puppies can be difficult to see for those looking in, particularly as there are overlapping titles on their slates and similarities in their underlying philosophy and concerns. Brad Torgersen (2015b) tried to make the distinction through tribalism, but also expressed resentment about what he viewed as the exclusion of his "outsider" tribe from WorldCon, home of the Hugos: "maybe just be wholly transparent and call it White American Liberals Con—An inclusive, diverse place where everyone talks about the same things, has the same tastes, votes the same way, and looks at the world through the same pair of eyes. *Whitelibbycon*." Meanwhile, Vox Day and his associates are more directly connected with trolling, and use a vocabulary and imagery that is explicitly destructive and matches with the "Evil Legion of Evil" label even as the group's rhetoric suggests that they view themselves as the righteous victims in the conflict.

In 2015, it looked as though this "Evil Legion of Evil" was winning, and a term had even been coined for the onslaught: PuppyGate. The Hugo Award nominees were announced following nominations by 2122 voters, nearly all of whom submitted online ("Announcing the 2015 Hugo Award Nominees" 2015). Miles Schneiderman reacted to the success of the Puppies in getting many of their nominees on the Hugo Slate in 2015:

> The Puppies aren't "taking back" speculative fiction; they are trying to mold a new speculative fiction in their own image. In their ideal world, the genre would be defined by the shallow rather than the meaningful, its most respected scions determined by mass popularity rather than thought provocation. (Schneiderman 2015)

The presence of so many Puppy nominations on the ballot had another effect: it reversed a trend towards close-to-equal gender representation among nominees, with only three women nominated in the fiction categories (Hines 2015). Ultimately, the Puppy slates were unsuccessful at winning awards: most of the nominees finished under "No Award" in votes, and in several categories no award was given at all (2015 Hugo Awards 2015). Gary K. Wolfe (2015) summed up the Hugo results:

> The outright rejection by Hugo voters of the Puppy slate—a few of whom, it must be said, might deserve recognition on their own merits—is not a rejection of a particular mode of writing, but of bullying and bad behavior—and,

frankly, bad fiction—and of an almost desperate effort to unravel the progress that has already been made, and that is still far from complete.

Meanwhile, Milo Yiannopoulos, a journalist best known for his role in and continual support of Gamergate, heralded the evening as a victory:

> Emboldened by the success of Gamergate in resisting cultural meddlers and authoritarians in video gaming, sci-fi fans resistant to identitarian politics are fighting back. Every year their numbers are growing, and they are more disciplined, more relentless and more determined than their social justice foes. (Yiannopoulos 2015)

The choice of "No Award" could be viewed by this lens as further evidence that the Hugo Awards had tried to resist the invaders through a self-destructive mechanism, forgoing giving any award rather than giving to a Puppies-supported nominee.

The ultimate fate of the Hugos is still in question: can a fairly open voting process work in an era of Internet campaigns and Puppy slates? Did it ever work in the first place, or was it always representative primarily of a small number of dedicated special-interest factions? George R.R. Martin (2015) has addressed the second question extensively as a veteran of the Hugo Awards, noting that "The Sad Puppies did not invent Hugo campaigning, by any means. But they escalated it … they ran the best organized, most focused, and most effective awards campaign in the history of our genre, and showed everyone else how it's done."

In 2016, that campaign succeeded despite prior warnings, in part thanks to attempts to legitimize the slate with the inclusion of big names (including Steven King)—of the 81 names they put forward on the Rabid Puppies slate, 64 were shortlisted for the Hugo award (Waldman 2016). However, the plan has backfired somewhat thanks to one surprising name on the list: Chuck Tingle, an author of satirical gay erotica, was included for his self-published pornographic sci-fi tale "Space Raptor Butt Invasion" (ibid.). The nomination seemed to be intended as a mockery of the Hugos and the entire open-nomination process, as noted sci-fi novelist N.K. Jemisin (2016) pointed out on Twitter: "CT is taking the place of some good writers. That's what the Rabbit Pubzees [sic] are up to—not just trolling, but trying to keep people + / who would have earned awards consideration based on the merit of their work from getting that consideration."

8 Conclusion: That's Not How Geek Masculinity Works! 193

However, Chuck Tingle (2016) took his moment in the spotlight as an opportunity to throw some shade back at the Rabid Puppies themselves: he took to Amazon, self-publishing a new work: *Slammed in the Butt By My Hugo Award Nomination*. His description parodies the entire event:

> When Tuck Bingle receives and email explaining that he's been nominated for science fiction literature's most prestigious award, he's left utterly confused. On one hand, Tuck is a successful writer of gay, science fiction erotic, but on the other, this email is addressed to someone by the name of Chuck Tingle. Tuck replies, but his message is not delivered because the recipient exists in another layer of The Tingleverse, a revelation that will take Tuck on a journey into the deepest realms of his butt's heart. Soon, Tuck is breaking fourth-walls and anal limits, pounded hard by a handsome sentient Hugo Award nomination named Kelpo and learning the true meaning of homoerotic love!

The cover (shown in Fig. 8.1) continued Tingle's tradition of good-looking, shirtless male models accompanied by surprising companions—in this case, a Hugo rocket with a face.

Tingle didn't end his mockery of the Puppies there: he announced that, in the event that he won the award, it would be accepted by Zoe Quinn, bringing the Puppies discourse right back to Gamergate's number one favorite victim (Romano 2016). He took it a step further by buying the domain "TheRabidPuppies.com" and using it to both showcase shirtless men and link to several campaigns: Zoe Quinn's social media attack victim support network Crash Override, fantasy writer Rach Swirsky's crowdfunding of LGBTQ health access and resources, and (perhaps in response to Jemisin's concerned tweets) Jemisin's own Hugo award-nominated novel (ibid.).

Meanwhile, PuppyGate joins Gamergate (which we discuss in Chap. 4) as an ideal case study of what geek masculinity looks like when members of the identity subculture deem themselves to be under siege. The overlap between the two groups is impossible fully to measure, as both rely on anonymous and pseudonymous members, but the alliance between Vox Day and Milo Yiannopoulos is clear. The rhetoric of both groups suggests a desire to "save" the past: to protect hypermasculine video games from feminist intervention, to keep science fiction clean of supposed political agendas and social metaphors, and in short to preserve geek cultural spaces for participants who share this same set of values without ever having those values tested or challenged.

Fig. 8.1 Chuck Tingle responds to his Hugo nomination, 2016

Defining Geek Fragility

PuppyGate and Gamergate are symptoms of the same condition: Geek Fragility. Robin DiAngelo (2011) defines White Fragility as a set of defensive reactions, "a state in which even a minimum amount of racial stress becomes intolerable, triggering a range of defensive moves. These moves include the outward display of emotions such as anger, fear, and guilt, and behaviors such as argumentation, silence, and leaving the stress-inducing situation. These behaviors, in turn, function to reinstate white racial equilibrium." We see these emotional displays everywhere in the geek community today: it's in the rants of angry comic creators plagued by fake geek girls,

8 Conclusion: That's Not How Geek Masculinity Works!   195

the tweets of gamers defending their medium against the alleged attacks of feminists, and the outcry of fanboys seeing female characters take over the lightsaber and legacy of *Star Wars*. And what is the nature of the geek equilibrium they seek to reinstate? It is a constructed fantasy, a world in which young white men outside the traditional definitions of masculinity are victims turned heroes, entitled to their rewards.

The texts of geek culture play a powerful role in creating aspirational models and providing heroes for readers, viewers, and players to identify with. We can see the power of these heroes in sales of merchandise, cosplay, and fan productions. We've examined many of these geek icons throughout this text. But geek culture is no longer an isolated subculture. Geek-oriented films are among the top-grossing films of all time. The Marvel cinematic universe has leapt out of comic books and taken over as the first example of a connected transmedia franchise on this scale, with a directed story team ensuring a consistency that offers continual rewards to dedicated viewers. Geek culture has made it into the mainstream, and it won't fit easily back into any box smaller than the Tardis.

With great visibility comes great pressure: the geek male hero of the 1980s and 1990s has been displaced. It is no longer enough to play arcade games to save the galaxy (as in *The Last Starfighter* 1984) or stop a global thermonuclear war triggered by your own hacking (ala *War Games* 1983). Male comic superheroes often come from geeky origins: Steve Roger's physical weakness is cured by a super solider serum. Hulk loses his calm scientist body and becomes a literal embodiment of uncontrolled rage. Iron Man dons a metal suit to augment his researcher-billionaire body into a war machine. These characters in their new incarnations combine mental skills and geek-valued abilities with hypermasculine strength, offering a vision of masculinity that draws upon both physical and mental traits.

Meanwhile, our obsession with the geeks who control a sizeable portion of the country's wealth and industry draws our gaze to Silicon Valley: from the HBO series to the many films probing the lives of Steve Jobs and Bill Gates, our geek heroes become themselves stories. Icons such as Mark Zuckerberg and even his elder statesmen Steve Jobs are even becoming fuel our superheroes. In a 2015 reboot of Marvel's *The Amazing Spider-Man*, Peter Parker takes his place among the rich as geek-turned-tech-tycoon. As Tim Carmody (2015) notes, "It doesn't seem like an accident that Spider-Man now joins Iron Man and Batman in the ranks of the rich, making three of the world's most popular superheroes wealthy inventor-entrepreneurs by day, crime fighters by night. It seems like a symptom." In a new age of geek-dominance, Peter Parker can be superhero by night, super-rich tech genius by day.

Mark Zuckerberg, played by a scrawny Jesse Eisenberg in *The Social Network* (Fincher 2010), lives out the ultimate Revenge of the Nerds fantasy as he outwits the muscular Harvard men of the varsity crew team. Yet in the opening scene, geek fragility is taken on directly through the words of a woman out with Mark Zuckerberg on a date:

> You are probably going to be a very successful computer person. But you're going to go through life thinking that girls don't like you because you're a nerd. And I want you to know, from the bottom of my heart, that that won't be true. It'll be because you're an asshole.

The woman's remark holds in it a reminder of years of stories in which nerds were depicted as challenged in romance. In the 1990s sitcom *Saved by the Bell*, geek Samuel Powers (called "Screech" by most) is a social reject in most respects, while academic failure star athletes Zach and AC ruled the school (Bobrick 1989–1993). However, the social norms that constructed these hierarchies are shifting, and Philip Veliz's (2015) study of attitudes among high school students towards success and popularity suggests that while characters like Screech might not be immediately popular, academic success is now expected as part of "coolness," even from athletes (70–71). And those same athletes are playing *Assassin's Creed* and *Gears of War*, going to see *Star Wars* and the next *Avengers*, and perhaps even picking up the latest young adult dystopian novel. Sheldon of *The Big Bang Theory* (discussed in Chap. 3) might be depicted as a social outsider, but he's one with clout and university funding. The space allotted to geeks in popular culture was once defined through external forces. However, the shift in balance in cultural power is now firmly skewed towards a tech industry that is predominately white and male (Jones and Trop 2015). With every major Hollywood franchise powered by special effects, animation, and digital tie-ins, Hollywood and Silicon Valley have become an inseparable powerhouse pairing. Geek identity has been commodified and commercialized through absorption into popular culture, but geekdom's defining myths haven't caught up with the power shift.

The Fandom Awakens

No recent film captures this shift in geek culture better than *Star Wars: The Force Awakens* (Abrams 2015). Geek masculinity is powerful and visible even in spaces where traditional masculinity dominates—the *Star Wars: Force Awakens* trailer premiered during half time of a Monday Night

8 Conclusion: That's Not How Geek Masculinity Works! 197

Football game, and tickets for opening night sold out across the nation and world in record times (Lang 2016). And to the surprise of many, the trailer brought the spotlight not to the franchise's established heroes (although Chewbacca, Han Solo, and Leia appeared), but to two new characters: Finn, a black Stormtrooper, and Reys, a young woman from a desert planet. As the film's marketing campaign stepped up, it became clear these two were going to bring something different to the universe, and the film itself did not disappoint.

The story of *The Force Awakens* is a familiar one, with a group of outsiders fighting against an Empire-esque army to bring a map vital to the Resistance and stop a Death Star-like planet destroying weapon in the process. But the characters provide some transformative elements to what could be a re-trod of familiar ground. In the final climactic battle of *The Force Awakens* Finn picks up Luke Skywalker's lightsaber and wields it against new villain Kylo Ren. Finn has demonstrated no real connection to the force, but this isn't his first time with the lightsaber during the film (he used it earlier against a skilled Stormtrooper), and Kylo Ren is wounded. However, the battle doesn't go well for Finn, and the lightsaber is knocked out of his hand. Kylo Ren reaches out with the force to collect it and we see the lightsaber slowly shaking in the snow, a direct echo of the first time Luke Skywalker reached out with the force. The lightsaber goes flying—right into Rey's waiting hands. In theatres around the world on opening night, that scene got a reaction: even though Rey's narrative had already clearly identified her as the future Jedi of the film, the sight of a lightsaber wielded competently in the hands of a main woman character was something unexpected. It was the realization of a promise Yoda made decades ago: "There is another," a phrase that left young women geeks hoping for a similar awakening that never came for Leia.

As of this writing, in early 2016, Rey's story is incomplete, her parentage a mystery (although speculations of her connection to Luke Skywalker are inevitable). The resolution to her story will be a long time in coming, as the second installment of the new *Star Wars* trilogy was pushed back, with some speculating that the script is being rewritten (Smith 2016). Rumors suggest that the rewrite is motivated by the need to further develop the stories of Rey and Finn, as well as Poe, a commander in the Resistance's Starfighter Corps and the third of the breakout characters of the new film (ibid.). Given Rey's clear centrality to the new universe, this seems surprising until we look at it through the lens of the changing currents of geek culture. Rey's importance aside, she has proven hard to find for fans seeking merchandise, and even been outright excluded from properties such as the *Force*

Awakens Monopoly game and a set of action figures sold at Target (Cox 2016). This has prompted fans to question "Where's Rey?" An anonymous industry insider suggested one answer: the exclusion of Rey was deliberate, as Disney executives told them "No boy wants to be given a product with a female character on it" (Boehm 2016). The insider further suggested that the diminishing of girl characters in marketing is common, which comes as no surprise to fans of characters such as Black Widow and Gamora, who have been similarly noted for their absence in merchandising (as we examined in Chap. 5). These omissions have been easier to explain, however: usually, such characters are the token woman within a team of men. As the new Jedi of the *Star Wars* universe, Rey makes for a much more obvious omission. But the reason behind her absence is even more striking: according to John Marcotte, Kylo Ren was expected to be the breakout character, and most of the merchandising for the film focuses on him (ibid.).

Kylo Ren is certainly the dominant young white male actor in the new cast: as the villain, he has arguably the coolest outfit as well as a Vader-esque mask that lends itself immediately to costuming. But more than that, he is himself a stand-in for a type of privileged geek masculinity that is demonstrated through his treatment of Rey and his many temper tantrums throughout the film:

> instead of treating Rey like a person, Kylo acts out of aggression, objectification, and self-centeredness. He immediately immobilizes her, Force-faints her, and then carries her, bridal-style, to his ship: old-fashioned, exploitative, and gross. His language towards her is incredibly patronizing: "So this is the girl I've heard so much about …" He proceeds to insult her friends and threaten and torture her: violating her mind, using her as a tool but also relishing the show of his own power and the taking of something personal by force. "I can take what I want" is simultaneously a threat, a statement of power/entitlement, and a declaration of how Kylo fundamentally views Rey: an object, something controllable to serve his purposes. When the tables turn and Rey reads him, he is incredibly shaken by the subversion of his own authority and control, and when she escapes, he storms around looking for her in a blind rage, pursuing her with a weapon. Even as she's beating him in the ensuing lightsaber battle, he has the gall to mansplain her own power to her: "YOU NEED A TEACHER!" (Bennion 2016)

Kylo Ren believes he is special. He will be the one to finish what Darth Vader started, as he confides to the burnt and twisted mask he talks to when there's no one else to listen. He wears a mask he doesn't even need in emulation of his idol. Comics writer Gail Simone (2015) sums up what makes him so terrifying in a tweet: "This is a harsh way to put it, but I think Kylo Ren is a school shooter. Think about it, that's his profile." Whether Disney's executives implied belief that Kylo Ren would be the breakout character of the film is accurate or not, there is no question what type of masculinity he reflects to the audience: a toxic, entitled, violent, and exploitative one. As Rich McCormick (2016) comments, "He's angry at the universe, but he's more angry at himself, especially after being beaten in a stand-up fight by an untrained scavenger using his idol's lightsaber"—and he takes out that anger on whatever is handy. He calls to mind *Jessica Jones* and Kilgrave (discussed in Chap. 5), particularly in his use of mental violation as a casual tactic.

Kylo Ren's parallels to voices within geek culture and particularly the various 'gates did not go unnoticed, and one individual immediately started an "Emo Kylo Ren" Twitter account to parody the character's mindset and origin story. As of January 23, 2016, the account had amassed 746,000 followers and sported the bio line "ren's right activist," demonstrating a very intentional parody of men's right activists. Notably, tweets from the account include "it's about ethics in Force journalism" (2015a), direct revision of Gamergate's motto, "what if men just have naturally different levels of force ability" (2015b), a twist on a common Men Right's Activist claim, and the appropriate "i suppose i was just born into the wrong era /that's all," which holds shades of Sad Puppy's desire to reclaim another era of science fiction (2015c). Of those tweets, the last is perhaps the most poignant, as it echoes a common thread within geek misogynist groups: the desire to return to a time when men were knights and heroes, women were a due reward (as with the white knights considered in Chap. 6), and life was appropriately simple.

The other men of the new *Star Wars* are not so simply painted as heroes of geek culture's hypermasculine tradition. Finn and Poe are both characters without any particularly misogynist actions. They have already been adopted by fandom as a shippable couple, dubbed "Stormpilot" by fans around the web. The popularity of Stormpilot as a slash pairing is grounded in canonical signifiers, as Andrew Wheeler (2016) writes:

> That famous jacket scene, in which Poe tells Finn to keep his jacket because it looks good on him, is a classic dramatization of attraction. Giving a guy your jacket and complimenting him on how it looks means you are *into him*. We wouldn't doubt the significance of that moment if one of the characters was a woman. And we certainly wouldn't doubt that lip bite.

The lip bite has become an iconic moment for fans of the film, as potent as any instance of queer-baiting on *Sherlock* or *Supernatural* (analyzed in Chap. 7).

And unlike in those shows, where such moments are usually followed by carefully scripted reminders of a character's heterosexuality, no current canonical text undermines readings of Poe's identity as queer. This is a significant move for a franchise previously founded on rescues of princesses and baby-focused heterosexual marriages.

Regardless of where Poe's story takes the character, he has become an icon for a different type of male hero: "In another movie, his character could have embodied *Top Gun* masculinity: cocky, smarmy, hothead, womanizing, self-centered, and aggressive. Instead, Poe is none of the above" (Bennion 2016). Unlike some of the classic geek heroes we analyzed earlier, the men of the new *Star Wars* point towards a more integrated, less toxic model of masculinity. Likewise, Finn is presented as a Stormtrooper driven to go against his training and escape to the outer reaches, but he is drawn back in by love of his friends. He is not the first black hero in the *Star Wars* universe: Lando Calrissian and to some extent the prequel's Mace Windu predate his appearance. However, he is the first to take such a prominent role in the narrative, a fact that allowed internet trolls and Men's Right Activist groups to start an apparent campaign to boycott the film over the absence of white men from the leading cast (Denham 2016).

Following closely on the heels of *The Force Awakens*, *Rogue One* (2016) spawned an immediate backlash with the announcement of the story's focus on another rebel woman, Jyn Erso. The Disney marketing team seemed to leap into action, releasing the names of man after man joining the cast, but even those names were not the usual suspects. By the film's release, it was clear this would feature the most diverse cast in the history of *Star Wars* films, although the deaths of most of the characters at the end of the film suddenly occupied a new metatextual layer as an explanation to what happened to the rebellion's diversity in the move to *Episode IV: A New Hope*. An explanation for why Darth Vader had forgotten to wield a lightsaber in the ensuing moments was not as easily forthcoming.

Revenge of the Geek

There are still a number of problematic aspects to the new *Star Wars* films and, indeed, to many of the franchises currently powering geek culture's decided move into the mainstream. But for standard-bearers of the old guard of geek masculinity, the steps towards becoming a mainstream standard is the opposite of progress. Many of geekdom's most iconic texts tell tales of the quest of the lone white male hero against an oppressive society, and this is no coincidence. The outsider mentality is deeply embedded into geek identity politics and cannot be easily dislodged. Leaders of movements dedicated to the preservation of geek masculinity adopt characteristics not unlike Kylo Ren's mask as part of campaigns of online intimidation, with Vox Day a notable example. Yet even as they do so, there is a clear implication that they believe that someday they will be seen as the heroes of the story.

Many like to argue that these individuals are simply trolls and should be ignored. It is easy to reduce this to a small group and say that they do not represent the whole of geek culture. They are out for laughs or attention or simply to see if they can piss someone off. They don't have a serious agenda that needs to be considered and questioned appropriately. Within Phillips' examination of trolling and mainstream culture, the author argues that even trolls come from somewhere: "First, trolls' privileging of cool rationality over emotionalism, coupled with their emphasis on 'wining' that is, successfully exerting dominance over a given adversary, represents a logical extension of androcentrism …" (ibid., 124). However, even if the troubles arise from a small group of trolls, as we have shown throughout the book, the culture of geekdom presents a definition of masculinity that allows for the fostering of these attitudes and fodder for their fights. The cultural trope of the geek as outcast helps to frame the arguments of the more abusive members of the community. According to this logic, geeks have already experienced personal pain and suffering as social outcasts of society and denying them their desires within the community is itself a form of abuse. Any actions they take to "protect" themselves or "defend" the community as they define it follows naturally from this perspective. This mentality that excuses abusive behaviors under the cover of past injuries was labelled The Victim by Lundy Bancroft. Very few geeks are deliberately abusive or making use of abusive tactics to harm others within the communities. But the mentalities that geek masculinity presents open the door to allow for these justifications to be used. In looking at the arguments of groups like the Puppies or Gamergate, these same arguments and justifications arise. One point that Bancroft (2002) points out from those engaging with this mentality is "When I point out this reality to the Victim, he describes a kind of paranoid fantasy in which women are behind the scenes secretly pulling the strings, largely by getting men to feel sorry for them" (96–98). This certainly seems similar to comments seen on supporting forums and social media sites for these movements. The focus on "ethics in journalism" that Gamergate has come from the idea that women were secretly running the media sites from behind or through trading promotion for sex. Each of these mentalities are not a binary yes or no but sliding scales of actions and justifications.

While these arguments may not represent the views of individual men and women within the community, they do arise as logical extensions of the cultural stances many take. In the Internet age, it becomes difficult to separate the memetic cultural interactions from the trolling that occurs.

As Phillips lays out, the generation of memes and selection of targets for trolling both rely upon objectifying the target (ibid., 118–119). It must be stripped from its cultural context and a location in space and time. Often this is easier on the Internet due to the nature of how many social media sites work, interspersing comments between other less serious content. It becomes easier to ignore the fact that a tweet or Facebook post occurs within a particular setting and make it an object floating in the void. When applied to people, it allows trolls to distance themselves from the human empathetic response and instead view their target as a thing. Things do not feel. They don't suffer. A thing is inherently othered because the self is always identified as a person, a class separate from thing.

Much of the angst being felt within these cultural spaces makes sense when viewed through the lens of social expectations and rewards. Engaging in these spaces and pursuits is meant to bring a sense of happiness or joy. Much like factions within the US political spectrum yearn for the perfect home life of the post-war era, geeks look towards the fabled golden age of geekdom that never was. Their unhappiness in finding that nostalgia is more potent than reality must be painted as belonging somewhere. As Sara Ahmed (2010) analyses in her book *The Promise of Happiness*:

> In the thick sociality of everyday spaces, feminists are thus attributed as the origin of bad feeling, as the ones who ruin the atmosphere, which is how the atmosphere might be imagined (retrospectively) as shared ... It is not just that feminists might not be happily affected by the object that are supposed to cause happiness but that their failure to be happy is read as sabotaging the happiness of others. (65–66)

Feminists, social justice warriors, and critics become easy targets for geeks' own unhappiness with their communities and lives. If uncritical appreciation of the different geek media is retrospectively considered to be the atmosphere of geekdom, then feminists, social justice warriors, and anyone different becomes an easy target for painting as the bad guy. Women and minority groups can't be part of these communities because even thinking about them as participants breaks the image of the geek as solitary, disliked male. If the important defining characteristics arise from some aspect inherent to white maleness, then any that ruin the groups' vision by being visibly different break the shared atmosphere.

These battles of identity have become so entrenched that the labels of geekdom are themselves being cast off. Thanks in large part to Gamergate, the label of "gamer" has become less desirable than ever, and women in particular are rejecting it: a Pew research study conducted in 2015 found that while American women and men play games in almost equal numbers, twice as many men as women identify as gamers (Duggan 2015). Furthermore, 60% of adults believe more men than women play games, suggesting that men's attempt at ownership of gamer identity has been successful as a marketing tactic if not as a way to actually drive women out of gaming (ibid.). While there has been no similar study of the label of "geek" itself, we speculate that the numbers may indeed be similar.

The demands of geek masculinity are in some ways greater than those of masculinity at large, which already charges a heavy toll for non-conformity. Intellectual ability is prized and apparent in the many heroes of geek fictions (as we examine in Chap. 2). Yet alongside this privileging of intellect and cultural knowledge come stories of geek heroes with extreme physical strength and games that encourage embodiment of hypermasculine avatars in world that offers very limited agency to women. This narrative, then, is a driving force in how geek masculinity is commodified and packaged both to geeks themselves and to outsiders: as these narratives change, the identity politics of geekdom must slowly change with them.

Heroes in a Dying Earth

Change is a difficult concept to come to grips with and involuntary change can often make a person feel disempowered. For those who have made geekdom the core of their identity, the cultural shifts that are in place can be frightening at best and overtly hostile to what they see as simply being themselves. Geek masculinity has made big assumptions about what benefits men may accrue through participation. Although this sense of entitlement may be unearned and disproportionate to their power and numbers, it is still a real emotion. The conflicts over defining what it means to be a geek and who rules geekdom are natural, but must be addressed to see change and growth in the future. Through examining geek masculinity and addressing the unbalanced nature of its presentation towards all participants within geekdom, some of these fears and feelings can be assuaged.

In Steven King's award-winning book series *The Dark Tower* (1982–2012) series, Roland Deschain, the main hero, portrays the classic caricature of the lone cowboy striving against a harsh world in a quest for redemption. Roland adventures through the varied world hunting down the Man in Black who harmed him and hurt those Roland loved. One thing that is quickly made clear, however, is that all is not right with the world Roland travels through. Following from his point of view, justice and sanity have fled in the wake of the Man in Black. Throughout the book the phrase "the world has moved on" is used to describe these changes, often in a negative fashion, reflecting upon how the good times used to be. Roland finds companions and loses them as he makes the hard choices about how to achieve his goals. He often causes just as much suffering as peace for those he crosses, despite his best intentions. It also becomes clear that Roland's memories of the past and his idyllic childhood are not the most accurate. The ending of the series is very controversial: Roland finally reaches the eponymous tower and his quest simply restarts back at the beginning. It is explained that being the hero is not what Roland or the world needs. He simply needs to learn to be human, to value the companions he meets along the way, and that causing harm in the name of good makes evil men of even the best.

Geek culture has moved on. Those who hold to the self-image of being a storied hero and fight their disappointment by holding tighter to the old world need to learn to let go. They will be forced to learn this lesson with increasing personal pain because the world cannot rewind. This process will not restore entitlements to those groups, but it will provide realistic expectations and interactions for living in a complex, mediated world. No longer will there need to be a fear of the feminists or social justice warriors in the new world order, but instead a better understanding how people help to form and shape culture. Perhaps it may be possible to move geekdom towards the creation of an actual safe space for those who do not feel like they fit in. It's not that the world no longer needs heroes, but they need to be ones that are aware of the world in which they live and the people they support.

References

Abrams, J.J. 2015. *Star wars: The force awakens*. Burbank, CA: Walt Disney Studios Motion Pictures. DVD.
Ahmed, Sara. 2010. *The promise of happiness*. Durham, NC: Duke University Press.
Announcing the 2015 Hugo Award Nominees. 2015. Tor, April 4. Accessed April7, 2015. http://www.tor.com/2015/04/04/2015-hugo-award-nominees/.
Bancroft, Lundy. 2002. *Why does he do that? Inside the minds of angry and controlling men*. New York: Putnam's Sons.

Bennion, Kate. 2016. The feminist message of the dudes in *Force Awakens*. *The Mary Sue*, January 19. Accessed October 12, 2016. https://www.themarysue.com/masculinity-the-force-awakens/.

Bobrick, Sam. 1989–1993. *Saved by the Bell*. NBC.

Boehm, Michael. 2016. Where's Rey? *Sweatpants and Coffee Blog*, January 19. Accessed March 12, 2016. http://sweatpantsandcoffee.com/rey/.

Carmody, Tim. 2015. Being rich isn't a superpower, and Steve Jobs isn't Spider-Man. *The Kernel*, September 27. Accessed October 12, 2015. http://kernelmag.dailydot.com/issue-sections/staff-editorials/14571/rich-spider-man-steve-jobs/#sthash.3Ly2uNjP.dpuf.

Cox, Carolyn. 2016. 8yo asks Hasbro Where's Rey, Hasbro responds pretty well, actually. *The Mary Sue*, January 5. Accessed January 5, 2016. https://www.themarysue.com/rey-is-on-her-way/.

Day, Vox. 2015a. *SJWs always lie: Taking down the thought police*. Kouvola, Finland: Castalia House.

Day, Vox. 2015b. Vox Popoli: In which tonight's events are contemplated. *Vox Day Blog*, August 22. Accessed August 23. https://voxday.blogspot.com/2015/08/in-which-tonights-events-are.html.

Day, Vox. 2015c. Vox Popoli: Rabid Puppies 2015. *Vox Day Blog*, February 2. Accessed February 4. https://voxday.blogspot.co.uk/2015/02/rabid-puppies-2015.html.

Denham, Jess. 2016. *Star Wars*: Men's rights activists claim boycott cost *The Force Awakens* $4.2 m. *The Independent*, January 4. Accessed February 2, 2016. https://www.independent.co.uk/arts-entertainment/films/news/star-wars-mens-rights-activists-claim-boycott-cost-the-force-awakens-42m-a6796146.html.

DiAngelo, Robin. 2011. White fragility. *The International Journal of Critical Pedagogy* 3 (3): 54–70. Paulo and Nita Freire International Project for Critical Pedagogy. doi:10.1177/02783649910382803.

Duggan, Maeve. 2015. Public debates about video games: Women players and violent behavior. *Gaming and Gamers Report—Pew Internet Research*, December 15. Accessed January 2, 2016. http://www.pewinternet.org/2015/12/15/public-debates-about-gaming-and-gamers/.

Fincher, David. 2010. *The social network*. DVD: Columbia Pictures.

Hines, Jim C. 2015. Gender balance in Hugo nominees. *Jim C. Hines Blog*, May 10. Accessed June 2, 2015. http://www.jimchines.com/2015/05/hugo-gender-balance/.

Hugo Awards. 2015. *The Hugo Awards*. Accessed January 3, 2016. http://www.thehugoawards.org/hugo-history/2015-hugo-awards/.

Jemision, NK. 2016. No title. *Twitter*, April 28. Accessed April 28, 2016. https://twitter.com/nkjemisin/status/725716394000666624.

Jones, Stacy and Jaclyn Trop. 2015. Tech company diversity: How do the big players compare? *Fortune*, July 3. Accessed July 4, 2015. http://fortune.com/2015/07/30/tech-companies-diveristy/.

KyloR3n. 2015a. No title. *Twitter*, December 21. Accessed December 21, 2015. https://twitter.com/KyloR3n/status/679123942330736640.

KyloR3n. 2015b. No title. *Twitter*, December 22. Accessed December 22, 2015. https://twitter.com/KyloR3n/status/679255772501557248.

KyloR3n. 2015c. No title. *Twitter*, December 22. Accessed December 22, 2015. https://twitter.com/KyloR3n/status/679283237605261312.

Lang, Brent. 2016. 'Star Wars: The Force Awakens' sets ticket sales record. *Variety*, October 20. Accessed October 22, 2016. https://variety.com/2015/film/news/star-wars-the-force-awakens-ticket-sales-1201621977/.

McCormick, Rich. 2016. Why is @EmoKyloRen so perfect? *The Verge*, January 1. Accessed January 2, 2016. https://www.theverge.com/2016/1/1/10698090/emo-kylo-ren-star-wars-parody-twitter.

Martin, George R.R. 2015. Blogging for rockets. *GRRM Blog*, April 9. Accessed May 12, 2016. http://grrm.livejournal.com/417812.html.

Romano, Aja. 2016. Satirical erotica author Chuck Tingle's massive troll of conservative sci-fi fans, explained. *Vox*, May 26. Accessed June 12, 2016. http://www.vox.com/2016/5/26/11759842/chuck-tingle-hugo-award-rabid-puppies-explained.

Schneiderman, Miles. 2015. Sad Puppies, rabid chauvinists: Will raging white guys succeed in hijacking sci-fi's biggest awards? *Yes!*, August 14. Accessed September 12, 2015. http://www.yesmagazine.org/peace-justice/sad-puppies-2015-hugo-awards-20150814.

Simone, Gail. 2015. No title. *Twitter*, December 22. Accessed December 22, 2015. https://twitter.com/GailSimone/status/679330673014870016.

Smith, Chris. 2016. New reports may reveal the reason 'Star Wars 8' was delayed. *BGR*, January 21. Accessed January 24, 2016. https://bgr.com/2016/01/21/star-wars-viii-working-title-screenplay/.

Tingle, Chuck. 2016. *Slammed in the Butt by My Hugo Award Nomination*. Amazon Kindle. https://www.amazon.com/Slammed-Butt-Hugo-Award-Nomination-ebook/dp/B01EUC93RE?ie=UTF8&*Version*=1&*entries*=0.

Torgersen, Brad. 2015a. Sad Puppies 3: The unraveling of an unreliable field. *Brad Torgersen Blog*, February 4. Accessed February 12, 2015. https://bradrtorgersen.wordpress.com/2015/02/04/sad-puppies-3-the-unraveling-of-an-unreliable-field/.

Torgersen, Brad. 2015b. Tribalism is as tribalism does. *Brad Torgersen Blog*, April 14. Accessed May 2, 2015. https://bradrtorgersen.wordpress.com/2015/04/14/tribalism-is-as-tribalism-does/.

Veliz, P. 2015. Too cool for school? *Contexts* 14 (3): 70–71. doi:10.1177/1536504215596952.

Waldman, Katy. 2016. Sad and Rabid Puppies are trying to game the Hugo Award shortlists again in 2016. *Slate*, April 29. Accessed May 2, 2016. http://www.slate.com/blogs/browbeat/2016/04/29/sad_and_rabid_puppies_are_trying_to_game_the_hugo_award_shortlists_again.html.

Wallace, Amy. 2015. Who won science fiction's Hugo Awards, and why it matters. *Wired*, August 23. Accessed September 13, 2015. https://www.wired.com/2015/08/won-science-fictions-hugo-awards-matters/.

Wheeler, Andrew. 2016. Super: Can we have nice things? The big gay Poe Dameron question. *Comics Alliance*, January 19. Accessed February 2, 2016. http://comicsalliance.com/super-poe-dameron-gay/.

Wolfe, Gary K. 2015. Hugo Awards: Rabid Puppies defeat reflects growing diversity in science fiction. *The Chicago Tribune*, May 28. Accessed June 12, 2015. http://www.chicagotribune.com/lifestyles/books/ct-prj-hugo-awards-controversy-science-fiction-20150828-story.html.

Yiannopoulos, Milo. 2015. Hugo Awards: SJWs just burned down the house. *Breitbart*, August 23. Accessed August 24, 2015. http://www.breitbart.com/big-government/2015/08/23/set-phasers-to-kill-sjws-burn-down-the-hugo-awards-to-prove-how-tolerant-and-welcoming-they-are/.

Index

A

Age 4, 10, 19, 28, 31, 57, 90, 115, 135, 139, 195, 202
Agent Carter 124
Alias 110, 121, 123
Alpha male. *See* Masculinity: alpha
Anime 139, 140
Ant Man 115
Assassin's Creed 196
Audience 3, 12, 18, 20, 21, 23, 26, 28, 29, 38, 40, 49–55, 74, 94, 105, 109, 112, 114, 119, 146–148, 153, 161, 170, 180, 183, 199
Avatar 2, 13, 75–77, 80, 82–84, 86, 88, 95, 112
Avengers franchise 107
  Age of Ultron 106
  Black Widow 106
  Captain America 23, 24, 39, 102, 112, 115, 122
  Carter, Peggy 115
  Iron Man/Tony Stark 37, 38, 40, 102, 105, 112, 115, 122, 195
  Potts, Pepper 37
  Thor 102, 115, 123

B

The Bard's Tale 131
Batman franchise 36, 102, 103, 108, 113, 116–118, 120, 123, 195
  Batgirl 110, 116–120, 123
  Batman 36, 102, 103, 108, 113, 117–121, 123, 195
  Batman Begins 121
  The Dark Knight 120
  Gordon, Barbara 116–118
  Gotham 118, 123
  The Killing Joke 116, 118
  Poison Ivy 120
  Quinn, Harley 120
Beauty and the Geek 46
The Big Bang Theory 1–3, 7, 9, 13, 21, 36, 48–56, 61, 62, 64, 67, 95, 109, 110, 147, 157, 196
  Penny 3, 9, 49–52, 55, 56, 147, 157
  Sheldon 1, 7, 9, 36, 48, 51, 52, 54–56, 157, 196
Bioshock franchise 78
Brogrammer 65, 67, 88
Brony 148. *See also My Little Pony*; Pegasister

© The Editor(s) (if applicable) and The Author(s) 2017
A. Salter and B. Blodgett, *Toxic Geek Masculinity in Media*,
DOI 10.1007/978-3-319-66077-6

C

Cage, Luke 121, 123
Campbell, Joseph 28
Cast roles 3
 primary 115
 secondary 18, 20, 27, 29, 159
Catwoman 113. *See also Batman* franchise
#ChangeTheCover 120
Chivalry 138, 141, 151, 152
Chuck 13, 14, 61–64, 95, 177, 178
 Nerd Herd 61–63
Comic books/graphic novels 3, 10, 11, 13, 14, 36, 49, 102, 104, 105, 107, 109–111, 120, 121, 133, 139, 147, 149, 195
Community 26, 29, 32, 73, 74, 76, 82, 84, 87, 89, 91, 92, 95, 103, 104, 124, 132, 134, 143, 146, 148, 152, 153, 157–159, 162, 166, 173, 174, 178–180, 182, 183, 194, 201, 202
 gaming 73, 74, 76, 81, 82, 84, 87, 89–91, 95, 132
 spaces 6, 7, 73, 82, 87, 90, 132, 159, 162, 183
Companionship 27–29, 31, 133, 168, 169, 193, 204. *See also Doctor Who*
Conformity 203
Control 19, 32, 35, 38, 60, 68, 104, 108, 120, 121, 133, 135, 136, 145, 158, 168, 195, 198
Conventions/ComicCons 52, 102, 103, 105, 110, 147, 166
 New York 105
 PAX East 81, 82
 San Diego 105

D

Damsel in distress 79, 80, 90, 131, 132, 141, 164, 167

The Dark Tower series 203
Day, Vox (Theodore Beale) 190, 191, 193, 201
DC Comics 101, 109, 119, 120, 123, 145
Demographics 86, 105, 106, 109
Dickwolf 82
Discourse communities 11
Doctor Who franchise 13, 14, 21, 27, 29, 31, 121, 145
 The Doctor 18, 19, 21, 25, 27, 29
 Oswald, Clara 21
 Pond, Amy 14, 21, 30, 31
 Song, River 14, 21, 29
 Tyler, Rose 18, 28
Doom 76, 80, 82, 83, 137
Doxxing 91
Duke Nukem franchise 9, 14, 26, 76, 79–83, 85, 90, 94, 95

E

Elektra 114
Emotion 25, 166, 167, 203

F

Family Matters (tv series) 67
Fans/fandom 4, 5, 12, 14, 15, 27, 29, 101–110, 112, 119, 123, 124, 132, 145–153, 158–162, 170, 171, 173–175, 177–183, 192, 196–199
 fanboy 5, 146, 153, 157, 195
 fangirl 5, 146, 149, 152, 153, 157, 168, 170, 180
Fantasy 2, 5, 9, 11, 13, 14, 20, 32, 34, 46, 49, 55, 61, 75, 76, 78, 102, 114, 122, 133, 135, 176, 181, 189, 190, 193, 195, 196, 201
Femininity 13–15, 25, 32, 35, 82, 104, 113, 120, 134, 161, 162, 180
Feminism 2, 74, 123
Fetish 113

Firefly 21, 30, 31
4chan 91, 148
Fragility 194, 196
    geek 194–196
    white 194, 195
Freaks and Geeks 64
Fridging 115, 117
Friends 1, 37, 45, 48, 49, 55, 56, 63, 64, 198, 200
Fruits Basket 140

G

Game development 87
Game industry 86–88
Game of Thrones 132, 135, 137, 138
Gamergate 12, 76, 91–94, 122, 132, 140, 141, 189, 191–194, 199, 201, 203
Gaming 11, 12, 26, 75–77, 79–83, 85, 89–94, 192, 203
    hardcore 73, 74, 82, 89
    shooter genre 79
    spaces 12. *See also* Community: spaces
Gaze 2, 14, 18, 75, 87, 110, 113, 114, 118, 124, 145, 149–151, 153, 158–160, 162, 172, 178, 180, 181, 183, 195
    female 2, 14, 87, 110, 111, 113, 146, 149–151, 159, 162, 180, 181, 183
    male 2, 75, 87, 110, 111, 145, 146, 153, 162, 178
Gears of War 78, 196
Geek Girls 12, 104, 105
Gender 8, 13–15, 17, 31, 46, 47, 49, 52, 56, 57, 60, 61, 65, 66, 74, 80, 82, 86, 88, 90, 91, 102, 104, 107, 110, 111, 124, 142, 143, 146–148, 150, 157, 159–162, 165, 190, 191
    representation 31, 86, 88, 111, 191
    roles 22, 26, 46, 48, 60, 76, 86, 110, 111, 134, 139, 180
Genre 20, 45, 53, 75, 77–79, 83, 166, 178, 189, 191, 192
#Girlswithtoys 57
Gotham. *See Batman* franchise: *Gotham*
Green Lantern 114
Guardians of the Galaxy 109

H

Hasbro 147
The Hawkeye Initiative 87, 113, 114
Heroism 9, 11, 12, 18, 21, 27, 64, 65, 75, 131, 132
    male 8, 9, 12, 18, 21, 75, 132
Heteronormativity 104, 139
Holmes, Sherlock. *See Sherlock Holmes* franchise: Holmes, Sherlock
Homophobia 27
Homosexuality 166
Homosocial 52, 53, 120
Hot wife trope 45, 50, 55
How I Met Your Mother 1, 48, 49
Hugo Awards 189. *See also* Sad Puppies; Rabid Puppies
Hulk 112, 115, 122, 195
Human/humanity 19, 20, 23, 27–30, 38, 39, 56, 58, 62, 75, 78, 86, 110, 113, 142, 146, 165, 167, 181, 202, 204
Hypermasculinity 4, 14, 22, 26, 27, 32, 33, 36, 37, 77, 85, 88, 111, 112, 120

I

Iconography 18
Identity 3, 5–12, 14, 15, 17, 19, 22, 24, 29, 32, 35, 36, 38, 40, 47, 48, 50, 53, 54, 58, 62, 64, 67, 68, 73–76, 78, 79, 82, 83, 85, 89–91, 93–95, 103, 113, 118, 135, 142–144,

147, 157–159, 161, 162, 166, 171, 193, 196, 200, 201, 203
construction 3, 11, 19, 24, 38, 75, 76, 79, 94, 167
oppositional 22, 31, 32, 35
performance 24
Intelligence 9, 30, 33, 34, 40, 56, 60

J

Jessica Jones 110, 121–124, 199
Kilgrave 121, 122, 199
Jones, Indiana 14, 21, 83

K

Kickstarter 84, 90
Kilgrave. *See Jessica Jones*: Kilgrave
King, Steven. *See The Dark Tower* series
King's Quest series 131
Knocked Up 45

L

Laffer, Larry (Leisure Suit Larry) 84
Lannister, Cersei (character *GoT*) 135
Leisure Suit Larry franchise 76, 79, 83–85, 90, 94
Lethal Weapon 21
Logic. *See* Rationality/logic
The Lord of the Rings 134
Aragorn 134
Lumberjanes 108

M

Marvel Cinematic Universe 40, 105, 112, 115, 123, 195
Masculinity 3–5, 8–11, 13, 17–23, 25, 26, 32–37, 39, 45–48, 52, 53, 63–68, 75, 76, 88, 93–95, 102–104, 112, 120–122, 124, 132, 134, 144, 148, 150, 159, 161, 162, 167, 168, 170, 173, 181, 193, 195, 196, 198–201, 203
alpha 17, 32, 34, 35

The Matrix 75
Medieval 133, 135, 138, 141
Men's Rights Activism 34, 93
Misogyny 27, 74, 92, 143
Motivations 38, 84, 144
My Little Pony 147. *See also* Brony; Pegasister

N

Narrative 4–6, 14, 15, 19, 26, 48, 53, 55, 56, 64, 77, 78, 93, 103, 113, 114, 116, 131, 138, 139, 144, 145, 151, 157, 165, 168, 170, 173, 181, 183, 190, 197, 200, 203
Neo 75
New 52 109, 118, 119, 145
Nintendo 77
Norms (cultural) 14, 89

O

Office Space 32–34

P

Parker, Peter 10, 112, 195
Participatory culture 7, 50, 102
Pegasister 148
Penny Arcade Expo. *See* Conventions/ComicCons: PAX East
Pitchford, Randy 81
Puella Magi Madoka Magica 139

Q

Queer 14, 94, 120, 122, 159–162, 164, 168, 176, 180, 183, 199, 200
Quinn, Zoe 91, 93, 141, 193

R

Rabid Puppies 189. *See also* Hugo Awards; Sad Puppies
Race 17, 19, 27, 30, 47, 78, 90, 112, 118, 165

Rationality/logic 124, 131, 190, 201
Rewards 32, 34, 48, 101, 131, 132, 142, 143, 195, 202
Rodgers, Elliot 140
Roles 2, 20, 32, 35, 55, 80, 87, 116, 120, 135
   gender 22, 26, 46, 109, 111, 134, 139, 180
   social 22, 32, 35, 46

S

Sad Puppies 189. *See also* Hugo Awards; Rabid Puppies
Sarkeesian, Anita 90, 92, 93. *See also* Gamergate
Scalzi, John 73
Science fiction 3–5, 9, 10, 13, 14, 17, 19–22, 28, 29, 31, 73, 75, 102, 189, 190, 193, 199
Scott Pilgrim Vs. the World 138
Sex/sexuality 8, 12, 20, 21, 26, 27, 31, 33, 54, 57, 66, 90, 104, 114, 118, 120, 140–143, 145–147, 159, 161, 167, 172, 180, 181, 201
   heteronormative 13, 20, 46, 111, 120, 123, 161
Sexism 66, 81, 89, 140–142, 149, 190
   benevolent 140–142, 149
Sexual abuse 14, 180
Sherlock Holmes franchise 4, 14, 25, 132, 143, 145, 160, 162–164, 167, 170–172
   Holmes, Sherlock 25, 145, 160, 162–164, 166, 167, 170, 171
Shrek franchise 132, 143, 145
Silicon Valley 5, 13, 47, 61, 64–67, 195, 196
Simone, Gail 115, 118, 198
The Social Network 196
A Song of Ice and Fire 135
Spider-Man franchise 9, 112, 143, 195
   Stacey, Gwen 115

Star Trek franchise 4, 14, 17, 19, 21, 49, 73
   Captain Kirk 17
Star Wars franchise 101, 195, 196, 199, 200
   Finn 197, 199, 200
   The Force Awakens 196, 197, 200
   Lando Calrissian 29, 200
   Luke Skywalker 197
   Princess Leia 49
   Ren, Kylo 197–199
   Rey 197, 198
   Skywalker, Luke 29
   Solo, Han 29, 197
STEM 13, 57, 88
Story/plot 5, 6, 18–21, 23, 25, 28–32, 37, 38, 40, 45, 49, 56, 60, 101, 112, 114–116, 119, 132, 134, 135, 138, 144, 145, 147, 163–167, 174, 177, 180–182, 190, 195, 197, 199–201
   arc 19, 20, 25, 32, 112
Subcultures 5, 22, 26, 27, 33, 103, 147
Suicide Squad 118. *See also* Batman franchise
Superbodies 110, 111, 124
Superman franchise 10, 18, 36, 40, 102, 108, 123
   Lane, Lois 115, 124
Supernatural 13, 14, 149–151, 153, 160, 162, 172–179, 181, 183, 199

T

Technology 1, 4, 6, 7, 27, 28, 37, 39, 48, 56, 57, 61, 68, 78
Ten Things I Hate About You 45
Threepwood, Guybrush 83
Tingle, Chuck 192–194
Tolkien, J.R.R. 159
Top Gun 21, 200
Traits 18–23, 25, 30, 32, 35, 37–39, 45, 47, 54–56, 58, 77, 157, 195

behavioral 22
physical 22, 23, 35–37, 45–47, 54, 55, 59, 157, 195
psychical 24
Transmedia 27, 77, 101, 132, 195
Tropes vs. Women series. *See* Sarkeesian, Anita
Twilight franchise 106, 148, 152, 179–181
Twi-hard 148, 179, 182

W
Watchmen 114
White knight 75, 141–144, 151–153, 164
syndrome 76, 141
Women 1–3, 8, 10, 12–15, 17, 19–21, 23, 26, 27, 30–32, 34, 37, 39, 45–48, 50, 53, 55–60, 65, 66, 68, 75, 79–94, 102–111, 113–116, 118, 120, 123, 124, 131–138, 140–149, 151, 152, 158–160, 164–166, 168, 170–174, 176, 180, 181, 190, 191, 197, 199, 201–203
objectification 79, 87, 113
Women in Refrigerators (WiR) 114, 116
Wonder Woman 9, 10, 108, 115
World of Warcraft 86, 95

Y
Yiannopoulos, Milo 93, 192, 193

Z
Zuckerberg, Mark. *See The Social Network*